Where Life Began

Rachel Carson starts her enthralling study at a point over two billion years ago. After the violent birth of the earth and its tidal moon, after molten rock and seething vapors had cooled, the rains fell and oceans formed in the great basins of the scarred planet. It was in these waters, carrying the salts and minerals of the earth, that protoplasmic life first made its miraculous appearance.

The enigmatic ocean-mother has always fascinated poets; here an eminent scientist presents a factual, informative, and comprehensive survey of the sea that retains the art and wonder of great poetry. Miss Carson describes the hidden mountains and canyons of the ocean deeps, how they are being mapped; tells of the ceaseless power of the winds, waves, and currents, and the paradox of the moving tides. She reveals the meaning of the ocean to man—the heritage of the sea that we carry in our bodies—and the riches to be found in its salty marshes. Presenting mystery after mystery with compelling imagination and expert knowledge, Miss Carson has produced the most illuminating and impressive book ever written about *the sea around us.*

THE
SEA
AROUND
US

REVISED EDITION

by RACHEL L. CARSON

Drawings by Katherine L. Howe

A MENTOR BOOK

NEW AMERICAN LIBRARY

TIMES MIRROR

NEW YORK AND SCARBOROUGH, ONTARIO

MENTOR TRADEMARK REG. U.S. PAT. OFF. AND FOREIGN COUNTRIES
REGISTERED TRADEMARK—MARCA REGISTRADA
HECHO EN CHICAGO, U.S.A.

SIGNET, SIGNET CLASSICS, MENTOR, PLUME, MERIDIAN AND NAL
BOOKS *are published in the United States
by The New American Library, Inc.,
1633 Broadway, New York, New York 10019,
in Canada by The New American Library of Canada Limited,
81 Mack Avenue, Scarborough, Ontario M1L 1M8*

27   28   29   30   31   32   33   34   35

PRINTED IN THE UNITED STATES OF AMERICA

To HENRY BRYANT BIGELOW

who by precept and example has guided all

others in the exploration of the sea

PREFACE TO THE REVISED EDITION

The sea has always challenged the minds and imagination of men and even today it remains the last great frontier of Earth. It is a realm so vast and so difficult of access that with all our efforts we have explored only a small fraction of its area. Not even the mighty technological developments of this, the Atomic Age, have greatly changed this situation. The awakening of active interest in the exploration of the sea came during the Second World War, when it became clear that our knowledge of the ocean was dangerously inadequate. We had only the most rudimentary notions of the geography of that undersea world over which our ships sailed and through which submarines moved. We knew even less about the dynamics of the sea in motion, although the ability to predict the actions of tides and currents and waves might easily determine the success or failure of military undertakings. The practical need having been so clearly established, the governments of the United States and of other leading sea powers began to devote increasing effort to the scientific study of the sea. Instruments and equipment, most of which had been born of urgent necessity, gave oceanographers the means of tracing the contours of the ocean bottom, of studying the movements of deep waters, and even of sampling the sea floor itself.

These vastly accelerated studies soon began to show that many of the old conceptions of the sea were faulty, and by the mid-point of the century a new picture had begun to emerge. But it was still like a huge canvas on which the artist has indicated the general scheme of his grand design but on which large blank areas await the clarifying touch of his brush.

This was the state of our knowledge of the ocean world when *The Sea Around Us* was written in 1951. Since that time the filling in of many of the blank areas has proceeded and new discoveries have been made. In this second edition of the book I have described the most important of the new findings in a series of notes which will be found in the Appendix. These notes are keyed to appropriate passages in the original text by reference numbers. For example, after the discussion of the Arctic ocean ending on page 63, the reader may go on to learn of recent discoveries in this area by turning to note 10 in the Appendix.

The 1950's have comprised an exciting decade in the science of the sea. During this period a manned vehicle has descended to the deepest hole in the ocean floor. During the 'fifties, also, the crossing of the entire Arctic basin was accomplished by submarines traveling under the ice. Many new features of the unseen floor of the sea have been described, including new mountain ranges that now appear to be linked with others to form the longest and mightiest mountains of the earth—a continuous chain encircling the globe. Deep, hidden rivers in the sea, subsurface currents with the volume of a thousand Mississippis, have been found. During the International Geophysical Year, 60 ships from 40 nations, as well as hundreds of stations on islands and seacoasts, co-operated in an enormously fruitful study of the sea.

Yet the present achievements, exciting though they are, must be considered only a beginning to what is yet to be achieved by probing the vast depths of water that cover most of the surface of the earth. In 1959 a group of distinguished scientists comprising the Committee on Oceanography of the National Academy of Sciences declared that "Man's knowledge of the oceans is meager indeed compared with their importance to him." The Committee recommended at least a doubling of basic research on the sea by the United States in the 1960's; anything less would, in its opinion, "jeopardize the position of oceanography in the United States" compared with other nations and "place us at a disadvantage in the future use of the relief of the lower slopes."

One of the most fascinating of the projects now planned for the future is an attempt to explore the interior of the earth by drilling a hole three or four miles deep in the bottom of the sea. This project, which is sponsored by the National Academy of Sciences, is designed to penetrate farther than instruments have ever before reached, to the boundary between the earth's crust and its mantle. This boundary is known to geologists as the Mohorovicic discontinuity (or more familiarly as the Moho) because it was discovered by a Yugoslavian of that name in 1912. The Moho is the point at which earthquake waves show a marked change in velocity, indicating a transition from one kind of material to something quite different. It lies much deeper under the continents than under the oceans, so, in spite of the obvious difficulties of drilling in deep water, an ocean site offers most promise. Above the Moho lies the crust of the earth, composed of relatively light rocks, below it the mantle, a layer some 1800 miles thick enclosing the hot core of the earth. The composition of the crust is not fully known and the nature of the mantle can be de-duced only by the most indirect methods. To penetrate these regions and bring back actual samples would therefore be an enormous step forward in understanding the nature of our earth, and would even advance our knowledge of the universe, since the deep structure of the earth may be assumed to be like that of other planets.

As we learn more about the sea through the combined studies of many specialists a new concept that is gradually taking form will almost certainly be strengthened. Even a decade or so ago it was the fashion to speak of the abyss as a place of eternal calm, its black recesses undisturbed by any movement of water more active than a slowly creeping current, a place isolated from the surface and from the very different world of the shallow sea. This picture is rapidly being replaced by one that shows the deep sea as a place of movement and change, an idea that is far more exciting and that possesses deep significance for some of the most pressing problems of our time.

In the new and more dynamic concept, the floor of the deep sea is shaped by racing turbidity currents or mud flows that pour down the slopes of the ocean basins at high speed; it is visited by submarine landslides and stirred by internal tides. The crests and ridges of some of the undersea mountains are swept bare of sediments by currents whose action, in the words of geologist Bruce Heezen, is comparable to "snow avalanches in the Alps (which) sweep down and smother the relief of the lower slopes."

Far from being isolated from the continents and the shallow seas that surround them, the abyssal plains are now known to receive sediments from the margins of the continents. The effect of the turbidity currents, over the vast stretches of geologic time, is to fill the trenches and the hollows of the abyssal floor with sediment. This concept helps us understand certain hitherto puzzling occurrences. Why, for example, have deposits of sand—surely a product of coastal erosion and the grinding of surf—appeared on the mid-ocean floor? Why have sediments at the mouths of submarine canyons, where they communicate with the abyss, been found to contain such reminders of the land as bits of wood and leaves, and why are there sands containing nuts, twigs, and the bark of trees even farther out on the plains of the abyss? In the powerful downrush of sediment-laden currents, triggered by storms or floods or earthquakes, we now have a mechanism that accounts for these once mysterious facts.

Although the beginnings of our present concept of a dynamic sea go back perhaps several decades, it is only the superb in-

struments of the past ten years that have allowed us to glimpse
the hidden movements of ocean waters. Now we suspect that
all those dark regions between the surface and the bottom are
stirred by currents. Even such mighty surface currents as the
Gulf Stream are not quite what we supposed them to be. Instead of a broad and steadily flowing river of water, the Gulf
Stream is now found to consist of narrow racing tongues of
warm water that curl back in swirls and eddies. And below the
surface currents are others unlike them, running at their own
speeds, in their own direction, with their own volume. And
below these are still others. Photographs of the sea bottom
taken at great depths formerly supposed to be eternally still
show ripple marks, a sign that moving waters are sorting over
sediments and carrying away the finer particles. Strong currents
have denuded the crest of much of the vast range of undersea
mountains known as the Atlantic Ridge, and every one of the
sea mounts that has been photographed reveals the work of
deep currents in ripple marks and scour marks.

Other photographs give fresh evidence of life at great depths.
Tracks and trails cross the sea floor and the bottom is studded
with small cones built by unknown forms of life or with holes
inhabited by small burrowers. The Danish research vessel
Galathea brought up living animals in dredges operated at
great depths, where only recently it was supposed life would be
too scanty to permit such sampling.

These findings of the dynamic nature of the sea are not aca-
demic; they are not merely dramatic details of a story that has
interest but no application. They have a direct and immediate
bearing on what has become a major problem of our time.

Although man's record as a steward of the natural resources
of the earth has been a discouraging one, there has long been a
certain comfort in the belief that the sea, at least, was inviolate,
beyond man's ability to change and to despoil. But this belief,
unfortunately, has proved to be naïve. In unlocking the secrets
of the atom, modern man has found himself confronted with a
frightening problem—what to do with the most dangerous
materials that have ever existed in all the earth's history, the by-
products of atomic fission. The stark problem that faces him is
whether he can dispose of these lethal substances without ren-
dering the earth uninhabitable.

No account of the sea today is complete unless it takes note
of this ominous problem. By its very vastness and its seeming
remoteness, the sea has invited the attention of those who have
the problem of disposal, and with very little discussion and
almost no public notice, at least until the late 'fifties, the sea
has been selected as a "natural" burying place for the con-

taminated rubbish and other "low-level wastes" of the Atomic Age. These wastes are placed in barrels lined with concrete and hauled out to sea, where they are dumped overboard at previously designated sites. Some have been taken out 100 miles or more; recently sites only 20 miles offshore have been suggested. In theory the containers are deposited at depths of about 1000 fathoms, but in practice they have at times been placed in much shallower waters. Supposedly the containers have a life of at least 10 years, after which whatever radioactive materials remain will be released to the sea. But again this is only in theory, and a representative of the Atomic Energy Commission, which either dumps the wastes or licenses others to do so, has publicly conceded that the containers are unlikely to maintain "their integrity" while sinking to the bottom. Indeed, in test conducted in California, some have been found to rupture under pressure at only a few hundred fathoms.

But it is only a matter of time until the contents of all such containers already deposited at sea will be free in the ocean waters, along with those yet to come as the applications of atomic science expand. To the packaged wastes so deposited there is now added the contaminated run-off from rivers that are serving as dumping grounds for atomic wastes, and the fallout from the testing of bombs, the greater part of which comes to rest on the vast surface of the sea.

The whole practice, despite protestations of safety by the regulatory agency, rests on the most insecure basis of fact. Oceanographers say they can make "only vague estimates" of the fate of radioactive elements introduced into the deep ocean. They declare that years of intensive study will be needed to provide understanding of what happens when such wastes are deposited in estuaries and coastal waters. As we have seen, all recent knowledge points to far greater activity at all levels of the sea than had ever been guessed at. The deep turbulence, the horizontal movements of vast rivers of ocean water streaming one above another in varying directions, the upwelling of water from the depths carrying with it minerals from the bottom, and the opposite downward sinking of great masses of surface water, all result in a gigantic mixing process that in time will bring about universal distribution of the radioactive contaminants.

And yet the actual transport of radioactive elements by the sea itself is only part of the problem. The concentration and distribution of radioisotopes by marine life may possibly have even greater importance from the standpoint of human hazard. It is known that plants and animals of the sea pick up and concentrate radiochemicals, but only vague information now exists as to details of the process. The minute life of the sea depends for its existence on the minerals in the water. If the normal supply of these is low, the organisms will utilize instead the radioisotope of the needed element if it is present, sometimes concentrating it as much as a million times beyond its abundance in sea water. What happens then to the careful calculation of a "maximum permissible level"? For the tiny organisms are eaten by larger ones and so on up the food chain to man. By such a process tuna over an area of a million square miles surrounding the Bikini bomb test developed a degree of radioactivity enormously higher than that of the sea water.

By their movements and migrations, marine creatures further upset the convenient theory that radioactive wastes remain in the area where they are deposited. The smaller organisms regularly make extensive vertical movements upward toward the surface of the sea at night, downward to great depths by day. And with them goes whatever radioactivity may be adhering to them or may have become incorporated into their bodies. The larger fauna, like fishes, seals, and whales, may migrate over enormous distances, again aiding in spreading and distributing the radioactive elements deposited at sea.

The problem, then, is far more complex and far more hazardous than has been admitted. Even in the comparatively short time since disposal began, research has shown that some of the assumptions on which it was based were dangerously inaccurate. The truth is that disposal has proceeded far more rapidly than our knowledge justifies. To dispose first and investigate later is an invitation to disaster, for once radioactive elements have been deposited at sea they are irretrievable. The mistakes that are made now are made for all time.

It is a curious situation that the sea, from which life first arose, should now be threatened by the activities of one form of that life. But the sea, though changed in a sinister way, will continue to exist; the threat is rather to life itself.

RACHEL CARSON

Silver Spring, Maryland
October 1960

ACKNOWLEDGMENTS

To cope alone and unaided with a subject so vast, so complex, and infinitely mysterious as the sea would be a task not only cheerless but impossible, and I have not attempted it. Instead, on every hand I have been given the most friendly and generous help by those whose work is the foundation and substance of our present knowledge of the sea. Specialists on many problems of the ocean have read chapters dealing with their fields of study and have made comments and suggestions based on their broad understanding. For such constructive help I am indebted to Henry B. Bigelow, Charles F. Brooks, and Henry C. Stetson of Harvard University; Martin W. Johnson, Walter H. Munk, and Francis P. Shepard of the Scripps Institution of Oceanography; Robert Cushman Murphy and Albert Eide Paar of the American Museum of Natural History; Carl O. Dunbar of Yale University; H. A. Marmer of the U.S. Coast and Geodetic Survey; R. C. Hussey of the University of Michigan; George Cohee of the U.S. Geological Survey; and Hilary B. Moore of the University of Miami.

Many others have cheerfully gone to great trouble to help locate elusive documents, have sent me unpublished information and comments, and in many other ways have lightened my task. Among these are H. U. Sverdrup of the Norsk Polarinstitutt in Oslo; L. H. W. Cooper of the Laboratory at Plymouth; Thor Heyerdahl of Oslo; J. W. Christensen, Jens Eggvin, and Gunnar Rollefsen of the Fiskeridirektoratets Havforskingsinstitutt in Bergen; H. Blegvad, Secretary General of the International Council for the Exploration of the Sea; Hans Pettersson of the Oceanografiska Institutet in Göteborg; and, in the United States, John Putnam Marble of the National Research Council; Richard Fleming of the Hydrographic Office; Daniel Merriman of the Bingham Oceanographic Laboratory; Edward H. Smith of the Woods Hole Oceanographic Institution; W. N. Bradley and H. S. Ladd of the U.S. Geological Survey; Maurice Ewing of Columbia University; and F. R. Fosberg of George Washington University.

The front end paper is reproduced from a portion of the map, *Il Mare di Amazones,* by permission of the New York Public Library. H. A. Marmer kindly provided a copy of the old Franklin chart of the Gulf Stream, which is here reproduced as the back end paper. The fathograms on pages 57 and 63 were furnished by the U.S. Fish and Wildlife Service and the U.S. Coast and Geodetic Survey, respectively. The drawings were prepared by Katherine L. Howe.

The library resources of many Government and private institutions have been placed freely at my disposal, and my especial thanks are due Ida K. Johnson, Reference Librarian of the Interior Department Library, whose tireless researches and thorough knowledge of the available literature have been unfailingly helpful.

My absorption in the mystery and meaning of the sea have been stimulated and the writing of this book aided by the friendship and encouragement of William Beebe.

The leisure to write the book and the means of carrying on some of the studies that contributed to it were in large part made possible by the award of the Eugene F. Saxton Memorial Fellowship.

R. L. C.

Silver Spring, Maryland
January 1951

CONTENTS

ILLUSTRATIONS

THE
SEA
AROUND
US

Part I

MOTHER SEA

The Gray Beginnings

AND THE EARTH WAS WITHOUT FORM, AND VOID; AND
DARKNESS WAS UPON THE FACE OF THE DEEP.
—GENESIS

Beginnings are apt to be shadowy, and so it is with the beginnings of that great mother of life, the sea. Many people have debated how and when the earth got its ocean, and it is not surprising that their explanations do not always agree. For the plain and inescapable truth is that no one was there to see, and in the absence of eyewitness accounts there is bound to be a certain amount of disagreement. So if I tell here the story of how the young planet Earth acquired an ocean, it must be a story pieced together from many sources and containing whole chapters the details of which we can only imagine. The story is founded on the testimony of the earth's most ancient rocks, which were young when the earth was young; on other evidence written on the face of the earth's satellite, the moon; and on hints contained in the history of the sun and the whole universe of star-filled space. For although no man was there to witness this cosmic birth, the stars and the moon and the rocks were there, and, indeed, had much to do with the fact that there is an ocean.

19

The events of which I write must have occurred somewhat more than 2 billion years ago. As nearly as science can tell, that is the approximate age of the earth, and the ocean must be very nearly as old. It is possible now to discover the age of the rocks that compose the crust of the earth by measuring the rate of decay of the radioactive materials they contain. The oldest rocks found anywhere on earth—in Manitoba—are about 2.3 billion years old. Allowing 100 million years or so for the cooling of the earth's materials to form a rocky crust, we arrive at the supposition that the tempestuous and violent events connected with our planet's birth occurred nearly 2½ billion years ago. But this is only a minimum estimate, for rocks indicating an even greater age may be found at any time.[1]

The new earth, freshly torn from its parent sun, was a ball of whirling gases, intensely hot, rushing through the black spaces of the universe on a path and at a speed controlled by immense forces. Gradually the ball of flaming gases cooled. The gases began to liquefy, and Earth became a molten mass. The materials of this mass eventually became sorted out in a definite pattern: the heaviest in the center, the less heavy surrounding them, and the least heavy forming the outer rim. This is the pattern which persists today—a central sphere of molten iron, very nearly as hot as it was 2 billion years ago, an intermediate sphere of semiplastic basalt, and a hard outer shell, relatively quite thin and composed of solid basalt and granite.

The outer shell of the young earth must have been a good many millions of years changing from the liquid to the solid state, and it is believed that, before this change was completed, an event of the greatest importance took place—the formation of the moon. The next time you stand on a beach at night, watching the moon's bright path across the water, and conscious of the moon-drawn tides, remember that the moon itself may have been born of a great tidal wave of earthly substance, torn off into space. And remember that if the moon was formed in this fashion, the event may have had much to do with shaping the ocean basins and the continents as we know them.

There were tides in the new earth, long before there was an ocean. In response to the pull of the sun the molten liquids of the earth's whole surface rose in tides that rolled unhindered around the globe and only gradually slackened and diminished as the earthly shell cooled, congealed, and hardened. Those who believe that the moon is a child of Earth say that during an early stage of the earth's development something happened that caused this rolling, viscid tide to gather speed and momentum and to rise to unimaginable heights. Apparently the force that created these greatest tides the earth has ever known was the force of resonance, for at this time the period of the solar tides had come to approach, then equal, the period of the free oscillation of the liquid earth. And so every sun tide was given increased momentum by the push of the earth's oscillation, and each of the twice-daily tides was larger than the one before it. Physicists have calculated that, after 500 years of such monstrous, steadily increasing tides, those on the side toward the sun became too high for stability, and a great wave was torn away and hurled into space. But immediately, of course, the newly created satellite became subject to physical laws that sent it spinning in an orbit of its own about the earth. This is what we call the moon.

There are reasons for believing that this event took place after the earth's crust had become slightly hardened, instead of during its partly liquid state. There is to this day a great scar on the surface of the globe. This scar or depression holds the Pacific Ocean. According to some geophysicists, the floor of the Pacific is composed of basalt, the substance of the earth's middle layer, while all other oceans are floored with a thin layer of granite, which makes up most of the earth's outer layer. We immediately wonder what became of the Pacific's granite covering and the most convenient assumption is that it was torn away when the moon was formed. There is supporting evidence. The mean density of the moon is much less than that of the earth (3.3 compared with 5.5), suggesting that the moon took away none of the earth's heavy iron core, but that it is composed only of the granite and some of the basalt of the outer layers.

The birth of the moon probably helped shape other regions of the world ocean besides the Pacific. When part of the crust was torn away, strains must have been set up in the remaining granite envelope. Perhaps the granite mass cracked open on the side opposite the moon scar. Perhaps, as the earth spun on its axis and rushed on its orbit through space, the cracks widened and the masses of granite began to drift apart, moving over a tarry, slowly hardening layer of basalt. Gradually the outer portions of the basalt layer became solid and the wandering continents came to rest, frozen into place with oceans between them. In spite of theories to the contrary, the weight of geologic evidence seems to be that the locations of the major ocean basins and the major continental land masses are today much the same as they have been since a very early period of the earth's history.

But this is to anticipate the story, for when the moon was born there was no ocean. The gradually cooling earth was enveloped in heavy layers of cloud, which contained much of the water of the new planet. For a long time its surface was so hot that no moisture could fall without immediately being reconverted to steam. This dense, perpetually renewed cloud covering must have been thick enough that no rays of sunlight could penetrate it. And so the rough outlines of the continents and the empty ocean basins were sculptured out of the surface of the earth in darkness, in a Stygian world of heated rock and swirling clouds and gloom.

As soon as the earth's crust cooled enough, the rains began to fall. Never have there been such rains since that time. They fell continuously, day and night, days passing into months, into years, into centuries. They poured into the waiting ocean basins, or, falling upon the continental masses, drained away to become sea.

That primeval ocean, growing in bulk as the rains slowly filled its basins, must have been only faintly salt. But the falling rains were the symbol of the dissolution of the continents. From the moment the rains began to fall, the lands began to be worn away and carried to the sea. It is an endless, inexorable process that has never stopped—the dissolving of the rocks, the leaching out of their contained minerals, the carrying of the rock fragments and dissolved minerals to the ocean. And over the eons of time, the sea has grown ever more bitter with the salt of the continents.

In what manner the sea produced the mysterious and wonderful stuff called protoplasm we cannot say. In its warm, dimly lit waters the unknown conditions of temperature and pressure and saltiness must have been the critical ones for the creation of life from non-life. At any rate they produced the result that neither the alchemists with their crucibles nor modern scientists in their laboratories have been able to achieve.

Before the first living cell was created, there may have been many trials and failures. It seems probable that, within the warm saltiness of the primeval sea, certain organic substances were fashioned from carbon dioxide, sulphur, nitrogen, phosphorus, potassium, and calcium. Perhaps these were transition steps from which the complex molecules of protoplasm arose—molecules that somehow acquired the ability to reproduce themselves and begin the endless stream of life. But at present no one is wise enough to be sure.

Those first living things may have been simple microorganisms rather like some of the bacteria we know today—mysterious borderline forms that were not quite plants, not quite animals, barely over the intangible line that separates the non-living from the living. It is doubtful that this first life possessed the substance chlorophyll, with which plants in sunlight transform lifeless chemicals into the living stuff of their tissues. Little sunshine could enter their dim world, penetrating the cloud banks from which fell the endless rains. Probably the sea's first children lived on the organic substances then present in the ocean waters, or, like the iron and sulphur bacteria that exist today, lived directly on inorganic food.

All the while the cloud cover was thinning, the darkness of the nights alternated with palely illumined days, and finally the sun for the first time shone through upon the sea. By this time some of the living things that floated in the sea must have developed the magic of chlorophyll. Now they were able to take the carbon dioxide of the air and the water of the sea and of these elements, in sunlight, build the organic substances they needed. So the first true plants came into being.

Another group of organisms, lacking the chlorophyll but needing organic food, found they could make a way of life for themselves by devouring the plants. So the first animals arose, and from that day to this, every animal in the world has followed the habit it learned in the ancient seas and depends, directly or through complex food chains, on the plants for food and life.

As the years passed, and the centuries, and the millions of years, the stream of life grew more and more complex. From simple, one-celled creatures, others that were aggregations of specialized cells arose, and then creatures with organs for feeding, digesting, breathing, reproducing. Sponges grew on the rocky bottom of the sea's edge and coral animals built their habitations in warm, clear waters. Jellyfish swam and drifted in the sea. Worms evolved, and starfish, and hard-shelled creatures with many-jointed legs, the arthropods. The plants, too, progressed, from the microscopic algae to branched and curiously fruiting seaweeds that swayed with the tides and were plucked from the coastal rocks by the surf and cast adrift.

During all this time the continents had no life. There was little to induce living things to come ashore, forsaking their all-providing, all-embracing mother sea. The lands must have been bleak and hostile beyond the power of words to describe. Imagine a whole continent of naked rock, across which no covering mantle of green had been drawn—a continent without soil, for there were no land plants to aid in its formation and bind it to the rocks with their roots. Imagine a land of stone, a silent land, except for the sound of the rains and winds that swept across it. For there was no living voice, and no living thing moved over the surface of the rocks.

Meanwhile, the gradual cooling of the planet, which had first given the earth its hard granite crust, was progressing into its deeper layers; and as the interior slowly cooled and contracted, it drew away from the outer shell. This shell, accommodating itself to the shrinking sphere within it, fell into folds and wrinkles—the earth's first mountain ranges.

Geologists tell us that there must have been at least two periods of mountain building (often called 'revolutions') in that dim period, so long ago that the rocks have no record of it, so long ago that the mountains themselves have long since been worn away. Then there came a third great period of upheaval and readjustment of the earth's crust, about a billion years ago, but of all its majestic mountains the only reminders today are the Laurentian hills of eastern Canada, and a great shield of granite over the flat country around Hudson Bay.

The epochs of mountain building only served to speed up the processes of erosion by which the continents were worn down and their crumbling rock and contained minerals returned to the sea. The uplifted masses of the mountains were prey to the bitter cold of the upper atmosphere and under the attacks of frost and snow and ice the rocks cracked and crumbled away. The rains beat with greater violence upon the slopes of the hills and carried away the substance of the mountains in torrential streams. There was still no plant covering to modify and resist the power of the rains.

And in the sea, life continued to evolve. The earliest forms have left no fossils by which we can identify them. Probably they were soft-bodied, with no hard parts that could be preserved. Then, too, the rock layers formed in those early days have since been so altered by enormous heat and pressure, under the foldings of the earth's crust, that any fossils they might have contained would have been destroyed.

For the past 500 million years, however, the rocks have preserved the fossil record. By the dawn of the Cambrian period, when the history of living things was first inscribed on rock pages, life in the sea had progressed so far that all the main groups of backboneless or invertebrate animals had been developed. But there were no animals with backbones, no insects or spiders, and still no plant or animal had been evolved that was capable of venturing onto the forbidding land. So for more than three-fourths of geologic time the continents were desolate and uninhabited, while the sea prepared the life that was later to invade them and make them habitable. Meanwhile, with violent tremblings of the earth and with the fire and smoke of roaring volcanoes, mountains rose and wore away, glaciers moved to and fro over the earth, and the sea crept over the continents and again receded.

It was not until Silurian time, some 350 million years ago, that the first pioneer of land life crept out on the shore. It was an arthropod, one of the great tribe that later produced crabs and lobsters and insects. It must have been something like a modern scorpion, but, unlike some of its descendants, it never wholly severed the ties that united it to the sea. It lived a strange life, half-terrestrial, half-aquatic, something like that of the ghost crabs that speed along the beaches today, now and then dashing into the surf to moisten their gills.

Fish, tapered of body and stream-molded by the press of running waters, were evolving in Silurian rivers. In times of drought, in the drying pools and lagoons, the shortage of oxygen forced them to develop swim bladders for the storage of air. One form that possessed an air-breathing lung was able to survive the dry periods by burying itself in mud, leaving a passage to the surface through which it breathed.

It is very doubtful that the animals alone would have succeeded in colonizing the land, for only the plants had the power to bring about the first amelioration of its harsh conditions. They helped make soil of the crumbling rocks, they held back the soil from the rains that would have swept it away, and little by little they softened and subdued the bare rock, the lifeless desert. We know very little about the first land plants, but they must have been closely related to some of the larger seaweeds that had learned to live in the coastal shallows, developing strengthened stems and grasping, rootlike holdfasts to resist the drag and pull of the waves. Perhaps it was in some coastal lowlands, periodically drained and flooded, that some such plants found it possible to survive, though separated from the sea. This also seems to have taken place in the Silurian period.

The mountains that had been thrown up by the Laurentian revolution gradually wore away, and as the sediments were

ERAS	PERIODS c. millions years ago (Holmes Scale) (Revised 1959)	Mountains	Volcanoes
CENOZOIC	Pleistocene 0—1	Coast ranges, western United States; this disturbance probably still in progress	
CENOZOIC	Tertiary 1—70	Alps, Himalayas, Apennines, Pyrenees, Caucasus	Great vulcanism in western United States formed Columbia Plateau (200,000 square miles of lava) Vesuvius and Etna began to erupt
MESOZOIC	Cretaceous 70—135	Rocky Mountains, Andes Rising of Panama Ridge indirect result — Gulf Stream	
MESOZOIC	Jurassic 135—180	Sierra Nevadas	
MESOZOIC	Triassic 180—225		Many volcanoes in western North America, also in New England
PALEOZOIC	Permian 225—270	Appalachians south of New England	Volcanic outpourings produced Deccan Plateau of India
PALEOZOIC	Carboniferous 270—350		
PALEOZOIC	Devonian 350—400	Northern Appalachians (this area never again covered by sea)	
PALEOZOIC	Silurian 400—440	Caledonian Mountains (Great Britain, Scandinavia, Greenland — only their roots remain)	Volcanoes in Maine and New Brunswick
PALEOZOIC	Ordovician 440—500		
PALEOZOIC	Cambrian 500—600		
PROTERO-ZOIC	600—3000±	Grenville Mountains of eastern North America (only their roots remain)— age 1000 million Penokean Mountains (Minnesota, Ontario) formerly Killarney—age 1700 million	
ARCHEO-ZOIC	3000±	Earliest known mountains (laurentian of Minnesota and Ontario—only traces remain—age 3600 million Earliest known sedimentary and volcanic rocks, much altered by heat and pressure, their history obscure	

Glaciers	Seas	DEVELOPMENT OF LIFE
Pleistocene glaciation — ice sheets over vast areas of North America and northern Europe	Sea level fluctuating because of glaciers	Rise of man Modern plants and animals
	Great submergence of lands Nummulitic limestone formed — later used in Pyramids	Higher mammals, except man Highest plants
	North of Europe and about half of North America submerged. Chalk cliffs of England formed	Last of dinosaurs and flying reptiles Reptiles dominant on land
	Last invasion of sea into eastern California and Oregon	First birds
		First dinosaurs Some reptiles return to sea Small, primitive mammals
Glaciers in broad equatorial belt India, Africa, Australia, South America	Extensive seas over western United States world's largest salt deposits formed in Germany	Primitive reptiles Amphibians declining Earliest cycads and conifers
	Central United States covered by sea for last time. Great coal beds formed	Amphibians developing rapidly First insects Coal-making plants
		Fishes dominate seas First amphibians (too?)
	Repeated invasions by sea. Salt beds formed in eastern United States	First life appeared on continents
	Greatest known submergence of North America — more than half of continent covered	Earliest known vertebrates Cephalopods common in seas
	Seas advance and withdraw, at one time covering most of United States	First clear fossil record dates from this period; all major groups of invertebrates established
Earliest known ice ages		Rise of invertebrates (inferred)
		Earliest life (inferred)

Chart of the History of the Earth and Its Life

washed from their summits and deposited on the lowlands, great areas of the continents sank under the load. The seas crept out of their basins and spread over the lands. Life fared well and was exceedingly abundant in those shallow, sunlit seas. But with the later retreat of the ocean water into the deeper basins, many creatures must have been left stranded in shallow, landlocked bays. Some of these animals found means to survive on land. The lakes, the shores of the rivers, and the coastal swamps of those days were the testing grounds in which plants and animals either became adapted to the new conditions or perished.

As the lands rose and the seas receded, a strange fishlike creature emerged on the land, and over the thousands of years its fins became legs, and instead of gills it developed lungs. In the Devonian sandstone this first amphibian left its footprint.

On land and sea the stream of life poured on. New forms evolved; some old ones declined and disappeared. On land the mosses and the ferns and the seed plants developed. The reptiles for a time dominated the earth, gigantic, grotesque, and terrifying. Birds learned to live and move in the ocean of air. The first small mammals lurked inconspicuously in hidden crannies of the earth as though in fear of the reptiles.

When they went ashore the animals that took up a land life carried with them a part of the sea in their bodies, a heritage which they passed on to their children and which even today links each land animal with its origin in the ancient sea. Fish, amphibian, and reptile, warm-blooded bird and mammal—each of us carries in our veins a salty stream in which the elements sodium, potassium, and calcium are combined in almost the same proportions as in sea water. This is our inheritance from the day, untold millions of years ago, when a remote ancestor, having progressed from the one-celled to the many-celled stage, first developed a circulatory system in which the fluid was merely the water of the sea. In the same way, our lime-hardened skeletons are a heritage from the calcium-rich ocean of Cambrian time. Even the protoplasm that streams within each cell of our bodies has the chemical structure impressed upon all living matter when the first simple creatures were brought forth in the ancient sea. And as life itself began in the sea, so each of us begins his individual life in a miniature ocean within his mother's womb, and in the stages of his embryonic development repeats the steps by which his race evolved, from gill-breathing inhabitants of a water world to creatures able to live on land.

Some of the land animals later returned to the ocean. After perhaps 50 million years of land life, a number of reptiles entered the sea about 170 million years ago, in the Triassic period. They were huge and formidable creatures. Some had oarlike limbs by which they rowed through the water; some were web-footed, with long, serpentine necks. These grotesque monsters disappeared millions of years ago, but we remember them when we come upon a large sea turtle swimming many miles at sea, its barnacle-encrusted shell eloquent of its marine life. Much later, perhaps no more than 50 million years ago, some of the mammals, too, abandoned a land life for the ocean. Their descendants are the sea lions, seals, sea elephants, and whales of today.

Among the land mammals there was a race of creatures that took to an arboreal existence. Their hands underwent remarkable development, becoming skilled in manipulating and examining objects, and along with this skill came a superior brain power that compensated for what these comparatively small mammals lacked in strength. At last, perhaps somewhere in the vast interior of Asia, they descended from the trees and became again terrestrial. The past million years have seen their transformation into beings with the body and brain and spirit of man.

Eventually man, too, found his way back to the sea. Standing on its shores, he must have looked out upon it with wonder and curiosity, compounded with an unconscious recognition of his lineage. He could not physically re-enter the ocean as the seals and whales had done. But over the centuries, with all the skill and ingenuity and reasoning powers of his mind, he has sought to explore and investigate even its most remote parts, so that he might re-enter it mentally and imaginatively.

He built boats to venture out on its surface. Later he found ways to descend to the shallow parts of its floor, carrying with him the air that, as a land mammal long unaccustomed to aquatic life, he needed to breathe. Moving in fascination over the deep sea he could not enter, he found ways to probe its depths, he let down nets to capture its life, he invented mechanical eyes and ears that could re-create for his senses a world long lost, but a world that, in the deepest part of his subconscious mind, he had never wholly forgotten.

And yet he has returned to his mother sea only on her own terms. He cannot control or change the ocean as, in his brief tenancy of earth, he has subdued and plundered the continents. In the artificial world of his cities and towns, he often forgets the true nature of his planet and the long vistas of its history, in which the existence of the race of men has occupied a mere moment of time. The sense of all these things comes to him most clearly in the course of a long ocean voyage, when he watches day after day the receding rim of the horizon, ridged and furrowed by waves; when at night he becomes aware of the earth's rotation as the stars pass overhead; or when, alone in this world of water and sky, he feels the loneliness of his earth in space. And then, as never on land, he knows the truth that his world is a water world, a planet dominated by its covering mantle of ocean, in which the continents are but transient intrusions of land above the surface of the all-encircling sea.

The Pattern of the Surface

THERE IS, ONE KNOWS NOT WHAT SWEET MYSTERY ABOUT
THIS SEA, WHOSE GENTLY AWFUL STIRRINGS SEEM
TO SPEAK OF SOME HIDDEN SOUL BENEATH.
—HERMAN MELVILLE

Nowhere in all the sea does life exist in such bewildering abundance as in the surface waters. From the deck of a vessel you may look down, hour after hour, on the shimmering discs of jellyfish, their gently pulsating bells dotting the surface as far as you can see. Or one day you may notice early in the morning that you are passing through a sea that has taken on a brick-red color from billions upon billions of microscopic creatures, each of which contains an orange pigment granule. At noon you are still moving through red seas, and when darkness falls the waters shine with an eerie glow from the phosphorescent fires of yet more billions and trillions of these same creatures.

And again you may glimpse not only the abundance but something of the fierce uncompromisingness of sea life when, as you look over the rail and down, down into water of a clear, deep green, suddenly there passes a silver shower of finger-long fishlets. The sun strikes a metallic gleam from their flanks as they streak by, driving deeper into the green depths with the desperate speed of the hunted. Perhaps you never see the hunters, but you sense their presence as you see the gulls hovering, with eager, mewing cries, waiting for the little fish to be driven to the surface.

Or again, perhaps, you may sail for days on end without seeing anything you could recognize as life or the indications of life, day after day of empty water and empty sky, and so you may reasonably conclude that there is no spot on earth so barren of life as the open ocean. But if you had the opportunity to tow a fine-meshed net through the seemingly lifeless water and then to examine the washings of the net, you would find that life is scattered almost everywhere through the surface waters like a fine dust. A cupful

31

of water may contain millions upon millions of diatoms, tiny plant cells, each of them far too small to be seen by the human eye; or it may swarm with an infinitude of animal creatures, none larger than a dust mote, which live on plant cells still smaller than themselves.

If you could be close to the surface waters of the ocean at night, you would realize that then they are alive with myriads of strange creatures never seen by day. They are alive with the moving lamps of small shrimplike beings that spend the daylight hours in the gloom of deep water, and with the shadowy forms of hungry fish and the dark shapes of squid. These things were seen, as few men have seen them, by the Norwegian ethnologist Thor Heyerdahl in the course of one of the most unusual journeys of modern times. In the summer of 1947 Heyerdahl and five companions drifted 4300 miles across the Pacific on a raft of balsa logs, to test a theory that the original inhabitants of Polynesia might have come from South America by raft. For 101 days and nights these men lived practically on the surface of the sea, driven by the trade wind, carried on the strong drift of the Equatorial Current, as much a part of the inexorable westward movement of wind and water as the creatures of the sea. Because of his enviable opportunity to observe the life of the surface while living as an actual part of it for so many weeks, I asked Mr. Heyerdahl about some of his impressions, especially of the sea at night, and he has written me as follows:

Chiefly at night, but occasionally in broad daylight, a shoal of small squids shot out of the water precisely like flying fish, gliding through the air as much as up to six feet above the surface, until they lost the speed accumulated below water, and fell down helplessly. In their gliding flight with flaps out they were so much like small flying fish at a distance, that we had no idea we saw anything unusual until a live squid flew right into one of the crew and fell down on deck. Almost every night we found one or two on the deck or on the roof of the bamboo hut.

It was my own definite impression that the marine life in general went deeper down in the daytime than during the nights, and that the darker the night was, the more life we had around us. At two different occasions, a snake-mackerel, Gempylus, never before seen by man except as skeletal remains washed ashore on South America and the Galapagos, came jumping clear out of the water and right up on the raft (once right into the hut). To judge from the huge eyes and the fact that the fish has never before been observed, I am inclined to suspect that it is a deep-sea fish that comes to the surface only at night.

On dark nights we could see much marine life which we were unable to identify. They seemed to be deep-sea fishes approaching the surface at night. Generally we saw it as vaguely phosphorescent bodies, often the size and shape of a dinner plate, but at least one night in the shape of three immense bodies of irregular and changing shape and dimensions which appeared to exceed those of the raft (KON-TIKI measured about 45 by 18 feet). Apart from these greater bodies, we observed occasionally great quantities of phosphorescent plankton, often containing illuminating copepods up to the size of a millimeter or more.

With these surface waters, through a series of delicately adjusted, interlocking relationships, the life of all parts of the sea is linked. What happens to a diatom in the upper, sunlit strata of the sea may well determine what happens to a cod lying on a ledge of some rocky canyon a hundred fathoms below, or to a bed of multicolored, gorgeously plumed seaworms carpeting an underlying shoal, or to a prawn creeping over the soft oozes of the sea floor in the blackness of mile-deep water.

The activities of the microscopic vegetables of the sea, of which the diatoms are most important, make the mineral wealth of the water available to the animals. Feeding directly on the diatoms and other groups of minute unicellular algae are the marine protozoa, many crustaceans, the young of crabs, barnacles, sea worms, and fishes. Hordes of the small carnivores, the first link in the chain of flesh eaters, move among these peaceful grazers. There are fierce little dragons half an inch long, the sharp-jawed arrowworms. There are gooseberrylike comb jellies, armed with grasping tentacles, and there are the shrimplike euphausiids that strain food from the water with their bristly appendages. Since they drift where the currents carry them, with no power or will to oppose that of the sea, this strange community of creatures and the marine plants that sustain them are called 'plankton,' a word derived from the Greek, meaning 'wandering.'

From the plankton the food chains lead on, to the schools of plankton-feeding fishes like the herring, menhaden, and mackerel; to the fish-eating fishes like the bluefish and tuna and sharks; to the pelagic squids that prey on fishes; to the great whales who, according to their species but not according to their size, may live on fishes, on shrimps, or on some of the smallest of the plankton creatures.

Unmarked and trackless though it may seem to us, the surface of the ocean is divided into definite zones, and the pattern of the surface water controls the distribution of its life. Fishes and plankton, whales and squids, birds and sea turtles, all are linked by unbreakable ties to certain kinds of water—to warm water or cold water, to clear or turbid water, to water rich in phosphates or in silicates. For the animals higher in the food chains the ties are less direct; they are bound to water where their food is plentiful, and the food animals are there because the water conditions are right.

The change from zone to zone may be abrupt. It may come upon us unseen, as our ship at night crosses an invisible boundary line. So Charles Darwin on H.M.S. *Beagle* one dark night off the coast of South America crossed from tropical water into that of the cool south. Instantly the vessel was surrounded by numerous seals and penguins, which made such a bedlam of strange noises that the officer on watch was deceived into thinking the ship had, by some miscalculation, run close inshore, and that the sounds he heard were the bellowing of cattle.

To the human senses, the most obvious patterning of the surface waters is indicated by color. The deep blue water of the open sea far from land is the color of emptiness and barrenness; the green water of the coastal areas, with all its varying hues, is the color of life. The sea is blue because the sunlight is reflected back to our eyes from the water molecules or from very minute particles suspended in the sea. In the journey of the light rays into deep water all the red rays and most of the yellow rays of the spectrum have been absorbed, so when the light returns to our eyes it is chiefly the cool blue rays that we see. Where the water is rich in plankton, it loses the glassy transparency that permits this deep penetration of the light rays. The yellow and brown and green hues of the coastal waters are derived from the minute algae and other microorganisms so abundant there. Seasonal abundance of certain forms containing reddish or brown pigments may cause the 'red water' known from ancient times in many parts of the world, and so common in this condition in some enclosed seas that they owe their names to it—the Red Sea and the Vermilion Sea are examples.

The colors of the sea are only the indirect signs of the presence or absence of conditions needed to support the surface life; other zones, invisible to the eye, are the ones that largely determine where marine creatures may live. For the sea is by no means a uniform solution of water; parts of it are more salty than others, and parts are warmer or colder.

The saltiest ocean water in the world is that of the Red Sea, where the burning sun and the fierce heat of the atmosphere produce such rapid evaporation that the salt content is 40 parts per thousand. The Sargasso Sea, an area of high air temperatures, receiving no inflow of river water or melting ice because of its remoteness from land, is the saltiest part of the Atlantic, which in turn is the saltiest of the oceans. The polar seas, as one would expect, are the least salty, because they are constantly being diluted by rain, snow, and melting ice. Along the Atlantic coast of the United States, the salinity range from about 33 parts per thousand off Cape Cod to about 36 off Florida is a difference easily perceptible to the senses of human bathers.

Ocean temperatures vary from about 28° F. in polar seas to 96° in the Persian Gulf, which contains the hottest ocean water in the world. To creatures of the sea, which with few exceptions must match in their own bodies the temperature of the surrounding water, this range is tremendous, and change of temperature is probably the most important single condition that controls the distribution of marine animals.

The beautiful reef corals are a perfect example of the way the inhabitable areas for any particular class of creatures may be established by temperatures. If you took a map of the world and drew a line 30° north of the equator and another 30° south of it, you would have outlined in general the waters where reef corals are found at the present time. It is true that the remains of ancient coral reefs have been discovered in arctic waters, but this means that in some past ages the climate of these northern seas was tropical. The calcareous structure of the coral reef can be fashioned only in water at least as warm as 70° Fahrenheit. We would have to make one northward extension of our map, where the Gulf Stream carries water warm enough for corals to Bermuda, at 32° north latitude. On the other hand, within our tropical belt, we would have to erase large areas on the west coasts of South America and Africa, where upwelling of cold water from lower ocean levels prevents the growth of corals. Most of the east coast of Florida has no coral reefs because of a cool inshore current, running southward between the coast and the Gulf Stream.

As between tropical and polar regions, the differences in the kinds and abundance of life are tremendous. The warm temperatures of the tropics speed up the processes of reproduction and growth, so that many generations are produced in the time required to bring one to maturity in cold seas. There is more opportunity for genetic mutations to be produced within a given time; hence the bewildering variety of tropical life. Yet in any species there are far fewer individuals than in the colder zones, where the mineral content of the water is richer, and there are no dense swarms of surface plankton, like the copepods of the Arctic. The pelagic, or free-swimming, forms of the tropics live deeper than those of the colder regions, and so there is less food for large surface-feeders. In the tropics, therefore, the sea birds do not compare in abundance with the clouds of shearwaters, fulmars, auks, whalebirds, albatrosses, and other birds seen over far northern or far southern fishing grounds.

In the cold-water communities of the polar seas, fewer of the animals have swimming larvae. Generation after generation settle down near the parents, so that large areas of bottom may be covered with the descendants of a very few animals. In the Barents Sea a research vessel once brought up more than a ton of one of the siliceous sponges at a single haul, and enormous patches of a single species of annelid worm carpet the east coast of Spitsbergen. Copepods and swimming snails fill the surface waters of the cold seas, and lure the herring and the mackerel, the flocks of sea birds, the whale, and the seals.

In the tropics, then, sea life is intense, vivid, and infinitely varied. In cold seas it proceeds at a pace slowed by the icy water in which it exists, but the mineral richness of these waters (largely a result of seasonal overturn and consequent mixing) makes possible the enormous abundance of the forms that inhabit them. For a good many years it has been said categorically that the total productivity of the colder temperate and polar seas is far greater than the tropical. Now it is becoming plain that there are important exceptions to this statement. In certain tropical and subtropical waters, there are areas where the sheer abundance of life rivals the Grand Banks or the Barents Sea or any antarctic whaling ground. Perhaps the best examples are the Humboldt Current, off the west coast of South America, and the Benguela Current, off the west coast of Africa. In both currents, upwelling of cold, mineral-laden water from deeper layers of the sea provides the fertilizing elements to sustain the great food chains. And wherever two currents meet, especially if they differ sharply in temperature or salinity, there are zones of great turbulence and unrest, with water sinking or rising up from the depths and with shifting eddies and foam lines at the surface. At such places the richness and abundance of marine life reveals itself most strikingly. This changing life, seen as his ship cut across the pathways of the great currents of the Pacific and the Atlantic, was described with vivid detail by S. C. Brooks:

Within a few degrees of the equator, the scattered cumulus clouds become thicker and grayer, a confused swell makes up, rain squalls come and go, and birds appear. At first there is only a greater abundance of storm petrels, with here and there petrels of other kinds hunting along utterly indifferent to the ship, or small groups of tropic birds flying along with the ship, off to one side or high overhead. Then scattered groups of various petrels appear, and finally for an hour or two there are birds on every hand. If one is not too far from land, a few hundred miles perhaps, as in the case of the south equatorial drift north of the Marquesas, one may also see multitudes of sooty or crested terns. Occasionally one sees the grayish blue form of a shark gliding along, or a big purplish-brown hammerhead lazily twisting around as though trying to get a better view of the ship. Flying fish, while not so closely localized as the birds, are breaking the water every few seconds, and bewitch the beholder by their myriad sizes, shapes, and antics, and their bewildering patterns and shades of deep brown, opal blue, yellow and purple. Then the sun comes out again, the sea takes on its deep tropical blue, the birds become more and more scarce, and gradually, as the ship moves on, the ocean resumes its desert aspect.

If it were daylight all the time, this same sequence might be seen in a more or less striking fashion twice or perhaps even three or four times. Inquiry soon reveals that this sequence marks the time of passing the edge of one of the great currents . . .

In the North Atlantic ship lanes the same play is staged with different actors. Instead of the equatorial currents there are the Gulf Stream and its continuation, the North Atlantic Drift, and the Arctic Current; instead of confused swell and squalls of rain there are slicks and fogs. Tropic-birds are replaced by jaegers and skuas; and different species of the petrel group, usually here spoken of as shearwaters and fulmars, are flying or swimming about, often in great flocks . . . Here, too, perhaps, one sees less of sharks and more of porpoise racing with the cut-water or doggedly hurrying, school after school, toward some unguessable objective. The flashing black and white of the young orcas, or the distant sudden spurt and lazy drift of a whale's spouting, lend life to the water, as do the antics of flying fish, distant though they be from their traditional home in the tropics . . . One may pass from the blue water of the Stream, with floating gulf weed (Sargassum), and perhaps here and there the iridescent float of a Portuguese man-of-war, into the gray-green water of the Arctic Current with its thousands of jelly fish, and in a few hours back again into the Stream. Each time, at the margin, one is likely to see the surface display of that abundance of life which has made the Grand Banks one of the great fisheries of the world.*

The mid-ocean regions, bounded by the currents that sweep around the ocean basins, are in general the deserts of the sea. There are few birds and few surface-feeding fishes, and indeed there is little surface plankton to attract them. The life of these regions is largely confined to deep water. The Sargasso Sea is an exception, not matched in the anticyclonic centers of other ocean basins. It is so different from any other place on earth that it may well be considered a definite geographic region. A line drawn from the mouth of Chesapeake Bay to Gibraltar would skirt its northern border; another from Haiti to Dakar would mark its southern boundary. It lies all about Bermuda and extends more than halfway across the Atlantic, its entire area being roughly as large as the United States. The Sargasso, with all its legendary terrors for sailing ships, is a creation of the great currents of the North Atlantic that encircle it and bring into it the millions of tons of floating sargassum weed from which the place derives its name, and all the weird assemblage of animals that live in the weed.

The Sargasso is a place forgotten by the winds, undisturbed by the strong flow of waters that girdle it as with a river. Under the seldom-clouded skies, its waters are warm and heavy with salt. Separated widely from coastal rivers and from polar ice, there is no inflow of fresh water to dilute its saltiness; the only influx is of saline water from the adjacent currents, especially from the Gulf Stream or North Atlantic Current as it crosses from America to Europe. And with the little, inflowing streams of surface water come the plants and animals that for months or years have drifted in the Gulf Stream.

The sargassum weeds are brown algae belonging to several species. Quantities of the weeds live attached to reefs or rocky outcroppings off the coasts of the West Indies and Florida. Many of the plants are torn away by storms, especially during the hurricane season. They are picked up by the Gulf Stream and are drifted northward. With the weeds go, as involuntary passengers, many small fishes, crabs, shrimps, and innumerable larvae of assorted species of marine creatures, whose home had been the coastal banks of sargassum weed.

Curious things happen to the animals that have ridden on the sargassum weed into a new home. Once they lived near the sea's edge, a few feet or a few fathoms below the surface, but never far above a firm bottom. They knew the rhythmic movements of waves and tides. They could leave the shelter of the weeds at will and creep or swim about over the bottom in search of food. Now, in the middle of the ocean, they are in a new world. The bottom lies two or three miles below them. Those who are poor swimmers must cling to the weed, which now represents a life raft, supporting them above the abyss. Over the ages since their ancestors came here, some species have developed special organs of attachment, either for themselves or for their eggs, so that they may not sink into the cold, dark water far below. The flying fish make nests of the weed to contain their eggs, which bear an amazing resemblance to the sargassum floats or 'berries.'

Indeed, many of the little marine beasts of the weedy jungle seem to be playing an elaborate game of disguise in which each is camouflaged to hide it from the others. The Sargasso sea slug—a snail without a shell—has a soft, shapeless brown body spotted with dark-edged circles and fringed with flaps and folds of skin, so that as it creeps over the weed in search of prey it can scarcely be distinguished from the vegetation. One of the fiercest carnivores of the place, the sargassum fish Pterophryne, has copied with utmost fidelity the branching fronds of the weed, its golden berries, its rich brown color, and even the white dots of encrusting worm tubes. All these elaborate bits of mimicry are indications of the fierce internecine wars of the Sargasso jungles, which go on without quarter and without mercy for the weak or the unwary.

In the science of the sea there has been a long-standing

controversy about the origin of the drifting weeds of the
Sargasso Sea. Some have held that the supply is maintained
by weeds recently torn away from coastal beds; others say
that the rather limited sargassum fields of the West Indies
and Florida cannot possibly supply the immense area of
the Sargasso. They believe that we find here a self-perpetuat-
ing community of plants that have become adapted to life
in the open sea, needing no roots or holdfasts for attachment, and able to propagate vegetatively. Probably there is
truth in both ideas. New plants do come in each year in
small numbers, and now cover an immense area because
of their very long life once they have reached this quiet
central region of the Atlantic.

It takes about half a year for the plants torn from West
Indian shores to reach the northern border of the Sargasso,
perhaps several years for them to be carried into the inner
parts of this area. Meanwhile, some have been swept onto
the shores of North America by storms, others have been
killed by cold during the passage from offshore New England across the Atlantic, where the Gulf Stream comes into
contact with waters from the Arctic. For the plants that
reach the calm of the Sargasso, there is virtual immortality.
A. E. Parr of the American Museum has recently suggested
that the individual plants may live, some for decades, other
for centuries, according to their species. It might well be
that some of the very weeds you would see if you visited
the place today were seen by Columbus and his men. Here,
in the heart of the Atlantic, the weed drifts endlessly, growing, reproducing vegetatively by a process of fragmentation.
Apparently almost the only plants that die are the ones
that drift into unfavorable conditions around the edges of
the Sargasso or are picked up by outward-moving currents.

Such losses are balanced, or possibly a little more than
balanced, by the annual addition of weeds from distant
coasts. It must have taken eons of time to accumulate the
present enormous quantities of weed, which Parr estimates
as about 10 million tons. But this, of course, is distributed
over so large an area that most of the Sargasso is open water.
The dense fields of weeds waiting to entrap a vessel never
existed except in the imaginations of sailors, and the gloomy
hulks of vessels doomed to endless drifting in the clinging
weed are only the ghosts of things that never were.

The Changing Year

For the sea as a whole, the alternation of day and night, the passage of the seasons, the procession of the years, are lost in its vastness, obliterated in its own changeless eternity. But the surface waters are different. The face of the sea is always changing. Crossed by colors, lights, and moving shadows, sparkling in the sun, mysterious in the twilight, its aspects and its moods vary hour by hour. The surface waters move with the tides, stir to the breath of the winds, and rise and fall to the endless, hurrying forms of the waves. Most of all, they change with the advance of the seasons. Spring moves over the temperate lands of our Northern Hemisphere in a tide of new life, of pushing green shoots and unfolding buds, all its mysteries and meanings symbolized in the northward migration of the birds, the awakening of sluggish amphibian life as the chorus of frogs rises again from the wet lands, the different sound of the wind which stirs the young leaves where a month ago it rattled the bare branches. These things we associate with the land, and it is easy to suppose that at sea there could be no such feeling of advancing spring. But the signs are there, and seen with understanding eye, they bring the same magical sense of awakening.

In the sea, as on land, spring is a time for the renewal of life. During the long months of winter in the temperate zones the surface waters have been absorbing the cold. Now the heavy water begins to sink, slipping down and displacing the warmer layers below. Rich stores of minerals have been accumulating on the floor of the continental shelf—some freighted down the rivers from the lands; some derived from sea creatures that have died and whose remains have drifted down to the bottom; some from the shells that once encased a diatom, the streaming protoplasm of a radiolarian, or the transparent tissues of a pteropod. Nothing is wasted in the sea; every particle of material is used over and over again, first by one creature, then by another. And when in spring the waters are deeply stirred, the warm bottom water brings to the surface a rich supply of minerals, ready for use by new forms of life.

Just as land plants depend on minerals in the soil for their growth, every marine plant, even the smallest, is dependent upon the nutrient salts or minerals in the sea water. Diatoms must have silica, the element of which their fragile shells are fashioned. For these and all other microplants, phosphorus is an indispensable mineral. Some of these elements are in short supply and in winter may be reduced below the minimum necessary for growth. The diatom population must tide itself over this season as best it can. It faces a stark problem of survival, with no opportunity to increase, a problem of keeping alive the spark of life by forming tough protective spores against the stringency of winter, a matter of existing in a dormant state in which no demands shall be made on an environment that already withholds all but the most meager necessities of life. So the diatoms hold their place in the winter sea, like seeds of wheat in a field under snow and ice, the seeds from which the spring growth will come.

These, then, are the elements of the vernal blooming of the sea: the 'seeds' of the dormant plants, the fertilizing chemicals, the warmth of the spring sun.

In a sudden awakening, incredible in its swiftness, the simplest plants of the sea begin to multiply. Their increase is of astronomical proportions. The spring sea belongs at first to the diatoms and to all the other microscopic plant life of the plankton. In the fierce intensity of their growth they cover vast areas of ocean with a living blanket of their cells. Mile after mile of water may appear red or brown or green, the whole surface taking on the color of the infinitesimal grains of pigment contained in each of the plant cells.

The plants have undisputed sway in the sea for only a short time. Almost at once their own burst of multiplication is matched by a similar increase in the small animals of the plankton. It is the spawning time of the copepod and the glassworm, the pelagic shrimp and the winged snail. Hungry swarms of these little beasts of the plankton roam through the waters, feeding on the abundant plants and themselves falling prey to larger creatures. Now in the spring the surface waters become a vast nursery. From the hills and valleys of the continent's edge lying far below, and from the scat-

tered shoals and banks, the eggs or young of many of the
bottom animals rise to the surface of the sea. Even those
which, in their maturity, will sink down to a sedentary life
on the bottom, spend the first weeks of life as freely swimming hunters of the plankton. So as spring progresses new
batches of larvae rise into the surface each day, the young
of fishes and crabs and mussels and tube worms, mingling for
a time with the regular members of the plankton.

Under the steady and voracious grazing, the grasslands
of the surface are soon depleted. The diatoms become more
and more scarce, and with them the other simple plants.
Still there are brief explosions of one or another form, when
in a sudden orgy of cell division it comes to claim whole
areas of the sea for its own. So, for a time each spring, the
waters may become blotched with brown, jellylike masses,
and the fishermen's nets come up dripping a brown slime and
containing no fish, for the herring have turned away from
these waters as though in loathing of the viscid, foul-smelling
algae. But in less time than passes between the full moon
and the new, the spring flowering of Phaeocystis is past and
the waters have cleared again.

In the spring the sea is filled with migrating fishes, some of
them bound for the mouths of great rivers, which they will
ascend to deposit their spawn. Such are the spring-run
chinooks coming in from the deep Pacific feeding grounds to
breast the rolling flood of the Columbia, the shad moving in
to the Chesapeake and the Hudson and the Connecticut, the
alewives seeking a hundred coastal streams of New England, the salmon feeling their way to the Penobscot and the
Kennebec. For months or years these fish have known only
the vast spaces of the ocean. Now the spring sea and the
maturing of their own bodies lead them back to the rivers of
their birth.

Other mysterious comings and goings are linked with the
advance of the year. Capelin gather in the deep, cold water
of the Barents Sea, their shoals followed and preyed upon by
flocks of auks, fulmars, and kittiwakes. Cod approach the
banks of Lofoten, and gather off the shores of Iceland. Birds
whose winter feeding territory may have encompassed the
whole Atlantic or the whole Pacific converge upon some
small island, the entire breeding population arriving within
the space of a few days. Whales suddenly appear off the
slopes of the coastal banks where the swarms of shrimplike
krill are spawning, the whales having come from no one
knows where, by no one knows what route.

With the subsiding of the diatoms and the completed

spawning of many of the plankton animals and most of the
fish, life in the surface waters slackens to the slower pace of
midsummer. Along the meeting places of the currents the
pale moon jelly Aurelia gathers in thousands, forming sin-
uous lines or windrows across miles of sea, and the birds see
their pale forms shimmering deep down in the green water.
By midsummer the large red jellyfish Cyanea may have grown
from the size of a thimble to that of an umbrella. The great
jellyfish moves through the sea with rhythmic pulsations,
trailing long tentacles and as likely as not shepherding a little
group of young cod or haddock, which find shelter under its
bell and travel with it.

A hard, brilliant, coruscating phosphorescence often illumi-
nates the summer sea. In waters where the protozoa Noctiluca
is abundant it is the chief source of this summer luminescence, causing fishes, squids, or dolphins to fill the water with
racing flames and to clothe themselves in a ghostly radiance.
Or again the summer sea may glitter with a thousand thousand
moving pinpricks of light, like an immense swarm of fireflies
moving through a dark wood. Such an effect is produced by a shoal of the brilliantly phosphorescent shrimp
Meganyctiphanes, a creature of cold and darkness and of the
places where icy water rolls upward from the depths and
bubbles with white ripplings at the surface.

Out over the plankton meadows of the North Atlantic the
dry twitter of the phalaropes, small brown birds, wheeling
and turning, dipping and rising, is heard for the first time
since early spring. The phalaropes have nested on the arctic
tundras, reared their young, and now the first of them are returning to the sea. Most of them will continue south over the
open water far from land, crossing the equator into the
South Atlantic. Here they will follow where the great whales
lead, for where the whales are, there also are the swarms of
plankton on which these strange little birds grow fat.

As the fall advances, there are other movements, some
in the surface, some hidden in the green depths, that betoken
the end of summer. In the fog-covered waters of Bering Sea,
down through the treacherous passes between the islands of
the Aleutian chain and southward into the open Pacific, the
herds of fur seals are moving. Left behind are two small
islands, treeless bits of volcanic soil thrust up into the waters of Bering Sea. The islands are silent now, but for the
several months of summer they resounded with the roar of
millions of seals come ashore to bear and rear their young—
all the fur seals of the eastern Pacific crowded into a few
square miles of bare rock and crumbling soil. Now once

more the seals turn south, to roam down along the sheer underwater cliffs of the continent's edge, where the rocky foundations fall away steeply into the deep sea. Here, in a blackness more absolute than that of arctic winter, the seals will find rich feeding as they swim down to prey on the fishes of this region of darkness.

Autumn comes to the sea with a fresh blaze of phosphorescence, when every wave crest is aflame. Here and there the whole surface may glow with sheets of cold fire, while below schools of fish pour through the water like molten metal. Often the autumnal phosphorescence is caused by a fall flowering of the dinoflagellates, multiplying furiously in a short-lived repetition of their vernal blooming.

Sometimes the meaning of the glowing water is ominous. Off the Pacific coast of North America, it may mean that the sea is filled with the dinoflagellate Gonyaulax, a minute plant that contains a poison of strange and terrible virulence. About four days after Gonyaulax comes to dominate the coastal plankton, some of the fishes and shellfish in the vicinity become toxic. This is because, in their normal feeding, they have strained the poisonous plankton out of the water. Mussels accumulate the Gonyaulax toxins in their livers, and the toxins react on the human nervous system with an effect similar to that of strychnine. Because of these facts, it is generally understood along the Pacific coast that it is unwise to eat shellfish taken from coasts exposed to the open sea where Gonyaulax may be abundant, in summer or early fall. For generations before the white men came, the Indians knew this. As soon as the red streaks appeared in the sea and the waves began to flicker at night with the mysterious blue-green fires, the tribal leaders forbade the taking of mussels until these warning signals should have passed. They even set guards at intervals along the beaches to warn inlanders who might come down for shellfish and be unable to read the language of the sea.

But usually the blaze and glitter of the sea, whatever its meaning for those who produce it, implies no menace to man. Seen from the deck of a vessel in open ocean, a tiny, man-made observation point in the vast world of sea and sky, it has an eerie and unearthly quality. Man, in his vanity, subconsciously attributes a human origin to any light not of moon or stars or sun. Lights on the shore, lights moving over the water, mean lights kindled and controlled by other men, serving purposes understandable to the human mind. Yet here are lights that flash and fade away, lights that come and go for reasons meaningless to man, lights that have been doing this very thing over the eons of time in which there were no men to stir in vague disquiet.

On such a night of phosphorescent display Charles Darwin stood on the deck of the *Beagle* as she plowed southward through the Atlantic off the coast of Brazil.

The sea from its extreme luminousness presented a wonderful and most beautiful appearance [he wrote in his diary]. Every part of the water which by day is seen as foam, glowed with a pale light. The vessel drove before her bows two billows of liquid phosphorus, and in her wake was a milky train. As far as the eye reached the crest of every wave was bright; and from the reflected light, the sky just above the horizon was not so utterly dark as the rest of the Heavens. It was impossible to behold this plain of matter, as if it were melted and consumed by heat, without being reminded of Milton's description of the regions of Chaos and Anarchy.*

Like the blazing colors of the autumn leaves before they wither and fall, the autumnal phosphorescence betokens the approach of winter. After their brief renewal of life the flagellates and the other minute algae dwindle away to a scattered few; so do the shrimps and the copepods, the glassworms and the comb jellies. The larvae of the bottom fauna have long since completed their development and drifted away to take up whatever existence is their lot. Even the roving fish schools have deserted the surface waters and have migrated into warmer latitudes or have found equivalent warmth in the deep, quiet waters along the edge of the continental shelf. There the torpor of semi-hibernation descends upon them and will possess them during the months of winter.

The surface waters now become the plaything of the winter gales. As the winds build up the giant storm waves and roar along their crests, lashing the water into foam and flying spray, it seems that life must forever have deserted this place.

For the mood of the winter sea, read Joseph Conrad's description:

The greyness of the whole immense surface, the wind furrows upon the faces of the waves, the great masses of

* From *Charles Darwin's Diary of the Voyage of H.M.S. Beagle,* edited by Nora Barlow, 1934 edition, Cambridge University Press, p. 107.

foam, tossed about and waving, like matted white locks, give to the sea in a gale an appearance of hoary age, lustreless, dull, without gleams, as though it had been created before light itself.*

But the symbols of hope are not lacking even in the grayness and bleakness of the winter sea. On land we know that the apparent lifelessness of winter is an illusion. Look closely at the bare branches of a tree, on which not the palest gleam of green can be discerned. Yet, spaced along each branch are the leaf buds, all the spring's magic of swelling green concealed and safely preserved under the insulating, overlapping layers. Pick off a piece of the rough bark of the trunk; there you will find hibernating insects. Dig down through the snow into the earth. There are the eggs of next summer's grasshoppers; there are the dormant seeds from which will come the grass, the herb, the oak tree.

So, too, the lifelessness, the hopelessness, the despair of the winter sea are an illusion. Everywhere are the assurances that the cycle has come to the full, containing the means of its own renewal. There is the promise of a new spring in the very iciness of the winter sea, in the chilling of the water, which must, before many weeks, become so heavy that it will plunge downward, precipitating the overturn that is the first act in the drama of spring. There is the promise of new life in the small plantlike things that cling to the rocks of the underlying bottom, the almost formless polyps from which, in spring, a new generation of jellyfish will bud off and rise into the surface waters. There is unconscious purpose in the sluggish forms of the copepods hibernating on the bottom, safe from the surface storms, life sustained in their tiny bodies by the extra store of fat with which they went into this winter sleep.

Already, from the gray shapes of cod that have moved, unseen by man, through the cold sea to their spawning places, the glassy globules of eggs are rising into the surface waters. Even in the harsh world of the winter sea, these eggs will begin the swift divisions by which a granule of protoplasm becomes a living fishlet.

Most of all, perhaps, there is assurance in the fine dust of life that remains in the surface waters, the invisible spores of the diatoms, needing only the touch of warming sun and fertilizing chemicals to repeat the magic of spring.

---

* From *The Mirror of the Sea*, Kent edition, 1925, Doubleday-Page, p. 71.

The Sunless Sea

WHERE GREAT WHALES COME SAILING BY,
SAIL AND SAIL, WITH UNSHUT EYE
—MATTHEW ARNOLD

Between the sunlit surface waters of the open sea and the hidden hills and valleys of the ocean floor lies the least-known region of the sea. These deep, dark waters, with all their mysteries and their unsolved problems, cover a very considerable part of the earth. The whole world ocean extends over about three-fourths of the surface of the globe. If we subtract the shallow areas of the continental shelves and the scattered banks and shoals, where at least the pale ghost of sunlight moves over the underlying bottom, there still remains about half the earth that is covered by miles-deep, lightless water, that has been dark since the world began.

This region has withheld its secrets more obstinately than any other. Man, with all his ingenuity, has been able to venture only to its threshold. Wearing a diving helmet, he can walk on the ocean floor about 10 fathoms down. He can descend to an extreme limit of about 500 feet in a complete diving suit, so heavily armored that movement is almost impossible, carrying with him a constant supply of oxygen. Only two men in all the history of the world have had the experience of descending, alive, beyond the range of visible light. These men are William Beebe and Otis Barton. In the bathysphere, they reached a depth of 3028 feet in the open ocean off Bermuda, in the year 1934. Barton alone, in a steel sphere known as the benthoscope, descended to the great depth of 4500 feet off California, in the summer of 1949.[2]

Although only a fortunate few can ever visit the deep sea, the precise instruments of the oceanographer, recording light penetration, pressure, salinity, and temperature, have given us the materials with which to reconstruct in imagination these eerie, forbidding regions. Unlike the surface waters, which are sensitive to every gust of wind, which know day and night, respond to the pull of sun and moon, and change as the seasons change, the deep waters are a place where change comes slowly, if at all. Down beyond the reach of the sun's rays, there is no alternation of light and darkness. There is rather an endless night, as old as the sea itself. For most of its creatures, groping their way endlessly through its black waters, it must be a place of hunger, where food is scarce and hard to find, a shelterless place where there is no sanctuary from ever-present enemies, where one can only move on and on, from birth to death, through the darkness, confined as in a prison to his own particular layer of the sea.

They used to say that nothing could live in the deep sea. It was a belief that must have been easy to accept, for without proof to the contrary, how could anyone conceive of life in such a place?

A century ago the British biologist Edward Forbes wrote: 'As we descend deeper and deeper into this region, the inhabitants become more and more modified, and fewer and fewer, indicating our approach to an abyss where life is either extinguished, or exhibits but a few sparks to mark its lingering presence.' Yet Forbes urged further exploration of 'this vast deep-sea region' to settle forever the question of the existence of life at great depths.

Even then, the evidence was accumulating. Sir John Ross, during his exploration of the arctic seas in 1818, had brought up from a depth of 1000 fathoms mud in which there were worms, 'thus proving there was animal life in the bed of the ocean notwithstanding the darkness, stillness, silence, and immense pressure produced by more than a mile of superincumbent water.'

Then from the surveying ship *Bulldog*, examining a proposed northern route for a cable from Faroe to Labrador in 1860, came another report. The *Bulldog*'s sounding line, which at one place had been allowed to lie for some time on the bottom at a depth of 1260 fathoms, came up with 13 starfish clinging to it. Through these starfish, the ship's naturalist wrote, 'the deep has sent forth the long coveted message.' But not all the zoologists of the day were prepared to accept the message. Some doubters asserted that the starfish had 'convulsively embraced' the line somewhere on the way back to the surface.

In the same year, 1860, a cable in the Mediterranean was raised for repairs from a depth of 1200 fathoms. It was found to be heavily encrusted with corals and other sessile animals that had attached themselves at an early stage of development and grown to maturity over a period of months or years. There was not the slightest chance that they had become entangled in the cable as it was being raised to the surface.

Then the *Challenger,* the first ship ever equipped for oceanographic exploration, set out from England in the year 1872 and traced a course around the globe. From bottoms lying under miles of water, from silent deeps carpeted with red clay ooze, and from all the lightless intermediate depths, net-haul after net-haul of strange and fantastic creatures came up and were spilled out on the decks. Poring over the weird beings thus brought up for the first time into the light of day, beings no man had ever seen before, the *Challenger* scientists realized that life existed even on the deepest floor of the abyss.

The recent discovery that a living cloud of some unknown creatures is spread over much of the ocean at a depth of several hundred fathoms below the surface is the most exciting thing that has been learned about the ocean for many years.

When, during the first quarter of the twentieth century, echo sounding was developed to allow ships while under way to record the depth of the bottom, probably no one suspected that it would also provide a means of learning something about deep-sea life. But operators of the new instruments soon discovered that the sound waves, directed downward from the ship like a beam of light, were reflected back from any solid object they met. Answering echoes were returned from intermediate depths, presumably from schools of fish, whales, or submarines; then a second echo was received from the bottom.

These facts were so well established by the late 1930's that fishermen had begun to talk about using their fathometers to search for schools of herring. Then the war brought the whole subject under strict security regulations, and little more was heard about it. In 1946, however, the United States Navy issued a significant bulletin. It was reported that several scientists, working with sonic equipment in deep water off the California coast, had discovered a widespread 'layer' of some sort, which gave back an answering echo to the sound waves. This reflecting layer, seemingly suspended between the surface and the floor of the Pacific, was found over an area 300 miles wide. It lay from 1000 to 1500 feet below the surface. The discovery was made by three scientists, C. F. Eyring, R. J. Christensen, and R. W. Raitt, aboard the U.S.S. *Jasper* in 1942, and for a time this mysterious phenomenon, of wholly unknown nature, was called the ECR layer. Then in 1945 Martin W. Johnson, marine biologist of the Scripps Institution of Oceanography, made a further discovery which gave the first clue to the nature of the layer. Working aboard the vessel *E. W. Scripps,* Johnson found that whatever sent back the echoes moved upward and downward in rhythmic fashion, being found near the surface at night, in deep water during the day. This discovery disposed of speculations that the reflections came from something inanimate, perhaps a mere physical discontinuity in the water, and showed that the layer is composed of living creatures capable of controlled movement.

From this time on, discoveries about the sea's 'phantom bottom' came rapidly. With widespread use of echo-sounding instruments, it has become clear that the phenomenon is not something peculiar to the coast of California alone. It occurs almost universally in the deep ocean basins—drifting by day at a depth of several hundred fathoms, at night rising to the surface, and again, before sunrise, sinking into the depths.

On the passage of the U.S.S. *Henderson* from San Diego to the Antarctic in 1947, the reflecting layer was detected during the greater part of each day, at depths varying from 150 to 450 fathoms, and on a later run from San Diego to Yokosuka, Japan, the *Henderson*'s fathometer again recorded the layer every day, suggesting that it exists almost continuously across the Pacific.

During July and August 1947, the U.S.S. *Nereus* made a continuous fathogram from Pearl Harbor to the Arctic and found the scattering layer over all deep waters along this course. It did not develop, however, in the shallow Bering and Chuckchee seas. Sometimes in the morning, the *Nereus* fathogram showed two layers, responding in different ways to the growing illumination of the water; both descended into deep water, but there was an interval of twenty minutes between the two descents.

Despite attempts to sample it or photograph it, no one is sure what the layer is, although the discovery may be made any day. There are three principal theories, each of which has its group of supporters. According to these theories, the sea's phantom bottom may consist of small planktonic shrimps, of fishes, or of squids.

As for the plankton theory, one of the most convincing arguments is the well-known fact that many plankton creatures make regular vertical migrations of hundreds of feet, rising toward the surface at night, sinking down below the zone of light penetration very early in the morning. This is, of course, exactly the behavior of the scattering layer. Whatever composes it is apparently strongly repelled by sunlight. The creatures of the layer seem almost to be held prisoner at the end—or beyond the end—of the sun's rays throughout the hours of daylight, waiting only for the welcome return of darkness to hurry upward into the surface waters. But what is the power that repels; and what the attraction that draws them surfaceward once the inhibiting force is removed? Is it comparative safety from enemies that makes them seek darkness? Is it more abundant food near the surface that lures them back under cover of night?

Those who say that fish are the reflectors of the sound waves usually account for the vertical migrations of the layer by suggesting that the fish are feeding on planktonic shrimp and are following their food. They believe that the air bladder of a fish is, of all structures concerned, most likely from its construction to return a strong echo. There is one outstanding difficulty in the way of accepting this theory: we have no other evidence that concentrations of fish are universally present in the oceans. In fact, almost everything else we know suggests that the really dense populations of fish live over the continental shelves or in certain very definitely determined zones of the open ocean where food is particularly abundant. If the reflecting layer is eventually proved to be composed of fish, the prevailing views of fish distribution will have to be radically revised.

The most startling theory (and the one that seems to have the fewest supporters) is that the layer consists of concentrations of squid, 'hovering below the illuminated zone of the sea and awaiting the arrival of darkness in which to resume their raids into the plankton-rich surface waters.' Proponents of this theory argue that squid are abundant enough, and of wide enough distribution, to give the echoes that have been picked up almost everywhere from the equator to the two poles. Squid are known to be the sole food of the sperm whale, found in the open oceans in all temperate and tropical waters. They also form the exclusive diet of the bottle-nosed whale and are eaten extensively by most other toothed whales, by seals, and by many sea birds. All these facts argue that they must be prodigiously abundant.

It is true that men who have worked close to the sea surface at night have received vivid impressions of the abundance and activity of squids in the surface waters in darkness. Long ago Johan Hjort wrote:

One night we were hauling long lines on the Faroe

slope, working with an electric lamp hanging over the side in order to see the line, when like lightning flashes one squid after another shot towards the light . . . In October 1902 we were one night steaming outside the slopes of the coast banks of Norway, and for many miles we could see the squids moving in the surface waters like luminous bubbles, resembling large milky white electric lamps being constantly lit and extinguished.*

Thor Heyerdahl reports that at night his raft was literally bombarded by squids; and Richard Fleming says that in his oceanographic work off the coast of Panama it was common to see immense schools of squid gathering at the surface at night and leaping upward toward the lights that were used by the men to operate their instruments. But equally spectacular surface displays of shrimp have been seen, and most people find it difficult to believe in the ocean-wide abundance of squid.

Deep-water photography holds much promise for the solution of the mystery of the phantom bottom. There are technical difficulties, such as the problem of holding a camera still as it swings at the end of a long cable, twisting and turning, suspended from a ship which itself moves with the sea. Some of the pictures so taken look as though the photographer has pointed his camera at a starry sky and swung it in an arc as he exposed the film. Yet the Norwegian biologist Gunnar Rollefson had an encouraging experience in correlating photography with echograms. On the research ship *Johan Hjort* off the Lofoten Islands, he persistently got reflection of sound from schools of fish in 20 to 30 fathoms. A specially constructed camera was lowered to the depth indicated by the echogram. When developed, the film showed moving shapes of fish at a distance, and a large and clearly recognizable cod appeared in the beam of light and hovered in front of the lens.

Direct sampling of the layer is the logical means of discovering its identity, but the problem is to develop large nets that can be operated rapidly enough to capture swift-moving animals. Scientists at Woods Hole, Massachusetts, have towed ordinary plankton nets in the layer and have found that euphausiid shrimps, glassworms, and other deep-water plankton are concentrated there; but there is still a possibility that the layer itself may actually be made up

* From *The Depths of the Ocean,* by Sir John Murray and Johan Hjort, 1912 edition, Macmillan & Co., p. 649.

of larger forms feeding on the shrimps—too large or swift
to be taken in the presently used nets. New nets may give
the answer. Television is another possibility.[3]

Shadowy and indefinite though they be, these recent indications of an abundant life at mid-depths agree with the reports of the only observers who have actually visited comparable depths and brought back eyewitness accounts of
what they saw. William Beebe's impressions from the
bathysphere were of a life far more abundant and varied
than he had been prepared to find, although, over a period
of six years, he had made many hundreds of net-hauls in
the same area. More than a quarter of a mile down, he reported aggregations of living things 'as thick as I have ever
seen them.' At half a mile—the deepest descent of the bathysphere—Dr. Beebe recalled that 'there was no instant when
a mist of plankton . . . was not swirling in the path of the
beam.'

The existence of an abundant deep-sea fauna was discovered, probably millions of years ago, by certain whales
and also, it now appears, by seals. The ancestors of all
whales, we know by fossil remains, were land mammals.
They must have been predatory beasts, if we are to judge
by their powerful jaws and teeth. Perhaps in their foragings
about the deltas of great rivers or around the edges of
shallow seas, they discovered the abundance of fish and
other marine life and over the centuries formed the habit
of following them farther and farther into the sea. Little
by little their bodies took on a form more suitable for
aquatic life; their hind limbs were reduced to rudiments,
which may be discovered in a modern whale by dissection,
and the forelimbs were modified into organs for steering
and balancing.

Eventually the whales, as though to divide the sea's food
resources among them, became separated into three groups:
the plankton-eaters, the fish-eaters, and the squid-eaters.
The plankton-eating whales can exist only where there are
dense masses of small shrimp or copepods to supply their
enormous food requirements. This limits them, except for
scattered areas, to arctic and antarctic waters and the high
temperate latitudes. Fish-eating whales may find food over a
somewhat wider range of ocean, but they are restricted to
places where there are enormous populations of schooling
fish. The blue water of the tropics and of the open ocean
basins offers little to either of these groups. But that immense, square-headed, formidably toothed whale known as
the cachalot or sperm whale discovered long ago what men

have known for only a short time—that hundreds of fathoms below the almost untenanted surface waters of these regions there is an abundant animal life. The sperm whale has taken these deep waters for his hunting grounds; his quarry is the deep-water population of squids, including the giant squid Architeuthis, which lives pelagically at depths of 1500 feet or more. The head of the sperm whale is often marked with long stripes, which consist of a great number of circular scars made by the suckers of the squid. From this evidence we can imagine the battles that go on, in the darkness of the deep water, between these two huge creatures—the sperm whale with its 70-ton bulk, the squid with a body as long as 30 feet, and writhing, grasping arms extending the total length of the animal to perhaps 50 feet.

The greatest depth at which the giant squid lives is not definitely known, but there is one instructive piece of evidence about the depth to which sperm whales descend, presumably in search of the squids. In April 1932, the cable repair ship *All America* was investigating an apparent break in the submarine cable between Balboa in the Canal Zone and Esmeraldas, Ecuador. The cable was brought to the surface off the coast of Colombia. Entangled in it was a dead 45-foot male sperm whale. The submarine cable was twisted around the lower jaw and was wrapped around one flipper, the body, and the caudal flukes. The cable was raised from a depth of 540 fathoms, or 3240 feet.[4]

Some of the seals also appear to have discovered the hidden food reserves of the deep ocean. It has long been something of a mystery where, and on what, the northern fur seals of the eastern Pacific feed during the winter, which they spend off the coast of North America from California to Alaska. There is no evidence that they are feeding to any great extent on sardines, mackerel, or other commercially important fishes. Presumably four million seals could not compete with commercial fishermen for the same species without the fact being known. But there is some evidence on the diet of the fur seals, and it is highly significant. Their stomachs have yielded the bones of a species of fish that has never been seen alive. Indeed, not even its remains have been found anywhere except in the stomachs of seals. Ichthyologists say that this 'seal fish' belongs to a group that typically inhabits very deep water, off the edge of the continental shelf.

How either whales or seals endure the tremendous pressure changes involved in dives of several hundred fathoms is not definitely known. They are warm-blooded mammals like ourselves. Caisson disease, which is caused by the rapid accumulation of nitrogen bubbles in the blood with sudden release of pressure, kills human divers if they are brought up rapidly from depths of 200 feet or so. Yet, according to the testimony of whalers, a baleen whale, when harpooned, can dive straight down to a depth of half a mile, as measured by the amount of line carried out. From these depths, where it has sustained a pressure of half a ton on every inch of body, it returns almost immediately to the surface. The most plausible explanation is that, unlike the diver, who has air pumped to him while he is under water, the whale has in its body only the limited supply it carries down, and does not have enough nitrogen in its blood to do serious harm. The plain truth is, however, that we really do not know, since it is obviously impossible to confine a living whale and experiment on it, and almost as difficult to dissect a dead one satisfactorily.

At first thought it seems a paradox that creatures of such great fragility as the glass sponge and the jellyfish can live under the conditions of immense pressure that prevail in deep water. For creatures at home in the deep sea, however, the saving fact is that the pressure inside their tissues is the same as that without, and, as long as this balance is preserved, they are no more inconvenienced by a pressure of a ton or so than we are by ordinary atmospheric pressure. And most abyssal creatures, it must be remembered, live out their whole lives in a comparatively restricted zone, and are never required to adjust themselves to extreme changes of pressure.

But of course there are exceptions, and the real miracle of sea life in relation to great pressure is not the animal that lives its whole life on the bottom, bearing a pressure of perhaps five or six tons, but those that regularly move up and down through hundreds or thousands of feet of vertical change. The small shrimps and other planktonic creatures that descend into deep water during the day are examples. Fish that possess air bladders, on the other hand, are vitally affected by abrupt changes of pressure, as anyone knows who has seen a trawler's net raised from a hundred fathoms. Apart from the accident of being captured in a net and hauled up through waters of rapidly diminishing pressures, fish may sometimes wander out of the zone to which they are adjusted and find themselves unable to return. Perhaps in their pursuit of food they roam upward to the ceiling of the zone that is theirs, and beyond whose invisible boundary they may not stray without meeting alien and inhospitable conditions. Moving from layer to layer of drifting plankton as they feed, they may pass beyond the boundary. In the lessened pressure of these upper waters the gas enclosed within the air bladder expands. The fish becomes lighter and more buoyant. Perhaps he tries to fight his way down again, opposing the upward lift with all the power of his muscles. If he does not succeed, he 'falls' to the surface, injured and dying, for the abrupt release of pressure from without causes distension and rupture of the tissues.

The compression of the sea under its own weight is relatively slight, and there is no basis for the old and picturesque belief that, at the deeper levels, the water resists the downward passage of objects from the surface. According to this belief, sinking ships, the bodies of drowned men, and presumably the bodies of the larger sea animals not consumed above by hungry scavengers, never reach the bottom, but come to rest at some level determined by the relation of their own weight to the compression of the water, there to drift forever. The fact is that anything will continue to sink as long as its specific gravity is greater than that of the surrounding water, and all large bodies descend, in a matter of a few days, to the ocean floor. As mute testimony to this fact, we bring up from the deepest ocean basins the teeth of sharks and the hard ear bones of whales.

Nevertheless the weight of sea water—the pressing down of miles of water upon all the underlying layers—does have a certain effect upon the water itself. If this downward compression could suddenly be relaxed by some miraculous suspension of natural laws, the sea level would rise about 93 feet all over the world. This would shift the Atlantic coastline of the United States westward a hundred miles or more and alter other familiar geographic outlines all over the world.

Immense pressure, then, is one of the governing conditions of life in the deep sea; darkness is another. The unrelieved darkness of the deep waters has produced weird and incredible modifications of the abyssal fauna. It is a blackness so divorced from the world of the sunlight that probably only the few men who have seen it with their own eyes can visualize it. We know that light fades out rapidly with descent below the surface. The red rays are gone at the end of the first 200 or 300 feet, and with them all the orange and yellow warmth of the sun. Then the greens fade out, and at 1000 feet only a deep, dark, brilliant blue is left. In very clear waters the violet rays of the spectrum

may penetrate another thousand feet. Beyond this is only
the blackness of the deep sea.

In a curious way, the colors of marine animals tend to
be related to the zone in which they live. Fishes of the
surface waters, like the mackerel and herring, often are blue
or green; so are the floats of the Portuguese men-of-war
and the azure-tinted wings of the swimming snails. Down
below the diatom meadows and the drifting sargassum weed,
where the water becomes ever more deeply, brilliantly blue,
many creatures are crystal clear. Their glassy, ghostly forms
blend with their surroundings and make it easier for them
to elude the ever-present, ever-hungry enemy. Such are the
transparent hordes of the arrowworms or glassworms, the
comb jellies, and the larvae of many fishes.

At a thousand feet, and on down to the very end of the
sun's rays, silvery fishes are common, and many others are
red, drab brown, or black. Pteropods are a dark violet.
Arrowworms, whose relatives in the upper layers are color-
less, are here a deep red. Jellyfish medusae, which above
would be transparent, at a depth of 1000 feet are a deep
brown.

At depths greater than 1500 feet, all the fishes are black,
deep violet, or brown, but the prawns wear amazing hues
of red, scarlet, and purple. Why, no one can say. Since all
the red rays are strained out of the water far above this
depth, the scarlet raiment of these creatures can only look
black to their neighbors.

The deep sea has its stars, and perhaps here and there
an eerie and transient equivalent of moonlight, for the mysterious phenomenon of luminescence is displayed by perhaps half of all the fishes that live in dimly lit or darkened
waters, and by many of the lower forms as well. Many
fishes carry luminous torches that can be turned on or off
at will, presumably helping them find or pursue their prey.
Others have rows of lights over their bodies, in patterns
that vary from species to species and may be a sort of
recognition mark or badge by which the bearer can be known
as friend or enemy. The deep-sea squid ejects a spurt of
fluid that becomes a luminous cloud, the counterpart of the
'ink' of his shallow-water relative.

Down beyond the reach of even the longest and strongest
of the sun's rays, the eyes of fishes become enlarged, as
though to make the most of any chance illumination of
whatever sort, or they may become telescopic, large of lens,
and protruding. In deep-sea fishes, hunting always in dark
waters, the eyes tend to lose the 'cones' or color-perceiving

cells of the retina, and to increase the 'rods,' which perceive dim light. Exactly the same modification is seen on land among the strictly nocturnal prowlers which, like abyssal fish, never see the sunlight.

In their world of darkness, it would seem likely that some of the animals might have become blind, as has happened to some cave fauna. So, indeed, many of them have, compensating for the lack of eyes with marvelously developed feelers and long, slender fins and processes with which they grope their way, like so many blind men with canes, their whole knowledge of friends, enemies, or food coming to them through the sense of touch.

The last traces of plant life are left behind in the thin upper layer of water, for no plant can live below about 600 feet even in very clear water, and few find enough sunlight for their food-manufacturing activities below 200 feet. Since no animal can make its own food, the creatures of the deeper waters live a strange, almost parasitic existence of utter dependence on the upper layers. These hungry carnivores prey fiercely and relentlessly upon each other, yet the whole community is ultimately dependent upon the slow rain of descending food particles from above. The components of this never-ending rain are the dead and dying plants and animals from the surface, or from one of the intermediate layers. For each of the horizontal zones or communities of the sea that lie, in tier after tier, between the surface and the sea bottom, the food supply is different and in general poorer than for the layer above. There is a hint of the fierce and uncompromising competition for food in the saber-toothed jaws of some of the small, dragonlike fishes of the deeper waters, in the immense mouths and in the elastic and distensible bodies that make it possible for a fish to swallow another several times its size, enjoying swift repletion after a long fast.

Pressure, darkness, and—we should have added only a few years ago—silence, are the conditions of life in the deep sea. But we know now that the conception of the sea as a silent place is wholly false. Wide experience with hydrophones and other listening devices for the detection of submarines has proved that, around the shore lines of much of the world, there is an extraordinary uproar produced by fishes, shrimps, porpoises, and probably other forms not yet identified. There has been little investigation as yet of sound in the deep, offshore areas, but when the crew of the *Atlantis* lowered a hydrophone into deep water off Bermuda, they recorded strange mewing sounds, shrieks, and ghostly moans, the sources of which have not been traced. But fish of shallower zones have been captured and confined in aquaria, where their voices have been recorded for comparison with sounds heard at sea, and in many cases satisfactory identification can be made.

During the Second World War the hydrophone network set up by the United States Navy to protect the entrance to Chesapeake Bay was temporarily made useless when, in the spring of 1942, the speakers at the surface began to give forth, every evening, a sound described as being like 'a pneumatic drill tearing up pavement.' The extraneous noises that came over the hydrophones completely masked the sounds of the passage of ships. Eventually it was discovered that the sounds were the voices of fish known as croakers, which in the spring move into Chesapeake Bay from their offshore wintering grounds. As soon as the noise had been identified and analyzed, it was possible to screen it out with an electric filter, so that once more only the sounds of ships came through the speakers.

Later in the same year, a chorus of croakers was discovered off the pier of the Scripps Institution at La Jolla. Every year from May until late September the evening chorus begins about sunset, and 'increases gradually to a steady uproar of harsh froggy croaks, with a background of soft drumming. This continues unabated for two to three hours and finally tapers off to individual outbursts at rare intervals.' Several species of croakers isolated in aquaria gave sounds similar to the 'froggy croaks,' but the authors of the soft background drumming—presumably another species of croaker—have not yet been discovered.

One of the most extraordinarily widespread sounds of the undersea is the crackling, sizzling sound, like dry twigs burning or fat frying, heard near beds of the snapping shrimp. This is a small, round shrimp, about half an inch in diameter, with one very large claw which it uses to stun its prey. The shrimp are forever clicking the two joints of this claw together, and it is the thousands of clicks that collectively produce the noise known as shrimp crackle. No one had any idea the little snapping shrimps were so abundant or so widely distributed until their signals began to be picked up on hydrophones. They had been heard all over a broad band that extends around the world, between latitudes 35° N and 35° S, (for example, from Cape Hatteras to Buenos Aires) in ocean waters less than 30 fathoms deep.

Mammals as well as fishes and crustaceans contribute to the undersea chorus. Biologists listening through a hydrophone in an estuary of the St. Lawrence River heard 'high-pitched resonant whistles and squeals, varied with the ticking and clucking sounds slightly reminiscent of a string orchestra tuning up, as well as mewing and occasional chirps.' This remarkable medley of sounds was heard only while schools of the white porpoise were seen passing up or down the river, and so was assumed to be produced by them.[5]

The mysteriousness, the eeriness, the ancient unchangingness of the great depths have led many people to suppose that some very old forms of life—some 'living fossils'—may be lurking undiscovered in the deep ocean. Some such hope may have been in the minds of the *Challenger* scientists. The forms they brought up in their nets were weird enough, and most of them had never before been seen by man. But basically they were modern types. There was nothing like the trilobites of Cambrian time or the sea scorpions of the Silurian, nothing reminiscent of the great marine reptiles that invaded the sea in the Mesozoic. Instead, there were modern fishes, squids, and shrimps, strangely and grotesquely modified, to be sure, for life in the difficult deep-sea world, but clearly types that have developed in rather recent geologic time.

Far from being the original home of life, the deep sea has probably been inhabited for a relatively short time. While life was developing and flourishing in the surface waters, along the shores, and perhaps in the rivers and swamps, two immense regions of the earth still forbade invasion by living things. These were the continents and the abyss. As we have seen, the immense difficulties of surviving on land were first overcome by colonists from the sea about 300 million years ago. The abyss, with its unending darkness, its crushing pressures, its glacial cold, presented even more formidable difficulties. Probably the successful invasion of this region—at least by higher forms of life—occurred somewhat later.

Yet in recent years there have been one or two significant happenings that have kept alive the hope that the deep sea may, after all, conceal strange links with the past. In December 1938, off the southeast tip of Africa, an amazing fish was caught alive in a trawl—a fish that was supposed to have been dead for at least 60 million years! This is to say, the last known fossil remains of its kind date from the Cretaceous, and no living example had been recognized in historic time until this lucky net-haul.

The fishermen who brought it up in their trawl from a

depth of only 40 fathoms realized that this five-foot, bright
blue fish, with its large head and strangely shaped scales,
fins, and tail, was different from anything they had ever
caught before, and on their return to port they took it to
the nearest museum. This single specimen of Latimeria, as
the fish was christened, is so far the only one that has been
captured, and it seems a reasonable guess that it may inhabit
depths below those ordinarily fished, and that the South
African specimen was a stray from its usual habitat.[6]

Occasionally a very primitive type of shark, known from
its puckered gills as a 'frillshark,' is taken in waters between
a quarter of a mile and half a mile down. Most of these
have been caught in Norwegian and Japanese waters—there
are only about 50 preserved in the museums of Europe and
America—but recently one was captured off Santa Barbara,
California. The frillshark has many anatomical features similar to those of the ancient sharks that lived 25 to 30 million
years ago. It has too many gills and too few dorsal fins for a
modern shark, and its teeth, like those of fossil sharks,
are three-pronged and briarlike. Some ichthyologists regard
it as a relic derived from very ancient shark ancestors that
have died out in the upper waters but, through this single
species, are still carrying on their struggle for earthly survival, in the quiet of the deep sea.

Possibly there are other such anachronisms lurking down
in these regions of which we know so little, but they are
likely to be few and scattered. The terms of existence in
these deep waters are far too uncompromising to support life
unless that life is plastic, molding itself constantly to the
harsh conditions, seizing every advantage that makes possible
the survival of living protoplasm in a world only a little less
hostile than the black reaches of interplanetary space.

Hidden Lands

The first European ever to sail across the wide Pacific was curious about the hidden worlds beneath his ship. Between the two coral islands of St. Paul and Los Tiburones in the Tuamotu Archipelago, Magellan ordered his sounding line to be lowered. It was the conventional line used by explorers of the day, no more than 200 fathoms long. It did not touch bottom, and Magellan declared that he was over the deepest part of the ocean. Of course he was completely mistaken, but the occasion was none the less historic. It was the first time in the history of the world that a navigator had attempted to sound the depths of the open ocean.

Three centuries later, in the year 1839, Sir James Clark Ross set out from England in command of two ships with names of dark foreboding, the *Erebus* and the *Terror*, bound for the 'utmost navigable limits of the Antarctic Ocean.' As he proceeded on his course he tried repeatedly to obtain soundings, but failed for lack of a proper line. Finally he had one constructed on board, of 'three thousand six hundred fathoms, or rather more than four miles in length. . . . On the 3rd of January, in latitude 27° 26′ S., longitude 17° 29′ W., the weather and all other circumstances being propitious, we succeeded in obtaining soundings with two thousand four hundred and twenty-five fathoms of line, a depression of the bed of the ocean beneath its surface very little short of the elevation of Mount Blanc above it.' This was the first successful abyssal sounding.

But taking soundings in the deep ocean was, and long remained, a laborious and time-consuming task, and knowledge of the undersea topography lagged considerably behind our acquaintance with the landscape of the near side of the moon. Over the years, methods were improved. For the heavy hemp line used by Ross, Maury of the United States Navy substituted a strong twine, and in 1870 Lord Kelvin used piano wire. Even with improved gear a deep-water sounding required several hours or sometimes an entire day. By 1854, when Maury collected all available records, only 180 deep soundings were available from the Atlantic, and by the time that modern echo sounding was developed, the total that had been taken from all the ocean basins of the world was only about 15,000. This is roughly one sounding for an area of 6000 square miles.

Now hundreds of vessels are equipped with sonic sounding instruments that trace a continuous profile of the bottom beneath the moving ship (although only a few can obtain profiles at depths greater than 2000 fathoms [7]). Soundings are accumulating much faster than they can be plotted on the charts. Little by little, like the details of a huge map being filled in by an artist, the hidden contours of the ocean are emerging. But, even with this recent progress, it will be years before an accurate and detailed relief map of the ocean basins can be constructed.

The general bottom topography is, however, well established. Once we have passed the tide lines, the three great geographic provinces of ocean are the continental shelves, the continental slopes, and the floor of the deep sea. Each of these regions is as different from the others as an arctic tundra from a range of the Rocky Mountains.

The continental shelf is of the sea, yet of all regions of the ocean it is most like the land. Sunlight penetrates to all but its deepest parts. Plants drift in the waters above it; seaweeds cling to its rocks and sway to the passage of the waves. Familiar fishes—unlike the weird monsters of the abyss—move over its plains like herds of cattle. Much of its substance is derived from the land—the sand and the rock fragments and the rich topsoil carried by running water to the sea and gently deposited on the shelf. Its submerged valleys and hills, in appropriate parts of the world, have been carved by glaciers into a topography much like the northern landscapes we know and the terrain is strewn with rocks and gravel deposited by the moving ice sheets. Indeed many parts (or perhaps all) of the shelf have been dry land in the geologic past, for a comparatively slight fall of sea level has sufficed, time and again, to expose it to wind and sun and rain. The Grand Banks of Newfoundland rose above the ancient seas and were submerged again. The Dogger Bank of the North Sea shelf was once a forested land inhabited by prehistoric beasts; now its 'forests' are seaweeds and its 'beasts' are fishes.

Of all parts of the sea, the continental shelves are perhaps most directly important to man as a source of material things. The great fisheries of the world, with only a few exceptions, are confined to the relatively shallow waters over the continental shelves. Seaweeds are gathered from their submerged plains to make scores of substances used in foods, drugs, and articles of commerce. As the petroleum reserves left on continental areas by ancient seas become depleted, petroleum geologists look more and more to the oil that may lie, as yet unmapped and unexploited, under these bordering lands of the sea.

The shelves begin at the tidelines and extend seaward as gently sloping plains. The 100-fathom contour used to be taken as the boundary between the continental shelf and the slope; now it is customary to place the division wherever the gentle declivity of the shelf changes abruptly to a steeper descent toward abyssal depths. The world over, the average depth at which this change occurs is about 72 fathoms; the greatest depth of any shelf is probably 200 to 300 fathoms.

Nowhere off the Pacific coast of the United States is the continental shelf much more than 20 miles wide—a narrowness characteristic of coasts bordered by young mountains perhaps still in the process of formation. On the American east coast, however, north of Cape Hatteras the shelf is as much as 150 miles wide. But at Hatteras and off southern Florida it is merely the narrowest of thresholds to the sea. Here its scant development seems to be related to the press of that great and rapidly flowing river-in-the-sea, the Gulf Stream, which at these places swings close inshore.

The widest shelves in all the world are those bordering the Arctic. The Barents Sea shelf is 750 miles across. It is also relatively deep, lying for the most part 100 to 200 fathoms below the surface, as though its floor had sagged and been down-warped under the load of glacial ice. It is scored by deep troughs between which banks and islands rise—further evidence of the work of the ice. The deepest shelves surround the Antarctic continent, where soundings in many areas show depths of several hundred fathoms near the coast and continuing out across the shelf.

Once beyond the edge of the shelf, as we visualize the steeper declivities of the continental slope, we begin to feel the mystery and the alien quality of the deep sea—the gathering darkness, the growing pressure, the starkness of a sea-scape in which all plant life has been left behind and there are only the unrelieved contours of rock and clay, of mud and sand.

Biologically the world of the continental slope, like that of the abyss, is a world of animals—a world of carnivores where each creature preys upon another. For no plants live here, and the only ones that drift down from above are the dead husks of the flora of the sunlit waters. Most of the slopes are below the zone of surface wave action, yet the moving water masses of the ocean currents press against them in their coastwise passage; the pulse of the tide beats against them; they feel the surge of the deep, internal waves.

Geographically, the slopes are the most imposing features of all the surface of the earth. They are the walls of the deep-sea basins. They are the farthermost bounds of the continents, the true place of beginning of the sea. The slopes are the longest and highest escarpments found anywhere on the earth; their average height is 12,000 feet, but in some places the reach the immense height of 30,000 feet. No continental mountain range has so great a difference of elevation between its foothills and its peaks.

Nor is the grandeur of slope topography confined to steepness and height. The slopes are the site of one of the most mysterious features of the sea. These are the submarine canyons with their steep cliffs and winding valleys cutting back into the walls of the continents. The canyons have now been found in so many parts of the world that when soundings have been taken in presently unexplored areas we shall probably find that they are of worldwide occurrence. Geologists say that some of the canyons were formed well within the most recent division of geologic time, the Cenozoic, most of them probably within the Pleistocene, a million years ago, or less. But how and by what they were carved, no one can say. Their origin is one of the most hotly disputed problems of the ocean.

Only the fact that the canyons are deeply hidden in the darkness of the sea (many extending a mile or more below present sea level) prevents them from being classed with the world's most spectacular scenery. The comparison with the Grand Canyon of the Colorado is irresistible. Like river-cut land canyons, sea canyons are deep and winding valleys, V-shaped in cross section, their walls sloping down at a steep angle to a narrow floor. The location of many of the largest ones suggests a past connection with some of the great rivers of the earth of our time. Hudson Canyon, one of the largest on the Atlantic coast, is separated by only a shallow sill from a long valley that wanders for more than a hundred miles across the continental shelf, originating at the entrance of New York Harbor and the estuary of the Hudson River. There are large canyons off the Congo, the Indus, the Ganges, the Columbia, the São Francisco, and the Mississippi, according to Francis Shepard, one of the principal students of the canyon problem. Monterey Canyon in California, Professor Shepard points out, is located off an old mouth of the Salinas River; the Cap Breton Canyon in France appears to have no relation to an existing river but actually lies off an old fifteenth-century mouth of the Adour River.

Their shape and apparent relation to existing rivers have led Shepard to suggest that the submarine canyons were cut by rivers at some time when their gorges were above sea level. The relative youth of the canyons seems to relate them to some happenings in the world of the Ice Age. It is generally agreed that sea level was lowered during the existence of the great glaciers, for water was withdrawn from the sea and frozen in the ice sheet. But most geologists say that the sea was lowered only a few hundred feet—not the mile that would be necessary to account for the canyons. According to one theory, there were heavy submarine mud flows during the times when the glaciers were advancing and sea level fell the lowest; mud stirred up by waves poured down the continental slopes and scoured out the canyons. Since none of the present evidence is conclusive, however, we simply do not know how the canyons came into being, and their mystery remains.[8]

The floor of the deep ocean basins is probably as old as the sea itself. In all the hundreds of millions of years that have intervened since the formation of the abyss, these deeper depressions have never, as far as we can learn, been drained of their covering waters. While the bordering shelves of the continents have known, in alternating geologic ages, now the surge of waves and again the eroding tools of rain and wind and frost, always the abyss has lain under the all-enveloping cover of miles-deep water.

But this does not mean that the contours of the abyss have remained unchanged since the day of its creation. The floor of the sea, like the stuff of the continents, is a thin crust over the plastic mantle of the earth. It is here thrust up into folds and wrinkles as the interior cools by imperceptible degrees and shrinks away from its covering layer; there it falls away into deep trenches in answer to the stresses and strains of crustal adjustment; and again it pushes up into the conelike shapes of undersea mountains as volcanoes boil upward from fissures in the crust.

Until very recent years, it has been the fashion of geographers and oceanographers to speak of the floor of the deep sea as a vast and comparatively level plain. The existence of certain topographic features was recognized, as, for, example, the Atlantic Ridge and a number of very deep depressions like the Mindanao Trench off the Philippines. But these were considered to be rather exceptional interruptions of a flat floor that otherwise showed little relief.

This legend of the flatness of the ocean floor was thoroughly destroyed by the Swedish Deep-Sea Expedition, which sailed from Goteborg in the summer of 1947 and spent the following 15 months exploring the bed of the ocean. While the Swedish *Albatross* was crossing the Atlantic in the direction of the Panama Canal, the scientists aboard were astonished by the extreme ruggedness of the ocean floor. Rarely did their fathometers reveal more than a few consecutive miles of level plain. Instead the bottom profile rose and fell in curious steps constructed on a Gargantuan scale, half a mile to several miles wide. In the Pacific, the uneven bottom contours made it difficult to use many of the oceanographic instruments. More than one coring tube was left behind, probably lodged in some undersea crevasse.

One of the exceptions to a hilly or mountainous floor was in the Indian Ocean, where, southeast of Ceylon, the *Albatross* ran for several hundred miles across a level plain. Attempts to take bottom samples from this plain had little success, for the corers were broken repeatedly, suggesting that the bottom was hardened lava and that the whole vast plateau might have been formed by the outpourings of submarine volcanoes on a stupendous scale. Perhaps this lava plain under the Indian Ocean is an undersea counterpart of the great basaltic plateau in the eastern part of the State of Washington, or of the Deccan plateau of India, built of basaltic rock 10,000 feet thick.

In parts of the Atlantic basin the Woods Hole Oceanographic Institutions's vessel *Atlantis* has found a flat plain occupying much of the ocean basin from Bermuda to the Atlantic Ridge and also to the east of the Ridge. Only a series of knolls, probably of volcanic origin, interrupts the even contours of the plains. These particular regions are so flat that it seems they must have remained largely undisturbed, receiving deposits of sediments over an immense period of time.

The deepest depressions on the floor of the sea occur not in the centers of the oceanic basis as might be expected, but near the continents. One of the deepest trenches of all, the

Mindanao, lies east of the Philippines and is an awesome pit in the sea, six and a half miles deep.[9] The Tuscarora Trench east of Japan, nearly as deep, is one of a series of long, narrow trenches that border the convex outer rim of a chain of islands including the Bonins, the Marianas, and the Palaus. On the seaward side of the Aleutian Islands is another group of trenches. The greatest deeps of the Atlantic lie adjacent to the islands of the West Indies, and also below Cape Horn, where other curving chains of islands go out like stepping stones into the Southern Ocean. And again in the Indian Ocean the curving island arcs of the East Indies have their accompanying deeps.

Always there is this association of island arcs and deep trenches, and always the two occur only in areas of volcanic unrest. The pattern, it is now agreed, is associated with mountain making and the sharp adjustments of the sea floor that accompany it. On the concave side of the island arcs are rows of volcanoes. On the convex side there is a sharp down-bending of the ocean floor, which results in the deep trenches with their broad V-shape. The two forces seem to be in a kind of uneasy balance: the upward folding of the earth's crust to form mountains, and the thrusting down of the crust of the sea floor into the basaltic substance of the underlying layer. Sometimes, it seems, the down-thrust mass of granite has shattered and risen again to form islands. Such is the supposed origin of Barbados in the West Indies and of Timor in the East Indies. Both have deep-sea deposits, as though they had once been part of the sea floor. Yet this must be exceptional. In the words of the great geologist Daly,

> Another property of the earth is its ability . . . to resist shearing pressures indefinitely . . . The continents, overlooking the sea bottom, stubbornly refuse to creep thither. The rock under the Pacific is strong enough to bear, with no known time limit, the huge stresses involved by the down-thrust of the crust at the Tonga Deep, and by the erection of the 10,000-meter dome of lavas and other volcanic products represented in the island of Hawaii.*

The least-known region of the ocean floor lies under the Arctic Sea. The physical difficulties of sounding here are enormous. A permanent sheet of ice, as much as fifteen feet

---

* From *The Changing World of the Ice Age*, 1934 edition, Yale University Press, p. 116.

thick, covers the whole central basin and is impenetrable to ships. Peary took several soundings in the course of his dash to the Pole by dog team in 1909. On one attempt a few miles from the Pole the wire broke with 1500 fathoms out. In 1927 Sir Hubert Wilkins landed his plane on the ice 550 miles north of Point Barrow and obtained a single echo sounding of 2975 fathoms, the deepest ever recorded from the Arctic Sea. Vessels deliberately frozen into the ice (such as the Norwegian *Fram* and the Russian *Sedov* and *Sadko*) in order to drift with it across the basin have obtained most of the depth records available for the central parts. In 1937 and 1938 Russian scientists were landed near the Pole and supplied by plane while they lived on the ice, drifting with it. These men took nearly a score of deep soundings.

The most daring plan for sounding the Arctic Sea was conceived by Wilkins, who actually set out in the submarine *Nautilus* in 1931 with the intention of traveling beneath the ice across the entire basin from Spitsbergen to Bering Strait. Mechanical failure of the diving equipment a few days after the *Nautilus* left Spitsbergen prevented the execution of the plan. By the middle 1940's, the total of soundings for deep arctic areas by all methods was only about 150, leaving most of the top of the world an unsounded sea whose contours can only be guessed. Soon after the close of the Second World War, the United States Navy began tests of a new method of obtaining soundings through the ice, which may provide the key to the arctic riddle. One interesting speculation to be tested by future soundings is that the mountain chain that bisects the Atlantic, and has been supposed to reach its northern terminus at Iceland, may actually continue across the arctic basin to the coast of Russia. The belt of earthquake epicenters that follows the Atlantic Ridge seems to extend across the Arctic Sea, and where there are submarine earthquakes it is at least reasonable to guess that there may be mountainous topography.[10]

A new feature on recent maps of undersea relief—something never included before the 1940's—is a group of about 160 curious, flat-topped sea mounts between Hawaii and the Marianas. It happened that a Princeton University geologist, H. H. Hess, was in command of the U.S.S. *Cape Johnson* during two years of the wartime cruising of this vessel in the Pacific. Hess was immediately struck by the number of these undersea mountains that appeared on the fathograms of the vessel. Time after time, as the moving pen of the fathometer traced the depth contours it would abruptly begin to rise in an outline of a steep-sided sea mount, standing solitarily on the bed of the sea. Unlike a typical volcanic cone, all of the mounts have broad, flat tops, as though the peaks had been cut off and planed down by waves. But the summits of the sea mounts are anywhere from half a mile to a mile or more below the surface of the sea. How they acquired their flat-topped contours is a mystery perhaps as great as that of the submarine canyons.

Unlike the scattered sea mounts, the long ranges of undersea mountains have been marked on the charts for a good many years. The Atlantic Ridge was discovered about a century ago. The early surveys for the route of the trans-Atlantic cable gave the first hint of its existence. The German oceanographic vessel *Meteor,* which crossed and recrossed the Atlantic during the 1920's, established the contours of much of the Ridge. The *Atlantis* of the Woods Hole Oceanographic Institution has spent several summers in an exhaustive study of the Ridge in the general vicinity of the Azores.

Now we can trace the outlines of this great mountain range, and dimly we begin to see the details of its hidden peaks and valleys. The Ridge rises in mid-Atlantic near Iceland. From this far-northern latitude it runs south midway between the continents, crosses the equator into the South Atlantic, and continues to about 50° south latitude, where it turns sharply eastward under the tip of Africa and runs toward the Indian Ocean. Its general course closely parallels the coastlines of the bordering continents, even to the definite flexure at the equator between the hump of Brazil and the eastward-curving coast of Africa. To some people this curvature has suggested that the Ridge was once part of a great continental mass, left behind in mid-ocean when, according to one theory, the continents of North and South America drifted away from Europe and Africa. However, recent work shows that on the floor of the Atlantic there are thick masses of sediments which must have required hundreds of millions of years for their accumulation.

Throughout much of its 10,000-mile length, the Atlantic Ridge is a place of disturbed and uneasy movements of the ocean floor, and the whole Ridge gives the impression of something formed by the interplay of great, opposing forces. From its western foothills across to where its slopes roll down into the eastern Atlantic basin, the range is about twice as wide as the Andes and several times the width of the Appalachians. Near the equator a deep gash cuts across it from east to west—the Romanche Trench. This is the only point of communication between the deep basins of the eastern and western Atlantic, although among its higher peaks there are other, lesser mountain passes.

The greater part of the Ridge is, of course, submerged. Its central backbone rises some 5000 to 10,000 feet above the sea floor, but another mile of water lies above most of its summits. Yet here and there a peak thrusts itself up out of the darkness of deep water and pushes above the surface of the ocean. These are the islands of the mid-Atlantic. The highest peak of the Ridge is Pico Island of the Azores. It rises 27,000 feet above the ocean floor, with only its upper 7000 to 8000 feet emergent. The sharpest peaks of the Ridge are the cluster of islets known as the Rocks of St. Paul, near the equator. The entire cluster of half a dozen islets is not more than a quarter of a mile across, and their rocky slopes drop off at so sheer an angle that water more than half a mile deep lies only a few feet off shore. The sultry volcanic bulk of Ascension is another peak of the Atlantic Ridge; so are Tristan da Cunha, Gough, and Bouvet.

But most of the Ridge lies forever hidden from human eyes. Its contours have been made out only indirectly by the marvelous probings of sound waves; bits of its substance have been brought up to us by corers and dredges; and some details of its landscape have been photographed with deep-sea cameras. With these aids our imaginations can picture the grandeur of the undersea mountains, with their sheer cliffs and rocky terraces, their deep valleys and towering peaks. If we are to compare the ocean's mountains with anything on the continents, we must think of terrestrial mountains far above the timber line, with their silent snow-filled valleys and their naked rocks swept by the winds. For the sea has an inverted 'timber line' or plant line, below which no vegetation can grow. The slopes of the undersea mountains are far beyond the reach of the sun's rays, and there are only the bare rocks, and, in the valleys, the deep drifts of sediments that have been silently piling up through the millions upon millions of years.

Neither the Pacific Ocean nor the Indian Ocean has any submerged mountains that compare in length with the Atlantic Ridge, but they have their smaller ranges. The Hawaiian Islands are the peaks of a mountain range that runs across the central Pacific basin for a distance of nearly 2000 miles. The Gilbert and Marshall islands stand on the shoulders of another mid-Pacific mountain chain. In the eastern Pacific, a broad plateau connects the coast of South America and the Tuamotu Islands in the mid-Pacific, and in the Indian Ocean a long ridge runs from India to Antarctica, for most of its length broader and deeper than the Atlantic Ridge.

One of the most fascinating fields for speculation is the age of the submarine mountains compared with that of past and present mountains of the continents. Looking back over the past ages of geologic time (page 26), we realize that mountains have been thrust up on the continents, to the accompaniment of volcanic outpourings and violent tremblings of the earth, only to crumble and wear away under the attacks of rain and frost and flood. What of the sea's mountains? Were they formed in the same way and do they, too, begin to die as soon as they are born?

There are indications that the earth's crust is no more stable under sea than on land. Quite a fair proportion of the world's earthquakes are traced through seismographs to sources under the oceans, and, as we shall see later, there are probably as many active volcanoes under water as on land. Apparently the Atlantic Ridge arose along a line of crustal shifting and rearrangement; although its volcanic fires seem to be largely quiescent, it is at present the site of most of the earthquakes in the Atlantic area. Almost the whole continental rim of the Pacific basin is aquiver with earthquakes and fiery with volcanoes, some frequently active, some extinct, some merely sleeping a centuries-long sleep between periods of explosive violence. From the high mountains that form an almost continuous border around the shores of the Pacific, the contours of the land slope abruptly down to very deep water. The deep trenches that lie off the coast of South America, from Alaska along the Aleutian Islands and across to Japan, and southward off Japan and the Philippines give the impression of a landscape in process of formation, of a zone of earth subject to great strains.

Yet the submarine mountains are earth's nearest approach to the 'eternal hills' of the poets. No sooner is a continental mountain thrust up than all the forces of nature conspire to level it. A mountain of the deep sea, in the years of its maturity, is beyond the reach of the ordinary erosive forces. It grows up on the ocean floor and may thrust volcanic peaks above the surface of the sea. These islands are attacked by the rains, and in time the young mountain is brought down within reach of the waves; in the tumult of the sea's attack it sinks again beneath the surface. Eventually the peak is worn down below the push and pull and drag of even the heaviest of storm waves. Here, in the twilight of the sea, in the calm of deep water, the mountain is secure from further attack. Here it is likely to remain almost unchanged, perhaps throughout the life of the earth.

Because of this virtual immortality, the oldest oceanic mountains must be infinitely older than any of the ranges left on land. Professor Hess, who discovered the sea mounts of the central Pacific, suggested that these 'drowned ancient islands' may have been formed before the Cambrian period, or somewhere between 500 million and 1 billion years ago. This would make them perhaps of an age with the continental mountains of the Laurentian upheaval. But the sea mounts have changed little if at all, comparing in elevation with modern terrestrial peaks like the Jungfrau, Mt. Etna, or Mt. Hood; while of the mountains of the Laurentian period scarcely a trace remains. The Pacific sea mounts, according to this theory, must have been of substantial age when the Appalachians were thrust up, 200 million years ago; they stood almost unchanged while the Appalachians wore down to mere wrinkles on the earth's face. The sea mounts were old, 60 million years ago, when the Alps and the Himalayas, the Rockies and the Andes, rose to their majestic heights. Yet it is probable that they will be standing unchanged in the deep sea when these, too, shall have crumbled away to dust.

As the hidden lands beneath the sea become better known, there recurs again and again the query: can the submerged masses of the undersea mountains be linked with the famed 'lost continents'? Shadowy and insubstantial as are the accounts of all such legendary lands—the fabled Lemuria of the Indian Ocean, St. Brendan's Island, the lost Atlantis—they persistently recur like some deeply rooted racial memory in the folklore of many parts of the world.

Best known is Atlantis, which according to Plato's account was a large island or continent beyond the Pillars of Hercules. Atlantis was the home of a warlike people ruled by powerful kings who made frequent attacks upon the mainlands of Africa and Europe, brought much of Libya under their power, roamed the Mediterranean coast of Europe, and finally attacked Athens. However, 'with great earthquakes and inundations, in a single day and one fatal night, all who had been warriors [against Greece] were swallowed up. The Island of Atlantis disappeared beneath the sea. Since that time the sea in these quarters has become unnavigable; vessels cannot press there because of the sands which extend over the site of the buried isle.'

The Atlantis legend has lived on through the centuries. As men became bold enough to sail out on the Atlantic, to cross it, and later to investigate its depths, they speculated about the location of the lost land. Various Atlantic islands have been said to be the remains of a land mass once more extensive. The lonely wave-washed Rocks of St. Paul, perhaps more often than any other, have been identified as the remains of Atlantis. During the past century, as the extent of the Atlantic Ridge became better known, speculations were often centered upon this great mass, far below the surface of the ocean.

Unfortunately for these picturesque imaginings, if the Ridge was ever exposed, it must have been at a time long before there were men to populate such an Atlantis. Some of the cores taken from the Ridge show a continuous series of sediments typical of open oceans, far from land, running back to a period some 60 million years ago. And man, even the most primitive type, has appeared only within the past million years or so.

Like other legends deeply rooted in folklore, the Atlantis story may have in it an element of truth. In the shadowy beginnings of human life on earth, primitive men here and there must have had knowledge of the sinking of an island or a peninsula, perhaps not with the dramatic suddenness attributed to Atlantis, but well within the time one man could observe. The witnesses of such a happening would have described it to their neighbors and children, and so the legend of a sinking continent might have been born.

Such a lost land lies today beneath the waters of the North Sea. Only a few scores of thousands of years ago, the Dogger Bank was dry land, but now the fishermen drag their nets over this famed fishing ground, catching cod and hake and flounders among its drowned tree trunks.

During the Pleistocene, when immense quantities of water were withdrawn from the ocean and locked up in the glaciers, the floor of the North Sea emerged and for a time became land. It was a low, wet land, covered with peat bogs; then little by little the forests from the neighboring high lands must have moved in, for there were willows and birches growing among the mosses and ferns. Animals moved down from the mainland and became established on this land recently won from the sea. There were bears and wolves and hyenas, the wild ox, the bison, the woolly rhinoceros, and the mammoth. Primitive men moved through the forests, carrying crude stone instruments; they stalked deer and other game and with their flints grubbed up the roots of the damp forest.

Then as the glaciers began to retreat and floods from the

melting ice poured into the sea and raised its level, this land became an island. Probably the men escaped to the mainland before the intervening channel had become too wide, leaving their stone implements behind. But most of the animals remained, perforce, and little by little their island shrank, and food became more and more scarce, but there was no escape. Finally the sea covered the island, claiming the land and all its life.

As for the men who escaped, perhaps in their primitive way they communicated this story to other men, who passed it down to others through the ages, until it became fixed in the memory of the race.

None of these facts were part of recorded history until, a generation ago, European fishermen moved out into the middle of the North Sea and began to trawl on the Dogger. They soon made out the contours of an irregular plateau nearly as large as Denmark, lying about 60 feet under water, but sloping off abruptly at its edges into much deeper water. Their trawls immediately began to bring up a great many things not found on any ordinary fishing bank. There were loose masses of peat, which the fishermen christened 'moorlog.' There were many bones, and, although the fishermen could not identify them, they seemed to belong to large land mammals. All of these objects damaged the nets and hindered fishing, so whenever possible the fishermen dragged them off the bank and sent them tumbling into deep water. But they brought back some of the bones, some of the moorlog and fragments of trees, and the crude stone implements; these specimens were turned over to scientists to identify. In this strange debris of the fishing nets the scientists recognized a whole Pleistocene fauna and flora, and the artifacts of Stone Age man. And remembering how once the North Sea had been dry land, they reconstructed the story of Dogger Bank, the lost island.

The Long Snowfall

A DEEP AND TREMULOUS EARTH-POETRY.
—LLEWELYN POWYS

Every part of earth or air or sea has an atmosphere peculiarly its own, a quality or characteristic that sets it apart from all others. When I think of the floor of the deep sea, the single, overwhelming fact that possesses my imagination is the accumulation of sediments. I see always the steady, unremitting, downward drift of materials from above, flake upon flake, layer upon layer—a drift that has continued for hundreds of millions of years, that will go on as long as there are seas and continents.

For the sediments are the materials of the most stupendous 'snowfall' the earth has ever seen. It began when the first rains fell on the barren rocks and set in motion the forces of erosion. It was accelerated when living creatures developed in the surface waters and the discarded little shells of lime or silica that had encased them in life began to drift downward to the bottom. Silently, endlessly, with the deliberation of earth processes that can afford to be slow because they have so much time for completion, the accumulation of the sediments has proceeded. So little in a year, or in a human lifetime, but so enormous an amount in the life of earth and sea.

The rains, the eroding away of the earth, the rush of sediment-laden waters have continued, with varying pulse and tempo, throughout all of geologic time. In addition to the silt load of every river that finds its way to the sea, there are other materials that compose the sediments. Volcanic dust, blown perhaps half way around the earth in the upper atmosphere, comes eventually to rest on the ocean, drifts in the currents, becomes waterlogged, and sinks. Sands from coastal deserts are carried seaward on offshore winds, fall to the sea, and sink. Gravel, pebbles, small

77

boulders, and shells are carried by icebergs and drift ice, to be released to the water when the ice melts. Fragments of iron, nickel, and other meteoric debris that enter the earth's atmosphere over the sea—these, too, become flakes of the great snowfall. But most widely distributed of all are the billions upon billions of tiny shells and skeletons, the limy or silicious remains of all the minute creatures that once lived in the upper waters.

The sediments are a sort of epic poem of the earth. When we are wise enough, perhaps we can read in them all of past history. For all is written here. In the nature of the materials that compose them and in the arrangement of their successive layers the sediments reflect all that has happened in the waters above them and on the surrounding lands. The dramatic and the catastrophic in earth history have left their trace in the sediments—the outpourings of volcanoes, the advance and retreat of the ice, the searing aridity of desert lands, the sweeping destruction of floods.

The book of the sediments has been opened only within the lifetime of the present generation of scientists, with the most exciting progress in collecting and deciphering samples made since 1945. Early oceanographers could scrape up surface layers of sediment from the sea bottom with dredges. But what was needed was an instrument, operated on the principle of an apple corer, that could be driven vertically into the bottom to remove a long sample or 'core' in which the order of the different layers was undisturbed. Such an instrument was invented by Dr. C. S. Piggot in 1935, and with the aid of this 'gun' he obtained a series of cores across the deep Atlantic from Newfoundland to Ireland. These cores averaged about 10 feet long. A piston core sampler, developed by the Swedish oceanographer Kullenberg about 10 years later, now takes undisturbed cores 70 feet long. The rate of sedimentation in the different parts of the ocean is not definitely known, but it is very slow; certainly such a sample represents millions of years of geologic history.

Another ingenious method for studying the sediments has been used by Professor W. Maurice Ewing of Columbia University and the Woods Hole Oceanographic Institution. Professor Ewing found that he could measure the thickness of the carpeting layer of sediments that overlies the rock of the ocean floor by exploding depth charges and recording their echoes; one echo is received from the top of the sediment layer (the apparent bottom of the sea), another from the 'bottom below the bottom' or the true rock floor.

The carrying and use of explosives at sea is hazardous and cannot be attempted by all vessels, but this method was used by the Swedish *Albatross* as well as by the *Atlantis* in its exploration of the Atlantic Ridge. Ewing on the *Atlantis* also used a seismic refraction technique by which sound waves are made to travel horizontally through the rock layers of the ocean floor, providing information about the nature of the rock.

Before these techniques were developed, we could only guess at the thickness of the sediment blanket over the floor of the sea. We might have expected the amount to be vast, if we thought back through the ages of gentle, unending fall—one sand grain at a time, one fragile shell after another, here a shark's tooth, there a meteorite fragment—but the whole continuing persistently, relentlessly, endlessly. It is, of course, a process similar to that which has built up the layers of rock that help to make our mountains, for they, too, were once soft sediments under the shallow seas that have overflowed the continents from time to time. The sediments eventually became consolidated and cemented and, as the seas retreated again, gave the continents their thick, covering layers of sedimentary rocks—layers which we can see uplifted, tilted, compressed, and broken by the vast earth movements. And we know that in places the sedimentary rocks are many thousands of feet thick. Yet most people felt a shock of surprise and wonder when Hans Pettersson, leader of the Swedish Deep Sea Expedition, announced that the *Albatross* measurements taken in the open Atlantic basin showed sediment layers as much as 12,000 feet thick.

If more than two miles of sediments have been deposited on the floor of the Atlantic, an interesting question arises: has the rocky floor sagged a corresponding distance under the terrific weight of the sediments? Geologists hold conflicting opinions. The recently discovered Pacific sea mounts may offer one piece of evidence that it has. If they are, as their discoverer called them, 'drowned ancient islands,' then they may have reached their present stand a mile or so below sea level through the sinking of the ocean floor. Hess believed the islands had been formed so long ago that coral animals had not yet evolved; otherwise the corals would presumably have settled on the flat, planed surfaces of the sea mounts and built them up as fast as their bases sank. In any event, it is hard to see how they could have been worn down so far below 'wave base' unless the crust of the earth sagged under its load.

One thing seems probable—the sediments have been un-

evenly distributed both in place and time. In contrast to
the 12,000-foot thickness found in parts of the Atlantic,
the Swedish oceanographers never found sediments thicker
than 1000 feet in the Pacific or in the Indian Ocean.
Perhaps a deep layer of lava, from ancient submarine eruptions on a stupendous scale, underlies the upper layers of
the sediments in these places and intercepts the sound waves.

Interesting variations in the thickness of the sediment
layer of the Atlantic Ridge and the approaches to the Ridge
from the American side were reported by Ewing. As the
bottom contours became less even and began to slope up
into the foothills of the Ridge, the sediments thickened,
as though piling up into mammoth drifts 1000 to 2000
feet deep against the slopes of the hills. Farther up in the
mountains of the Ridge, where there are many level terraces from a few to a score of miles wide, the sediments
were even deeper, measuring up to 3000 feet. But along
the backbone of the Ridge, on the steep slopes and peaks
and pinnacles, the bare rock emerged, swept clean of sediments.[11]

Reflecting on these differences in thickness and distribution, our minds return inevitably to the simile of the long
snowfall. We may think of the abyssal snowstorm in terms
of a bleak and blizzard-ridden arctic tundra. Long days of
storm visit this place, when driving snow fills the air; then
a lull comes in the blizzard, and the snowfall is light.
In the snowfall of the sediments, also, there is an alternation of light and heavy falls. The heavy falls correspond
to the periods of mountain building on the continents, when
the lands are lifted high and the rain rushes down their
slopes, carrying mud and rock fragments to the sea; the
light falls mark the lulls between the mountain-building periods, when the continents are flat and erosion is slowed.
And again, on our imaginary tundra, the winds blow the snow
into deep drifts, filling in all the valleys between the ridges,
piling the snow up and up until the contours of the land are
obliterated, but scouring the ridges clear. In the drifting
sediments on the floor of the ocean we see the work of the
'winds,' which may be the deep ocean currents, distributing
the sediments according to laws of their own, not as yet
grasped by human minds.

We have known the general pattern of the sediment carpet, however, for a good many years. Around the foundations of the continents, in the deep waters off the borders
of the continental slopes, are the muds of terrestrial origin.
There are muds of many colors—blue, green, red, black, and

white—apparently varying with climatic changes as well as with the dominant soils and rocks of the lands of their origin. Farther at sea are the oozes of predominantly marine origin—the remains of the trillions of tiny sea creatures. Over great areas of the temperate oceans the sea floor is largely covered with the remains of unicellular creatures known as foraminifera, of which the most abundant genus is Globigerina. The shells of Globigerina may be recognized in very ancient sediments as well as in modern ones, but over the ages the species have varied. Knowing this, we can date approximately the deposits in which they occur. But always they have been simple animals, living in an intricately sculptured shell of carbonate of lime, the whole so small you would need a microscope to see its details. After the fashion of unicellular beings, the individual Globigerina normally did not die, but by the division of its substance became two. At each division, the old shell was abandoned, and two new ones were formed. In warm, lime-rich seas these tiny creatures have always multiplied prodigiously, and so, although each is so minute, their innumerable shells blanket millions of square miles of ocean bottom, and to a depth of thousands of feet.

In the great depths of the ocean, however, the immense pressures and the high carbon-dioxide content of deep water dissolve much of the lime long before it reaches the bottom and return it to the great chemical reservoir of the sea. Silica is more resistant to solution. It is one of the curious paradoxes of the ocean that the bulk of the organic remains that reach the great depths intact belong to unicellular creatures seemingly of the most delicate construction. The radiolarians remind us irresistibly of snow flakes, as infinitely varied in pattern, as lacy, and as intricately made. Yet because their shells are fashioned of silica instead of carbonate of lime, they can descend unchanged into the abyssal depths. So there are broad bands of radiolarian ooze in the deep tropical waters of the North Pacific, underlying the surface zones where the living radiolarians occur most numerously.

Two other kinds of organic sediments are named for the creatures whose remains compose them. Diatoms, the microscopic plant life of the sea, flourish most abundantly in cold waters. There is a broad belt of diatom ooze on the floor of the Antarctic Ocean, outside the zone of glacial debris dropped by the ice pack. There is another across the North Pacific, along the chain of great deeps that run from Alaska to Japan. Both are zones where nutrient-laden water wells up from the depths, sustaining a rich growth of plants. The diatoms, like the radiolarians are encased in silicious coverings—small, boxlike cases of varied shape and meticulously etched design.

Then, in relatively shallow parts of the open Atlantic, there are patches of ooze composed of the remains of delicate swimming snails, called pteropods. These winged mollusks, possessing transparent shells of great beauty, are here and there incredibly abundant. Pteropod ooze is the characteristic bottom deposit in the vicinity of Bermuda, and a large patch occurs in the South Atlantic.

Mysterious and eerie are the immense areas, especially in the North Pacific, carpeted with a soft, red sediment in which there are no organic remains except sharks' teeth and the ear bones of whales. This red clay occurs at great depths. Perhaps all the materials of the other sediments are dissolved before they can reach this zone of immense pressures and glacial cold.

The reading of the story contained in the sediments has only begun. When more cores are collected and examined we shall certainly decipher many exciting chapters. Geologists have pointed out that a series of cores from the Mediterranean might settle several controversial problems concerning the history of the ocean and of the lands around the Mediterranean basin. For example, somewhere in the layers of sediment under this sea there must be evidence, in a sharply defined layer of sand, of the time when the deserts of the Sahara were formed and the hot, dry winds began to skim off the shifting surface layers and carry them seaward. Long cores recently obtained in the western Mediterranean off Algeria have given a record of volcanic activity extending back through thousands of years, and including great prehistoric eruptions of which we know nothing.

The Atlantic cores taken more than a decade ago by Piggot from the cable ship *Lord Kelvin* have been thoroughly studied by geologists. From their analysis it is possible to look back into the past 10,000 years or so and to sense the pulse of the earth's climatic rhythms; for the cores were composed of layers of coldwater Globigerina faunas (and hence glacial stage sediments), alternating with Globigerina ooze characteristic of warmer waters. From the clues furnished by these cores we can visualize interglacial stages when there were periods of mild climates, with warm water overlying the sea bottom and warmth-loving creatures living in the ocean. Between these periods the sea grew chill. Clouds gathered, the snows fell, and on the North American continent the great ice sheets grew and the ice mountains moved out to the coast. The glaciers reached the sea along a wide front; there they produced icebergs by the thousand. The slow-moving, majestic processions of the bergs passed out to sea, and because of the coldness of much of the earth they penetrated farther south than any but stray bergs do today. When finally they melted, they relinquished their loads of silt and sand and gravel and rock fragments that had become frozen into their under surfaces as they made their grinding way over the land. And so a layer of glacial sediment came to overlie the normal Globigerina ooze, and the record of an Ice Age was inscribed.

Then the sea grew warmer again, the glaciers melted and retreated, and once more the warmer-water species of Globigerina lived in the sea—lived and died and drifted down to build another layer of Globigerina ooze, this time over the clays and gravels from the glaciers. And the record of warmth and mildness was again written in the sediments. From the Piggot cores it has been possible to reconstruct four different periods of the advance of the ice, separated by periods of warm climate.

It is interesting to think that even now, in our own lifetime, the flakes of a new snow storm are falling, falling, one by one, out there on the ocean floor. The billions of Globigerina are drifting down, writing their unequivocal record that this, our present world, is on the whole a world of mild and temperate climate. Who will read their record, ten thousand years from now?

The Birth of an Island

MANY A GREEN ISLE NEEDS MUST BE
IN THE DEEP, WIDE SEA . . .
—SHELLEY

Millions of years ago, a volcano built a mountain on the floor of the Atlantic. In eruption after eruption, it pushed up a great pile of volcanic rock, until it had accumulated a mass a hundred miles across at its base, reaching upward toward the surface of the sea. Finally its cone emerged as an island with an area of about 200 square miles. Thousands of years passed, and thousands of thousands. Eventually the waves of the Atlantic cut down the cone and reduced it to a shoal—all of it, that is, but a small fragment which remained above water. This fragment we know as Bermuda.

With variations, the life story of Bermuda has been repeated by almost every one of the islands that interrupt the watery expanses of the oceans far from land. For these isolated islands in the sea are fundamentally different from the continents. The major land masses and the ocean basins are today much as they have been throughout the greater part of geologic time. But islands are ephemeral, created today, destroyed tomorrow. With few exceptions, they are the result of the violent, explosive, earth-shaking eruptions of submarine volcanoes, working perhaps for millions of years to achieve their end. It is one of the paradoxes in the ways of earth and sea that a process seemingly so destructive, so catastrophic in nature, can result in an act of creation.

Islands have always fascinated the human mind. Perhaps it is the instinctive response of man, the land animal, welcoming a brief intrusion of earth in the vast, overwhelming expanse of sea. Here in a great ocean basin, a thousand miles from the nearest continent, with miles of water under our vessel, we come upon an island. Our imaginations can follow its slopes down through darkening waters to where it rests on the sea floor. We wonder why and how it arose here in the midst of the ocean.

The birth of a volcanic island is an event marked by prolonged and violent travail: the forces of the earth striving to create, and all the forces of the sea opposing. The sea floor, where an island begins, is probably nowhere more than about fifty miles thick—a thin covering over the vast bulk of the earth. In it are deep cracks and fissures, the results of unequal cooling and shrinkage in past ages. Along such lines of weakness the molten lava from the earth's interior presses up and finally bursts forth into the sea. But a submarine volcano is different from a terrestrial eruption, where the lava, molten rocks, gases, and other ejecta are hurled into the air through an open crater. Here on the bottom of the ocean the volcano has resisting it all the weight of the ocean water above it. Despite the immense pressure of, it may be, two or three miles of sea water, the new volcanic cone builds upward toward the surface, in flow after flow of lava. Once within reach of the waves, its soft ash and tuff are violently attacked, and for a long period the potential island may remain a shoal, unable to emerge. But, eventually, in new eruptions, the cone is pushed up into the air and a rampart against the attacks of the waves is built of hardened lava.

Navigators' charts are marked with numerous, recently discovered submarine mountains. Many of these are the submerged remnants of the islands of a geologic yesterday. The same charts show islands that emerged from the sea at least fifty million years ago, and others that arose within our own memory. Among the undersea mountains marked on the charts may be the islands of tomorrow, which at this moment are forming, unseen, on the floor of the ocean and are growing upward toward its surface.

For the sea is by no means done with submarine eruptions; they occur fairly commonly, sometimes detected only by instruments, sometimes obvious to the most casual observer. Ships in volcanic zones may suddenly find themselves in violently disturbed water. There are heavy discharges of steam. The sea appears to bubble or boil in a furious turbulence. Fountains spring from its surface. Floating up from the deep, hidden places of the actual eruption come the bodies of fishes and other deep-sea creatures, and quantities of volcanic ash and pumice.

One of the youngest of the large volcanic islands of the world is Ascension in the South Atlantic. During the Second World War the American airmen sang

If we don't find Ascension
Our wives will get a pension

this island being the only piece of dry land between the hump of Brazil and the bulge of Africa. It is a forbidding mass of cinders, in which the vents of no less than forty extinct volcanoes can be counted. It has not always been so barren, for its slopes have yielded the fossil remains of trees. What happened to the forests no one knows; the first men to explore the island, about the year 1500, found it treeless, and today it has no natural greenness except on its highest peak, known as Green Mountain.

In modern times we have never seen the birth of an island as large as Ascension. But now and then there is a report of a small island appearing where none was before. Perhaps a month, a year, five years later, the island has disappeared into the sea again. These are the little, stillborn islands, doomed to only a brief emergence above the sea.

About 1830 such an island suddenly appeared in the Mediterranean between Sicily and the coast of Africa, rising from 100-fathom depths after there had been signs of volcanic activity in the area. It was little more than a black cinder pile, perhaps 200 feet high. Waves, wind, and rain attacked it. Its soft and porous materials were easily eroded; its substance was rapidly eaten away and it sank beneath the sea. Now it is a shoal, marked on the charts as Graham's Reef.

Falcon Island, the tip of a volcano projecting above the Pacific nearly two thousand miles east of Australia, suddenly disappeared in 1913. Thirteen years later, after violent eruptions in the vicinity, it as suddenly rose again above the surface and remained as a physical bit of the British Empire until 1949. Then it was reported by the Colonial Under Secretary to be missing again.

Almost from the moment of its creation, a volcanic island is foredoomed to destruction. It has in itself the seeds of its own dissolution, for new explosions, or landslides of the soft soil, may violently accelerate its disintegration. Whether the destruction of an island comes quickly or only after long ages of geologic time may also depend on external forces: the rains that wear away the loftiest of land mountains, the sea, and even man himself.

South Trinidad, or in the Portuguese spelling, 'Ilha Trinidade,' is an example of an island that has been sculptured into bizarre forms through centuries of weathering—an island in which the signs of dissolution are clearly apparent.

This group of volcanic peaks lies in the open Atlantic, about a thousand miles northeast of Rio de Janeiro. E. F. Knight wrote in 1907 that Trinidad 'is rotten throughout, its substance has been disintegrated by volcanic fires and by the action of water, so that it is everywhere tumbling to pieces.' During an interval of nine years between Knight's visits, a whole mountainside had collapsed in a great landslide of broken rocks and volcanic debris.

Sometimes the disintegration takes abrupt and violent form. The greatest explosion of historic time was the literal evisceration of the island of Krakatoa. In 1680 there had been a premonitory eruption on this small island in Sunda Strait, between Java and Sumatra in the Netherlands Indies. Two hundred years later there had been a series of earthquakes. In the spring of 1883, smoke and steam began to ascend from fissures in the volcanic cone. The ground became noticeably warm, and warning rumblings and hissings came from the volcano. Then, on 27 August, Krakatoa literally exploded. In an appalling series of eruptions, that lasted two days, the whole northern half of the cone was carried away. The sudden inrush of ocean water added the fury of superheated steam to the cauldron. When the inferno of white-hot lava, molten rock, steam, and smoke had finally subsided, the island that had stood 1400 feet above the sea had become a cavity a thousand feet below sea level. Only along one edge of the former crater did a remnant of the island remain.

Krakatoa, in its destruction, became known to the entire world. The eruption gave rise to a hundred-foot wave that wiped out villages along the Strait and killed people by tens of thousands. The wave was felt on the shores of the Indian Ocean and at Cape Horn; rounding the Cape into the Atlantic, it sped northward and retained its identity even as far as the English Channel. The sound of the explosions was heard in the Philippine Islands, in Australia, and on the Island of Madagascar, nearly 3000 miles away. And clouds of volcanic dust, the pulverized rock that had been torn from the heart of Krakatoa, ascended into the stratosphere and were carried around the globe to give rise to a series of spectacular sunsets in every country of the world for nearly a year.

Although Krakatoa's dramatic passing was the most violent eruption that modern man has witnessed, Krakatoa itself seems to have been the product of an even greater one. There is evidence that an immense volcano once stood where the waters of Sunda Strait now lie. In some remote period a titanic explosion blew it away, leaving only its base represented by a broken ring of islands. The largest of these was

Krakatoa, which, in its own demise, carried away what was left of the original crater ring. But in 1929 a new volcanic island arose in this place—Anak Krakatoa, Child of Krakatoa.

Subterranean fires and deep unrest disturb the whole area occupied by the Aleutians. The islands themselves are the peaks of a thousand-mile chain of undersea mountains, of which volcanic action was the chief architect. The geologic structure of the ridge is little known, but it rises abruptly from oceanic depths of about a mile on one side and two miles on the other. Apparently this long narrow ridge indicates a deep fracture of the earth's crust. On many of the islands volcanoes are now active, or only temporarily quiescent. In the short history of modern navigation in this region, it has often happened that a new island has been reported but perhaps only the following year could not be found.

The small island of Bogoslof, since it was first observed in 1796, has altered its shape and position several times and has even disappeared completely, only to emerge again. The original island was a mass of black rock, sculptured into fantastic, towerlike shapes. Explorers and sealers coming upon it in the fog were reminded of a castle and named it Castle Rock. At the present time there remain only one or two pinnacles of the castle, a long spit of black rocks where sea lions haul out, and a cluster of higher rocks resounding with the cries of thousands of sea birds. Each time the parent volcano erupts, as it has done at least half a dozen times since men have been observing it, new masses of steaming rocks emerge from the heated waters, some to reach heights of several hundred feet before they are destroyed in fresh explosions. Each new cone that appears is, as described by the volcanologist Jaggar, 'the live crest, equivalent to a crater, of a great submarine heap of lava six thousand feet high, piled above the floor of Bering Sea where the Aleutian mountains fall off to the deep sea.'

One of the few exceptions to the almost universal rule that oceanic islands have a volcanic origin seems to be the remarkable and fascinating group of islets known as the Rocks of St. Paul. Lying in the open Atlantic between Brazil and Africa, St. Paul's Rocks are an obstruction thrust up from the floor of the ocean into the midst of the racing Equatorial Current, a mass against which the seas, which have rolled a thousand miles unhindered, break in sudden violence. The entire cluster of rocks covers not more than a quarter of a mile, running in a curved line like a horseshoe. The highest rock is no more than sixty feet above the sea; spray wets it to the summit. Abruptly the rocks dip under water and slope steeply down into great depths. Geologists since the time of Darwin have puzzled over the origin of these black, wave-washed islets. Most of them agree that they are composed of material like that of the sea floor itself. In some remote period, inconceivable stresses in the earth's crust must have pushed a solid rock mass upward more than two miles.

So bare and desolate that not even a lichen grows on them, St. Paul's Rocks would seem one of the most unpromising places in the world to look for a spider, spinning its web in arachnidan hope of snaring passing insects. Yet Darwin found spiders when he visited the Rocks in 1833, and forty years later the naturalists of H.M.S. *Challenger* also reported them, busy at their web-spinning. A few insects are there, too, some as parasites on the sea birds, three species of which nest on the Rocks. One of the insects is a small brown moth that lives on feathers. This very nearly completes the inventory of the inhabitants of St. Paul's Rocks, except for the grotesque crabs that swarm over the islets, living chiefly on the flying fish brought by the birds to their young.

St. Paul's Rocks are not alone in having an extraordinary assortment of inhabitants, for the faunas and floras of oceanic islands are amazingly different from those of the continents. The pattern of island life is peculiar and significant. Aside from forms recently introduced by man, islands remote from the continents are never inhabited by any land mammals, except sometimes the one mammal that has learned to fly—the bat. There are never any frogs, salamanders, or other amphibians. Of reptiles, there may be a few snakes, lizards, and turtles, but the more remote the island from a major land mass, the fewer reptiles there are, and the really isolated islands have none. There are usually a few species of land birds, some insects, and some spiders. So remote an island as Tristan da Cunha in the South Atlantic, 1500 miles from the nearest continent, has no land animals but these: three species of land birds, a few insects, and several small snails.

With so selective a list, it is hard to see how, as some biologists believe, the islands could have been colonized by migration across land bridges, even if there were good evidence for the existence of the bridges. The very animals missing from the islands are the ones that would have had to come dry-shod, over the hypothetical bridges. The plants and animals that we find on oceanic islands, on the other hand, are the ones that could have come by wind or water. As an alternative, then, we must suppose that the stocking of the islands has been accomplished by the strangest migration in earth's history—a migration that began long before man appeared on earth and is still continuing, a migration that seems more like a series of cosmic accidents than an orderly process of nature.

We can only guess how long after its emergence from the sea an oceanic island may lie uninhabited. Certainly in its original state it is a land bare, harsh, and repelling beyond human experience. No living thing moves over the slopes of its volcanic hills; no plants cover its naked lava fields. But little by little, riding on the winds, drifting on the currents, or rafting in on logs, floating brush, or trees, the plants and animals that are to colonize it arrive from the distant continents.

So deliberate, so unhurried, so inexorable are the ways of nature that the stocking of an island may require thousands or millions of years. It may be that no more than half a dozen times in all these eons does a particular form, such as a tortoise, make a successful landing upon its shores. To wonder impatiently why man is not a constant witness of such arrivals is to fail to understand the majestic pace of the process.

Yet we have occasional glimpses of the method. Natural rafts of uprooted trees and matted vegetation have frequently been seen adrift at sea, more than a thousand miles off the mouths of such great tropical rivers as the Congo, the Ganges, the Amazon, and the Orinoco. Such rafts could easily carry an assortment of insect, reptile, or mollusk passengers. Some of the involuntary passengers might be able to withstand long weeks at sea; others would die during the first stages of the journey. Probably the ones best adapted for travel by raft are the wood-boring insects, which, of all the insect tribe, are most commonly found on oceanic islands. The poorest raft travelers must be the mammals. But even a mammal might cover short interisland distances. A few days after the explosion of Krakatoa, a small monkey was rescued from some drifting timber in Sundra Strait. She had been terribly burned, but survived the experience.

No less than the water, the winds and the air currents play their part in bringing habitants to the islands. The upper atmosphere, even during the ages before man entered it in his machines, was a place of congested traffic. Thousands of feet above the earth, the air is crowded with living creatures, drifting, flying, gliding, ballooning, or involuntarily swirling along on the high winds. Discovery of this rich aerial plankton had to wait until man himself had found means to make physical invasion of these regions. With special nets and traps, scientists have now collected from the upper atmosphere many of the forms that inhabit oceanic islands. Spiders, whose almost invariable presence on these islands is a fascinating problem, have been captured nearly three miles above the earth's surface. Airmen have passed through great numbers of the white, silken filaments of spiders' 'parachutes' at heights of two to three miles. At altitudes of 6000 to 16,000 feet, and with wind velocities reaching 45 miles an hour, many living insects have been taken. At such heights and on such strong winds, they might well have been carried hundreds of miles. Seeds have been collected at altitudes up to 5000 feet. Among those commonly taken are members of the Composite family, especially the so-called 'thistle-down' typical of oceanic islands.

An interesting point about transport of living plants and animals by wind is the fact that in the upper layers of the earth's atmosphere the winds do not necessarily blow in the same direction as at the earth's surface. The trade winds are notably shallow, so that a man standing on the cliffs of St. Helena, a thousand feet above the sea, is above the wind, which blows with great force below him. Once drawn into the upper air, insects, seeds, and the like can easily be carried in a direction contrary to that of the winds prevailing at island level.

The wide-ranging birds that visit islands of the ocean in migration may also have a good deal to do with the distribution of plants, and perhaps even of some insects and minute land shells. From a ball of mud taken from a bird's plumage, Charles Darwin raised eighty-two separate plants, belonging to five distinct species! Many plant seeds have hooks or prickles, ideal for attachment to feathers. Such birds as the Pacific golden plover, which annually flies from the mainland of Alaska to the Hawaiian Islands and even beyond, probably figure in many riddles of plant distribution.

The catastrophe of Krakatoa gave naturalists a perfect opportunity to observe the colonization of an island. With most of the island itself destroyed, and the remnant covered with a deep layer of lava and ash that remained hot for weeks, Krakatoa after the explosive eruptions of 1883 was, from a biological standpoint, a new volcanic island. As soon as it was possible to visit it, scientists searched for signs of life, although it was hard to imagine how any living thing could have survived. Not a single plant or animal could be found. It was not until nine months after the eruption that the naturalist Cotteau was able to report: 'I only discovered one microscopic spider—only one. This strange pioneer of the renovation was busy spinning its web.' Since there were no insects on the island, the web-spinning of the bold little spider was presumably in vain, and except for a few blades of grass, practically nothing lived on Krakatoa for a quarter of a century. Then the colonists began to arrive—a few mammals in 1908; a number of birds, lizards, and snakes; various mollusks, insects, and earthworms. Ninety per cent of Krakatoa's new inhabitants, Dutch scientists found, were forms that could have arrived by air.

Isolated from the great mass of life on the continents, with no opportunity for the crossbreeding that tends to preserve the average and to eliminate the new and unusual, island life has developed in a remarkable manner. On these remote bits of earth, nature has excelled in the creation of strange and wonderful forms. As though to prove her incredible versatility, almost every island has developed species that are endemic—that is, they are peculiar to it alone and are duplicated nowhere else on earth.

It was from the pages of earth's history written on the lava fields of the Galapagos that young Charles Darwin got his first inkling of the great truths of the origin of species. Observing the strange plants and animals—giant tortoises, black, amazing lizards that hunted their food in the surf, sea lions, birds in extraordinary variety—Darwin was struck by their vague similarity to mainland species of South and Central America, yet was haunted by the differences, differences that distinguish them not only from the mainland species but from those on other islands of the archipelago. Years later he was to write in reminiscence: 'Both in space and time, we seem to be brought somewhat near to that great fact—that mystery of mysteries—the first appearance of new beings on earth.'

Of the 'new beings' evolved on islands, some of the most striking examples have been birds. In some remote age before there were men, a small, pigeonlike bird found its way to the island of Mauritius, in the Indian Ocean. By processes of change at which we can only guess, this bird lost the power of flight, developed short, stout legs, and grew larger until it reached the size of a modern turkey. Such was the origin of the fabulous dodo, which did not long survive the advent of man on Mauritius. New Zealand was the sole home of the moas. One species of these ostrich-like birds stood twelve feet high. Moas had roamed New Zealand from the early part of the Tertiary; those that remained when the Maoris arrived soon died out.

Other island forms besides the dodo and the moas have tended to become large. Perhaps the Galapagos tortoise became a giant after its arrival on the islands, although fossil remains on the continents cast doubt on this. The loss of wing use and even of the wings themselves (the moas had none) are common results of insular life. Insects on small, wind-swept islands tend to lose the power of flight—those that retain it are in danger of being blown out to sea. The Galapagos Islands have a flightless cormorant. There have been at least fourteen species of flightless rails on the islands of the Pacific alone.

One of the most interesting and engaging characteristics of island species is their extraordinary tameness—a lack of sophistication in dealings with the human race, which even the bitter teachings of experience do not quickly alter. When Robert Cushman Murphy visited the island of South Trinidad in 1913 with a party from the brig *Daisy*, terns alighted on the heads of the men in the whaleboat and peered inquiringly into their faces. Albatrosses on Laysan, whose habits include wonderful ceremonial dances, allowed naturalists to walk among their colonies and responded with a grave bow to similar polite greetings from the visitors. When the British ornithologist David Lack visited the Galapagos Islands, a century after Darwin, he found that the hawks allowed themselves to be touched, and the flycatchers tried to remove hair from the heads of the men for nesting material. 'It is a curious pleasure,' he wrote, 'to have the birds of the wilderness settling upon one's shoulders, and the pleasure could be much less rare were man less destructive.'

But man, unhappily, has written one of his blackest records as a destroyer on the oceanic islands. He has seldom set foot on an island that he has not brought about disastrous changes. He has destroyed environments by cutting, clearing, and burning; he has brought with him as a chance associate the nefarious rat; and almost invariably he has turned loose upon the islands a whole Noah's Ark of goats, hogs, cattle, dogs, cats, and other non-native animals as well as plants. Upon species after species of island life, the black night of extinction has fallen.

In all the world of living things, it is doubtful whether there is a more delicately balanced relationship than that of island life to its environment. This environment is a remarkably uniform one. In the midst of a great ocean, ruled by currents and winds that rarely shift their course, climate changes little. There are few natural enemies, perhaps none at all. The harsh struggle for existence that is the normal lot of continental life is softened on the islands. When this gentle pattern of life is abruptly changed, the island creatures have little ability to make the adjustments necessary for survival.

Ernst Mayr tells of a steamer wrecked off Lord Howe Island east of Australia in 1918. Its rats swam ashore. In two years they had so nearly exterminated the native birds that an islander wrote, 'This paradise of birds has become a wilderness, and the quietness of death reigns where all was melody.'

On Tristan da Cunha almost all of the unique land birds that had evolved there in the course of the ages were exterminated by hogs and rats. The native fauna of the island of Tahiti is losing ground against the horde of alien species that man has introduced. The Hawaiian Islands, which have have lost their native plants and animals faster than almost any other area in the world, are a classic example of the results of interfering with natural balances. Certain relations of animal to plant, and of plant to soil, had grown up through the centuries. When man came in and rudely disturbed this balance, he set off a whole series of chain reactions.

Vancouver brought cattle and goats to the Hawaiian Islands, and the resulting damage to forests and other vegetation was enormous. Many plant introductions were as bad. A plant known as the pamakani was brought in many years ago, according to report, by a Captain Makee for his beautiful gardens on the island of Maui. The pamakani, which has light, wind-borne seeds, quickly escaped from the captain's gardens, ruined the pasture lands on Maui, and proceeded to hop from island to island. The CCC boys were at one time put to work to clear it out of the Honouliuli Forest Reserve, but as fast as they destroyed it, the seeds of new plants arrived on the wind. Lantana was another plant brought in as an ornamental species. Now it covers thousands of acres with a thorny, scrambling growth—despite large sums of money spent to import parasitic insects to control it.

There was once a society in Hawaii for the special purpose of introducing exotic birds. Today when you go to the islands, you see, instead of the exquisite native birds that greeted Captain Cook, mynas from India, cardinals from the United States or Brazil, doves from Asia, weavers from Australia, skylarks from Europe, and titmice from Japan. Most of the original bird life has been wiped out, and to find its fugitive remnants you would have to search assiduously in the most remote hills.

Some of the island species have, at best, the most tenuous hold on life. The Laysan teal is found nowhere in the world but on the one small island of Laysan. Even on this island it occurs only on one end, where there is a seepage of fresh water. Probably the total population of this species does not exceed fifty individuals. Destruction of the small swampy bit of land that is its home, or the introduction of a hostile or competing species, could easily snap the slender thread of life.

Most of man's habitual tampering with nature's balance by introducing exotic species has been done in ignorance of the fatal chain of events that would follow. But in modern times, at least, we might profit by history. About the year 1513, the Portuguese introduced goats onto the recently discovered island of St. Helena, which had developed a magnificent forest of gumwood, ebony, and brazilwood. By 1560 or thereabouts, the goats had so multiplied that they wandered over the island by the thousand, in flocks a mile long. They trampled the young trees and ate the seedlings. By this time the colonists had begun to cut and burn the forests, so that it is hard to say whether men or goats were the more responsible for the destruction. But of the result there was no doubt. By the early 1800's the forests were gone, and the naturalist Alfred Wallace later described this once beautiful, forest-clad volcanic island as a 'rocky desert,' in which the remnants of the original flora persisted only in the most inaccessible peaks and crater ridges.

When the astronomer Halley visited the islands of the Atlantic about 1700, he put a few goats ashore on South Trinidad. This time, without the further aid of man, the work of deforestation proceeded so rapidly that it was nearly completed within the century. Today Trinidad's slopes are the place of a ghost forest, strewn with the fallen and decaying trunks of long-dead trees; its soft volcanic soils, no longer held by the interlacing roots, are sliding away into the sea.

One of the most interesting of the Pacific islands was Laysan, a tiny scrap of soil which is a far outrider of the Hawaiian chain. It once supported a forest of sandalwood and fanleaf palms and had five land birds, all peculiar to Laysan alone. One of them was the Laysan rail, a charming, gnomelike creature no more than six inches high, with wings that seemed too small (and were never used as wings), and feet that seemed too large, and a voice like distant, tinkling bells. About 1887, the captain of a visiting ship moved some of the rails to Midway, about 300 miles to the west, establishing a second colony. It seemed a fortunate move, for soon thereafter rabbits were introduced on Laysan. Within a quarter of a century, the rabbits had killed off the vegetation of the tiny island, reduced it to a sandy desert, and all but exterminated themselves. As for the rails, the devastation of their island was fatal, and the last rail died about 1924.

Perhaps the Laysan colony could later have been restored from the Midway group had not tragedy struck there also. During the war in the Pacific, rats went ashore to island after island from ships and landing craft. They invaded Midway in 1943. The adult rails were slaughtered. The eggs were eaten, and the young birds killed. The world's last Laysan rail was seen in 1944.

The tragedy of the oceanic islands lies in the uniqueness, the irreplaceability of the species they have developed by the slow processes of the ages. In a reasonable world men would have treated these islands as precious possessions, as natural museums filled with beautiful and curious works of creation, valuable beyond price because nowhere in the world are they duplicated. W. H. Hudson's lament for the birds of the Argentine pampas might even more truly have been spoken of the islands: 'The beautiful has vanished and returns not.'

The Shape of Ancient Seas

TILL THE SLOW SEA RISE AND THE SHEER CLIFF CRUMBLE,
TILL TERRACE AND MEADOW THE DEEP GULFS DRINK.
—SWINBURNE

We live in an age of rising seas. Along all the coasts of the United States a continuing rise of sea level has been perceptible on the tide gauges of the Coast and Geodetic Survey since 1930. For the thousand-mile stretch from Massachusetts to Florida, and on the coast of the Gulf of Mexico, the rise amounted to about a third of a foot between 1930 and 1948. The water is also rising (but more slowly) along the Pacific shores. These records of the tide gauges do not include the transient advances and retreats of the water caused by winds and storms, but signify a steady, continuing advance of the sea upon the land.

This evidence of a rising sea is an interesting and even an exciting thing because it is rare that, in the short span of human life, we can actually observe and measure the progress of one of the great earth rhythms. What is happening is nothing new. Over the long span of geologic time, the ocean waters have come in over North America many times and have again retreated into their basins. For the boundary between sea and land is the most fleeting and transitory feature of the earth, and the sea is forever repeating its encroachments upon the continents. It rises and falls like a great tide, sometimes engulfing half a continent in its flood, reluctant in its ebb, moving in a rhythm mysterious and infinitely deliberate.

Now once again the ocean is overfull. It is spilling over the rims of its basins. It fills the shallow seas that border the continents, like the Barents, Bering, and China seas. Here and there it has advanced into the interior and lies in such inland seas as Hudson Bay, the St. Lawrence embayment, the Baltic, and the Sunda Sea. On the Atlantic coast of the United States the mouths of many rivers, like the Hudson and the Susquehanna, have been drowned by the advancing flood; the old, submerged channels are hidden under bays like the Chesapeake and the Delaware.

The advance noted so clearly on the tide gauges may be part of a long rise that began thousands of years ago —perhaps when the glaciers of the most recent Ice Age began to melt. But it is only within recent decades that there have been instruments to measure it in any part of the world. Even now the gauges are few and scattered, considering the world as a whole. Because of the scarcity of world records, it is not known whether the rise observed in the United States since 1930 is being duplicated on all other continents.

Where and when the ocean will halt its present advance and begin again its slow retreat into its basin, no one can say. If the rise over the continent of North America should amount to a hundred feet (and there is more than enough water now frozen in land ice to provide such a rise) most of the Atlantic seaboard, with its cities and towns, would be submerged. The surf would break against the foothills of the Appalachians. The coastal plain of the Gulf of Mexico would lie under water; the lower part of the Mississippi Valley would be submerged.

If, however, the rise should be as much as 600 feet, large areas in the eastern half of the continent would disappear under the waters. The Appalachians would become a chain of mountainous islands. The Gulf of Mexico would creep north, finally meeting in mid-continent with the flood that had entered from the Atlantic into the Great Lakes, through the valley of the St. Lawrence. Much of northern Canada would be covered by water from the Arctic Ocean and Hudson Bay.

All of this would seem to us extraordinary and catastrophic, but the truth is that North America and most other continents have known even more extensive invasions by the sea than the one we have just imagined. Probably the greatest submergence in the history of the earth took place in the Cretaceous period, about 100 million years ago. Then the ocean waters advanced upon North America from the north, south, and east, finally forming an inland sea about 1000 miles wide that extended from the Arctic to the Gulf of Mexico, and then spread eastward to cover the coastal plain from the Gulf to New Jersey. At the height of the Cretaceous flood about half of North America was submerged. All over the world the seas rose. They covered most of the British Isles, except for scattered outcroppings of ancient rocks. In southern Europe only the old, rocky highlands stood above the sea, which intruded in long bays and gulfs even into the central highlands of the continent. The ocean moved into Africa and laid down deposits of sandstones; later weathering of these rocks provided the desert sands of the Sahara. From a drowned Sweden, an inland sea flowed across Russia, covered the Caspian Sea, and extended to the Himalayas. Parts of India were submerged, and of Australia, Japan, and Siberia. On the South American continent, the area where later the Andes were to rise was covered by sea.

With variations of extent and detail, these events have been repeated again and again. The very ancient Ordovician seas, some 400 million years ago, submerged more than half of North America, leaving only a few large islands marking the borderlands of the continent, and a scattering of smaller ones rising out of the inland sea. The marine transgressions of Devonian and Silurian time were almost as extensive. But each time the pattern of invasion was a little different, and it is doubtful that there is any part of the continent that at some time has not lain at the bottom of one of these shallow seas.

You do not have to travel to find the sea, for the traces of its ancient stands are everywhere about. Though you may be a thousand miles inland, you can easily find reminders that will reconstruct for the eye and ear of the mind the processions of its ghostly waves and the roar of its surf, far back in time. So, on a mountain top in Pennsylvania, I have sat on rocks of whitened limestone, fashioned of the shells of billions upon billions of minute sea creatures. Once they had lived and died in an arm of the ocean that overlay this place, and their limy remains had settled to the bottom. There, after eons of time, they had become compacted into rock and the sea had receded; after yet more eons the rock had been uplifted by bucklings of the earth's crust and now it formed the backbone of a long mountain range.

Far in the interior of the Florida Everglades I have wondered at the feeling of the sea that came to me—wondered until I realized that here were the same flatness, the same immense spaces, the same dominance of the sky and its moving, changing clouds; wondered until I remembered that the hard rocky floor on which I stood, its flatness interrupted by upthrust masses of jagged coral rock, had been only recently constructed by the busy architects of the coral reefs under a warm sea. Now the rock is thinly covered with grass and water; but everywhere is the feeling that the land has formed only the thinnest veneer over the underlying platform of the sea, that at any moment the process might be reversed and the sea reclaim its own.

So in all lands we may sense the former presence of the sea. There are outcroppings of marine limestone in the Himalayas, now at an elevation of 20,000 feet. These rocks are reminders of a warm, clear sea that lay over southern Europe and northern Africa and extended into southwestern Asia. This was some 50 million years ago. Immense numbers of a large protozoan known as nummulites swarmed in this sea and each, in death, contributed to the building of a thick layer of nummulitic limestone. Eons later, the ancient Egyptians were to carve their Sphinx from a mass of this rock; other deposits of the same stone they quarried to obtain material to build their pyramids.

The famous white cliffs of Dover are composed of chalk deposited by the seas of the Cretaceous period, during that great inundation we have spoken of. The chalk extends from Ireland through Denmark and Germany, and forms its thickest beds in south Russia. It consists of shells of those minute sea creatures called foraminifera, the shells being cemented together with a fine-textured deposit of calcium carbonate. In contrast to the foraminiferal ooze that covers large areas of ocean bottom at moderate depths, the chalk seems to be a shallow-water deposit, but it is so pure in texture that the surrounding lands must have been low deserts, from which little material was carried seaward. Grains of wind-borne quartz sand, which frequently occur in the chalk, support this view. At certain levels the chalk contains nodules of flint. Stone Age men mined the flint for weapons and tools and also used this relic of the Cretaceous sea to light their fires.

Many of the natural wonders of the earth owe their existence to the fact that once the sea crept over the land, laid down its deposits of sediments, and then withdrew. There is Mammoth Cave in Kentucky, for example, where one may wander through miles of underground passages and enter rooms with ceilings 250 feet overhead. Caves and passageways have been dissolved by ground water out of an immense thickness of limestone, deposited by a Paleozoic sea. In the same way, the story of Niagara Falls goes back to Silurian time, when a vast embayment of the Arctic Sea crept southward over the continent. Its waters were clear, for the borderlands were low and little sediment or silt was carried into the inland sea. It deposited large beds of the hard rock called dolomite, and in time they formed a long escarpment near the present border between Canada and the United States. Millions of years later, floods of water released from melting glaciers poured over this cliff, cutting away the soft shales that underlay the dolomite, and causing mass after mass of the undercut rock to break away. In this fashion Niagara Falls and its gorge were created.

Some of these inland seas were immense and important features of their world, although all of them were shallow compared with the central basin where, since earliest time, the bulk of the ocean waters have resided. Some may have been as much as 600 feet deep, about the same as the depths over the outer edge of the continental shelf. No one knows the pattern of their currents, but often they must have carried the warmth of the tropics into far northern lands. During the Cretaceous period, for example, breadfruit, cinnamon, laurel, and fig trees grew in Greenland. When the continents were reduced to groups of island there must have been few places that possessed a continental type of climate with its harsh extremes of heat and cold; mild oceanic climates must rather have been the rule.

Geologists say that each of the grander divisions of earth history consists of three phases: in the first the continents are high, erosion is active, and the seas are largely confined to their basins; in the second the continents are lowest and the seas have invaded them broadly; in the third the continents have begun once more to rise. According to the late Charles Schuchert, who devoted much of his distinguished career as a geologist to mapping the ancient seas and lands: 'Today we are living in the beginning of a new cycle, when the continents are largest, highest, and scenically grandest. The oceans, however, have begun another invasion upon North America.'

What brings the ocean out of its deep basins, where it has been contained for eons of time, to invade the lands? Probably there has always been not one alone, but a combination of causes.

The mobility of the earth's crust is inseparably linked with the changing relations of sea and land—the warping upward or downward of that surprisingly plastic substance which forms the outer covering of our earth. The crustal movements affect both land and sea bottom but are most marked near the continental margins. They may involve one or both shores of an ocean, one or all coasts of a continent. They proceed in a slow and mysterious cycle, one phase of which may require millions of years for its completion. Each downward movement of the continental crust is accompanied by a slow flooding of the land by the sea, each upward buckling by the retreat of the water.

But the movements of the earth's crust are not alone responsible for the invading seas. There are other important causes. Certainly one of them is the displacement of ocean water by land sediments. Every grain of sand or silt carried out by the rivers and deposited at sea displaces a corresponding amount of water. Disintegration of the land and the seaward freighting of its substance have gone on without interruption since the beginning of geologic time. It might be thought that the sea level would have been rising continuously, but the matter is not so simple. As they lose substance the continents tend to rise higher, like a ship relieved of part of its cargo. The ocean floor, to which the sediments are transferred, sags under its load. The exact combination of all these conditions that will result in a rising ocean level is a very complex matter, not easily recognized or predicted.

Then there is the growth of the great submarine volcanoes, which build up immense lava cones on the floor of the ocean. Some geologists believe these may have an important effect on the changing level of the sea. The bulk of some of these volcanoes is impressive. Bermuda is one of the smallest, but its volume beneath the surface is about 2500 cubic miles. The Hawaiian chain of volcanic islands extends for nearly 2000 miles across the Pacific and contains several islands of great size; its total displacement of water must be tremendous. Perhaps it is more than coincidence that this chain arose in Cretaceous time, when the greatest flood the world has ever seen advanced upon the continents.

For the past million years, all other causes of marine transgressions have been dwarfed by the dominating role of the glaciers. The Pleistocene period was marked by alternating advances and retreats of a great ice sheet. Four times the ice caps formed and grew deep over the land, pressing southward into the valleys and over the plains. And four times the ice melted and shrank and withdrew from the lands it had covered. We live now in the last stages of this fourth withdrawal. About half the ice formed in the last Pleistocene glaciation remains in the ice caps of Greenland and Antarctica and the scattered glaciers of certain mountains.

Each time the ice sheet thickened and expanded with the

unmelted snows of winter after winter, its growth meant a corresponding lowering of the ocean level. For directly or indirectly, the moisture that falls on the earth's surface as rain or snow has been withdrawn from the reservoir of the sea. Ordinarily, the withdrawal is a temporary one, the water being returned via the normal runoff of rain and melting snow. But in the glacial period the summers were cool, and the snows of any winter did not melt entirely but were carried over to the succeeding winter, when the new snows found and covered them. So little by little the level of the sea dropped as the glaciers robbed it of its water, and at the climax of each of the major glaciations the ocean all over the world stood at a very low level.

Today, if you look in the right places, you will see the evidences of some of these old stands of the sea. Of course the strand marks left by the extreme low levels are now deeply covered by water and may be discovered only indirectly by sounding. But where, in past ages, the water level stood higher than it does today you can find its traces. In Samoa, at the foot of a cliff wall now 15 feet above the present level of the sea, you can find benches cut in the rocks by waves. You will find the same thing on other Pacific islands, and on St. Helena in the South Atlantic, on islands of the Indian Ocean, in the West Indies, and around the Cape of Good Hope.

Sea caves in cliffs now high above the battering assault and the flung spray of the waves that cut them are eloquent of the changed relation of sea and land. You will find such caves widely scattered over the world. On the west coast of Norway there is a remarkable, wave-cut tunnel. Out of the hard granite of the island of Torghattan, the pounding surf of a flooding interglacial sea cut a passageway through the island, a distance of about 530 feet, and in so doing removed nearly 5 million cubic feet of rock. The tunnel now stands 400 feet above the sea. Its elevation is due in part to the elastic, upward rebound of the crust after the melting of the ice.

During the other half of the cycle, when the seas sank lower and lower as the glaciers grew in thickness, the world's shorelines were undergoing changes even more far-reaching and dramatic. Every river felt the effect of the lowering sea; its waters were speeded in their course to the ocean and given new strength for the deepening and cutting of its channel. Following the downward-moving shorelines, the rivers extended their courses over the drying sands and muds of what only recently had been the sloping sea bottom. Here the rushing torrents—swollen with melting glacier water—picked up great quantities of loose mud and sand and rolled into the sea as a turgid flood.

During one or more of the Pleistocene lowerings of sea level, the floor of the North Sea was drained of its water and for a time became dry land. The rivers of northern Europe and of the British Isles followed the retreating waters seaward. Eventually the Rhine captured the whole drainage system of the Thames. The Elbe and the Weser became one river. The Seine rolled through what is now the English Channel and cut itself a trough out across the continental shelf—perhaps the same drowned channel now discernible by soundings beyond Lands End.

The greatest of all Pleistocene glaciations came rather late in the period—probably only about 200 thousand years ago, and well within the time of man. The tremendous lowering of sea level must have affected the life of Paleolithic man. Certainly he was able, at more than one period, to walk across a wide bridge at Bering Strait, which became dry land when the level of the ocean dropped below this shallow shelf. There were other land bridges, created in the same way. As the ocean receded from the coast of India, a long submarine bank became a shoal, then finally emerged, and primitive man walked across 'Adam's Bridge' to the island of Ceylon.

Many of the settlements of ancient man must have been located on the seacoast or near the great deltas of the rivers, and relics of his civilization may lie in caves long since covered by the rising ocean. Our meager knowledge of Paleolithic man might be increased by searching along these old drowned shorelines. One archaeologist has recommended searching shallow portions of the Adriatic Sea, with 'submarine boats casting strong electric lights' or even with glass-bottomed boats and artificial light in the hope of discovering the outlines of shell heaps—the kitchen middens of the early men who once lived here. Professor R. A. Daly has pointed out:

The last Glacial stage was the Reindeer Age of French history. Men then lived in the famous caves overlooking the channels of the French rivers, and hunted the reindeer which throve on the cool plains of France south of the ice border. The Late-Glacial rise of general sea level was necessarily accompanied by a rise of the river waters downstream. Hence the lowest caves are likely to have been partly or wholly drowned . . . There the search for more relics of Paleolithic man should be pursued.*

Some of our Stone Age ancestors must have known the rigors of life near the glaciers. While men as well as plants and animals moved southward before the ice, some must have remained within sight and sound of the great frozen wall. To these the world was a place of storm and blizzard, with bitter winds roaring down out of the blue mountain of ice that dominated the horizon and reached upward into gray skies, all filled with the roaring tumult of the advancing glacier, and with the thunder of moving tons of ice breaking away and plunging into the sea.

But those who lived half the earth away, on some sunny coast of the Indian Ocean, walked and hunted on dry land over which the sea, only recently, had rolled deeply. These men knew nothing of the distant glaciers, nor did they understand that they walked and hunted where they did because quantities of ocean water were frozen as ice and snow in a distant land.

In any imaginative reconstruction of the world of the Ice Age, we are plagued by one tantalizing uncertainty: how low did the ocean level fall during the period of greatest spread of the glaciers, when unknown quantities of water were frozen in the ice? Was it only a moderate fall of 200 or 300 feet—a change paralleled many times in geologic history in the ebb and flow of the epicontinental seas? Or was it a dramatic drawing down of the ocean by 2000, even 3000 feet?

Each of these various levels has been suggested as an actual possibility by one or more geologists. Perhaps it is not surprising that there should be such radical disagreement. It has been only about a century since Louis Agassiz gave the world its first understanding of the moving mountains of ice and their dominating effect on the Pleistocene world. Since then, men in all parts of the earth have been patiently accumulating the facts and reconstructing the events of those four successive advances and retreats of the ice. Only the present generation of scientists, led by such daring thinkers as Daly, have understood that each thickening of the ice sheets meant a corresponding lowering of the ocean, and that with each retreat of the melting ice a returning flood of water raised the sea level.

Of this 'alternate robbery and restitution' most geologists

---

* From *The Changing World of the Ice Age,* 1934 edition, Yale University Press, p. 210.

have taken a conservative view and said that the greatest lowering of the sea level could not have amounted to more than 400 feet, possibly only half as much. Most of those who argue that the drawing down was much greater base their reasoning upon the submarine canyons, those deep gorges cut in the continental slopes. The deeper canyons lie a mile or more below the present level of the sea. Geologists who maintain that at least the upper parts of the canyons were stream-cut say that the sea level must have fallen enough to permit this during the Pleistocene glaciation.

This question of the farthest retreat of the sea into its basins must await further searchings into the mysteries of the ocean. We seem on the verge of exciting new discoveries. Now oceanographers and geologists have better instruments than ever before to probe the depths of the sea, to sample its rocks and deeply layered sediments, and to read with greater clarity the dim pages of past history.

Meanwhile, the sea ebbs and flows in these grander tides of earth, whose stages are measurable not in hours but in millennia—tides so vast they are invisible and uncomprehended by the senses of man. Their ultimate cause, should it ever be discovered, may be found to be deep within the fiery center of the earth, or it may lie somewhere in the dark spaces of the universe.

Part **II**

THE RESTLESS SEA

Wind and Water

THE WIND'S FEET SHINE ALONG THE SEA.
—SWINBURNE

As the waves roll in toward Lands End on the westernmost tip of England they bring the feel of the distant places of the Atlantic. Moving shoreward above the steeply rising floor of the deep sea, from dark blue water into troubled green, they pass the edge of 'soundings' and roll up over the continental shelf in confused ripplings and turbulence. Over the shoaling bottom they sweep landward, breaking on the Seven Stones of the channel between the Scilly Isles and Lands End, coming in over the sunken ledges and the rocks that roll out their glistening backs at low water. As they approach the rocky tip of Lands End, they pass over a strange instrument lying on the sea bottom. By the fluctuating pressure of their rise and fall they tell this instrument many things of the distant Atlantic waters from which they have come, and their messages are translated by its mechanisms into symbols understandable to the human mind.

If you visited this place and talked to the meteorologist in charge, he could tell you the life histories of the waves that are rolling in, minute by minute and hour after hour, bringing their messages of far-off places. He could tell you where the waves were created by the action of wind on water, the strength of the winds that produced them, how fast the storm is moving, and how soon, if at all, it will become necessary to raise storm warnings along the coast of England. Most of the waves that roll over the recorder at Lands End, he would tell you, are born in the stormy North Atlantic eastward from Newfoundland and south of Greenland. Some can be traced to tropical storms on the opposite side of the Atlantic, moving through the West Indies and along the coast of Florida. A few have rolled up from the southernmost part of the world, taking a great-circle course all the way from Cape Horn to Lands End, a journey of 6000 miles.

On the coast of California wave recorders have detected swell from as great a distance, for some of the surf that breaks on that coast in summer is born in the west-wind belt of the Southern Hemisphere. The Cornwall recorders and those in California, as well as a few on the east coast of America, have been in use since the end of the Second World War. These experiments have several objects, among them the development of a new kind of weather forecasting. In the countries bordering the North Atlantic there is no practical need to turn to the waves for weather information because meteorological stations are numerous and strategically placed. The areas in which the wave recorders are presently used have served rather as a testing laboratory to develop the method. It will soon be ready for use in other parts of the world, for which there are no meteorological data except those the waves bring. Especially in the Southern Hemisphere, many coasts are washed by waves that have come from lonely, unvisited parts of the ocean, seldom crossed by vessels, off the normal routes of the air lines. Storms may develop in these remote places, unobserved, and sweep down suddenly on midocean islands or exposed coasts. Over the millions of years the waves, running ahead of the storms, have been crying a warning, but only now are we learning to read their language. Or only now, at least, are we learning to do so scientifically. There is a basis in folklore for these modern achievements in wave research. To generations of Pacific Island natives, a certain kind of swell has signaled the approach of a typhoon. And centuries ago, when peasants on the lonely shores of Ireland saw the long swells that herald a storm rolling in upon their coasts, they shuddered and talked of death waves.

Now our study of waves has come of age, and on all sides we can find evidence that modern man is turning to the waves of the sea for practical purposes. Off the Fishing

Pier at Long Branch, New Jersey, at the end of a quarter-mile pipeline on the bed of the ocean, a wave-recording instrument silently and continuously takes note of the arrival of waves from the open Atlantic. By electric impulses transmitted through the pipeline, the height of each wave and the interval between succeeding crests are transmitted to a shore station and automatically recorded as a graph. These records are carefully studied by the Beach Erosion Board of the Army Corps of Engineers, which is concerned about the rate of erosion along the New Jersey coast.

Off the coast of Africa, high-flying planes recently took a series of overlapping photographs of the surf and the areas immediately offshore. From these photographs, trained men determined the speed of the waves moving in toward the shore. Then they applied a mathematical formula that relates the behavior of waves advancing into shallow water to the depths beneath them. All this information provided the British government with usable surveys of the depths off the coast of an almost inaccessible part of its empire, which could have been sounded in the ordinary way only at great expense and with endless difficulty. Like much of our new knowledge of waves, this practical method was born of wartime necessity.

Forecasts of the state of the sea and particularly the height of the surf became regular preliminaries to invasion in the Second World War, especially on the exposed beaches of Europe and Africa. But application of theory to practical conditions was at first difficult; so was the interpretation of the actual effect of any predicted height of surf or roughness of sea surface on the transfer of men and supplies between boats or from boats to beaches. This first attempt at practical military oceanography was, as one naval officer put it, a 'most frightening lesson' concerning the 'almost desperate lack of basic information on the fundamentals of the nature of the sea.'

As long as there has been an earth, the moving masses of air that we call winds have swept back and forth across its surface. And as long as there has been an ocean, its waters have stirred to the passage of the winds. Most waves are the result of the action of wind on water. There are exceptions, such as the tidal waves sometimes produced by earthquakes under the sea. But the waves most of us know best are wind waves.

It is a confused pattern that the waves make in the open sea—a mixture of countless different wave trains, intermingling, overtaking, passing, or sometimes engulfing one another; each group differing from the others in the place and manner of its origin, in its speed, its direction of movement; some doomed never to reach any shore, others destined to roll across half an ocean before they dissolve in thunder on a distant beach.

Out of such seemingly hopeless confusion the patient study of many men over many years has brought a surprising amount of order. While there is still much to be learned about waves, and much to be done to apply what is known to man's advantage, there is a solid basis of fact on which to reconstruct the life history of a wave, predict its behavior under all the changing circumstances of its life, and foretell its effect on human affairs.

Before constructing an imaginary life history of a typical wave, we need to become familiar with some of its physical characteristics. A wave has height, from trough to crest. It has length, the distance from its crest to that of the following wave. The period of the wave refers to the time required for succeeding crests to pass a fixed point. None of these dimensions is static; all change, but bear definite relations to the wind, the depth of the water, and many other matters. Furthermore, the water that composes a wave does not advance with it across the sea; each water particle describes a circular or elliptical orbit with the passage of the wave form, but returns very nearly to its original position. And it is fortunate that this is so, for if the huge masses of water that comprise a wave actually moved across the sea, navigation would be impossible. Those who deal professionally in the lore of waves make frequent use of a picturesque expression —the 'length of fetch.' The 'fetch' is the distance that the waves have run, under the drive of a wind blowing in a constant direction, without obstruction. The greater the fetch, the higher the waves. Really large waves cannot be generated within the confined space of a bay or a small area. A fetch of perhaps 600 to 800 miles, with winds of gale velocity, is required to get up the largest ocean waves.

Now let us suppose that, after a period of calm, a storm develops far out in the Atlantic, perhaps a thousand miles from the New Jersey coast where we are spending a summer holiday. Its winds blow irregularly, with sudden gusts, shifting direction but in general blowing shoreward. The sheet of water under the wind responds to the changing pressures. It is no longer a level surface; it becomes furrowed with alternating troughs and ridges. The waves move toward the coast, and the wind that created them controls their destiny. As the storm continues and the waves move shoreward, they receive energy from the wind and increase in height. Up to a point they will continue to take to themselves the fierce energy of the wind, growing in height as the strength of the gale is absorbed, but when a wave becomes about a seventh as high from trough to crest as the distance to the next crest it will begin to topple in foaming whitecaps. Winds of hurricane force often blow the tops off the waves by their sheer violence; in such a storm the highest waves may develop after the wind has begun to subside.

But to return to our typical wave, born of wind and water far out in the Atlantic, grown to its full height on the energy of the winds, with its fellow waves forming a confused, irregular pattern known as a 'sea.' As the waves gradually pass out of the storm area their height diminishes, the distance between successive crests increases, and the 'sea' becomes a 'swell,' moving at an average speed of about 15 miles an hour. Near the coast a pattern of long, regular swells is substituted for the turbulence of open ocean. But as the swell enters shallow water a startling transformation takes place. For the first time in its existence, the wave feels the drag of shoaling bottom. Its speed slackens, crests of following waves crowd in toward it, abruptly its height increases and the wave form steepens. Then with a spilling, tumbling rush of water falling down into its trough, it dissolves in a seething confusion of foam.

An observer sitting on a beach can make at least an intelligent guess whether the surf spilling out onto the sand before him has been produced by a gale close offshore or by a distant storm. Young waves, only recently shaped by the wind, have a steep, peaked shape even well out at sea. From far out on the horizon you can see them forming whitecaps as they come in; bits of foam are spilling down their fronts and boiling and bubbling over the advancing face, and the final breaking of the wave is a prolonged and deliberate process. But if a wave, on coming into the surf zone, rears high as though gathering all its strength for the final act of its life, if the crest forms all along its advancing front and then begins to curl forward, if the whole mass of water plunges suddenly with a booming roar into its trough— then you may take it that these waves are visitors from some very distant part of the ocean, that they have traveled long and far before their final dissolution at your feet.

What is true of the Atlantic wave we have followed is true, in general, of wind waves the world over. The incidents in the life of a wave are many. How long it will live, how far it will travel, to what manner of end it will come are all determined, in large measure, by the conditions it meets in its progression across the face of the sea. For the one essential quality of a wave is that it moves; anything that retards or stops its motion dooms it to dissolution and death.

Forces within the sea itself may affect a wave most profoundly. Some of the most terrible furies of the ocean are unleashed when tidal currents cross the path of the waves or move in direct opposition to them. This is the cause of the famous 'roosts' of Scotland, like the one off Sumburgh Head, at the southernmost tip of the Shetland Islands. During northeasterly winds the roost is quiescent, but when the wind-born waves roll in from any other quarter they encounter the tidal currents, either streaming shoreward in flood or seaward on the ebb. It is like the meeting of two wild beasts. The battle of the waves and tides is fought over an area of sea that may be three miles wide when the tides are running at full strength, first off Sumburgh Head, then gradually shifting seaward, subsiding only with the temporary slackening of the tide. 'In this confused, tumbling, and bursting sea, vessels often become entirely unmanageable and sometimes founder,' says the *British Islands Pilot*, 'while others have been tossed about for days together.' Such dangerous waters have been personified in many parts of the world by names that are handed down through generations of seafaring men. As in the time of our grandfathers and of their grandfathers, the Bore of Duncansby and the Merry Men of Mey rage at opposite ends of the Pentland Firth, which separates the Orkney Islands from the northern tip of Scotland. The sailing directions for the Firth in the *North Sea Pilot* for 1875 contained a warning to mariners, which is repeated verbatim in the modern *Pilot*:

> Before entering the Pentland Firth all vessels should be prepared to batten down, and the hatches of small vessels ought to be secured even in the finest weather, as it is difficult to see what may be going on in the distance, and the transition from smooth water to a broken sea is so sudden that no time is given for making arrangements.

Both roosts are caused by the meeting of swells from the open ocean and opposing tidal currents, so that at the east end of the Firth the Bore of Duncansby is to be feared with easterly swells and a flood tide, and at the west end the Merry Men of Mey stage their revelries with the ebb tides and a westerly swell. Then, according to the *Pilot*, 'a sea is

Andreas Feininger

Fossil remains of a trilobite, an ancient crustacean of Cambrian seas

Photo by Fritz Goro (Life)

Above: Sargassum fish in seaweed

Right, above: In summer seas, billions of tiny Noctiluca gleam like stars

Right, below: Camera reveals living creatures, tracks, and holes on sea floor

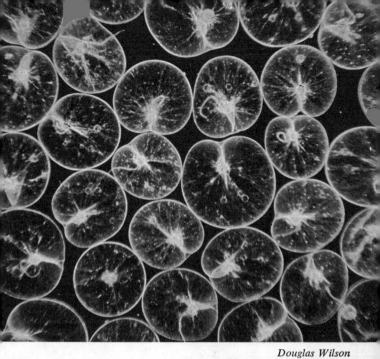

Douglas Wilson

Lamont Geological Observatory (Columbia University)

In the bathyscaphe *Trieste* men first penetrated
the greatest depths of the sea

Lamont Geological Observatory (Columbia University)

Above: Coring tube being lowered for sample of bottom

Right, above: This sea mount was discovered by the U.S. Coast and Geodetic Survey's *Pathfinder* in the Gulf of Alaska; it rises 9600 feet from the ocean floor and is 857 fathoms below the surface

Right, below: The U.S.S. *Albatross III* traced this profile of Lydonia Canyon where it cuts across the outer edge of Georges Bank

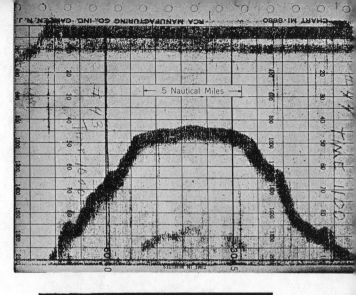

←—— 5 Nautical Miles ——→

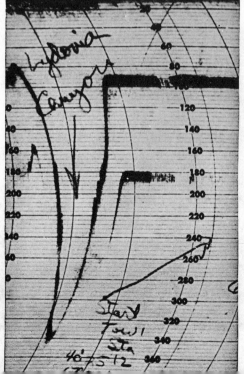

Wide World Photos

The birth of an island

Countless billions of tiny shells compose the cliffs of Dover

Paul Popper, Ltd.

Right: Minot's Light withstands raging surf on the Massachusetts coast

Below: Surf pounds endlessly on the shores of the world

Ludwig Schuster

Paul Popper, Ltd.

Above: Waves cut away softer rock,
leaving chimney-like stack
Right: The face of the sea in a storm

Philip Gendreau

Above: Coral rock, once formed beneath the sea, now is sculptured by waves

Right: Seismic sea waves of April 1, 1946, carried away a lighthouse at Scotch Cap, Alaska, 90 feet above the sea, and also
smashed shore structures on Hawaiian Islands

Official U.S. Coast Guard Photo
United Press International Photo

Clouds draw heat energy from tropical seas to fuel the wind
systems of the globe

PRINTED IN THE UNITED STATES OF AMERICA

raised which cannot be imagined by those who have never experienced it.'

Such a rip may offer protection to the near-by coast by the very fury and uncompromisingness of the struggle between waves and tide. Thomas Stevenson long ago observed that as long as the Sumburgh roost was breaking and cresting heavily off the Head there was little surf on shore; once the strength of the tide was spent and it could no longer run down the seas a heavy surf rolled in against the coast and rose to great heights on the cliffs. And in the western Atlantic, the confused and swiftly running tidal currents at the mouth of the Bay of Fundy offer such strong opposition to waves approaching from any quarter from southwest to southeast that such surf as develops within the Bay is almost entirely local in its origin.

Out in the open sea, a train of waves encountering a hostile wind may be rapidly destroyed, for the power that created a wave may also destroy it. So a fresh trade wind in the Atlantic has often flattened out the swells as they rolled down from Iceland toward Africa. Or a friendly wind, suddenly springing up to blow in the direction the waves are moving, may cause their height to increase at the rate of a foot or two per minute. Once a group of moving ridges has been created, the wind has only to fall into the troughs between them to push up their crests rapidly.

Rocky ledges, shoals of sand or clay or rock, and coastal islands in the mouths of bays all play their part in the fate of the waves that advance toward shore. The long swells that roll from the open ocean toward the shores of northern New England seldom reach it in full strength. Their energy is spent in passing over that great submerged highland known as Georges Bank, the crests of whose highest hills approach the surface over the Cultivator Shoals. The hindrance of these submarine hills, and of the tidal currents that swirl around and across them, robs the long ocean swells of their power. Or islands scattered within a bay or about its mouth may so absorb the strength of the waves that the head of the bay is free from surf. Even scattered reefs off a coast may offer it great protection, by causing the highest waves to break there, so that they never reach the shore.

Ice, snow, rain—all are enemies of the waves and under proper conditions may knock down a sea or cushion the force of surf on a beach. Within loose pack ice a vessel may count on smooth seas even if a gale is raging and surf is breaking heavily about the edges of the pack. Ice crystals forming in the sea will smooth the waves by increasing the friction between water particles; even the delicate, crystalline form of a snowflake has such an effect on a smaller scale. A hail storm will knock down a rough sea, and even a sudden downpour of rain may often turn the surface of the ocean to oiled-silk smoothness, rippling to the passage of the swells.

The divers of ancient times who carried oil in their mouths to release beneath the surface when rough water made their work difficult were applying what every seaman today knows —that oil appears to have a calming effect on the free waves of the open ocean. Instructions for the use of oil in emergencies at sea are carried by most official sailing directions of maritime nations. Oil has little effect on surf, however, once the dissolution of the wave form has begun.

In the Southern Ocean where the waves are not destroyed by breaking on any beach, the great swells produced by the westerly winds roll around and around the world. Here the longest waves, and those with the greatest sidewise expanse of crest, are formed. Here, it might be supposed, the highest waves would also be found. Yet there is no evidence that the waves of the Southern Ocean surpass the giants of any other ocean. A long series of reports culled from the publications of engineers and ships' officers show that waves higher than 25 feet from trough to crest are rare in all oceans. Storm waves may grow twice as high, and if a full gale blows long enough in one direction to have a fetch of 600 to 800 miles, the resulting waves may be even higher. The greatest possible height of storm waves at sea is a much debated question, with most textbooks citing a conservative 60 feet, and mariners stubbornly describing much higher waves. Throughout the century that has followed the report of Dumont d'Urville that he encountered a wave 100 feet high off the Cape of Good Hope, science generally has viewed such figures with skepticism. Yet there is one record of a giant wave which, because of the method of measurement, seems to be accepted as reliable.

In February 1933 the U.S.S. *Ramapo,* while proceeding from Manila to San Diego, encountered seven days of stormy weather. The storm was part of a weather disturbance that extended all the way from Kamchatka to New York and permitted the winds an unbroken fetch of thousands of miles. During the height of the storm the *Ramapo* maintained a course running down the wind and with the sea. On 6 February the gale reached its fiercest intensity. Winds of 68 knots came in gusts and squalls, and the seas reached mountainous height. While standing watch on the bridge during the early hours of that day, one of the officers of the *Ramapo* saw, in the moonlight, a great sea rising astern to a level above an iron strap on the crow's nest of the mainmast. The *Ramapo* was on even keel and her stern was in the trough of the sea. These circumstances made possible an exact line of sight from the bridge to the crest of the wave, and simple mathematical calculations based on the dimensions of the ship gave the height of the wave. It was 112 feet.

Waves have taken their toll of shipping and of human life on the open sea, but it is around the shorelines of the world they are most destructive. Whatever the height of storm waves at sea, there is abundant evidence, as some of the case histories that follow will show, that breaking surf and the upward-leaping water masses from thundering breakers may engulf lighthouses, shatter buildings, and hurl stones through lighthouse windows anywhere from 100 to 300 feet above the sea. Before the power of such surf, piers and breakwaters and other shore installations are fragile as a child's toys.

Almost every coast of the world is visited periodically by violent storm surf, but there are some that have never known the sea in its milder moods. 'There is not in the world a coast more terrible than this!' exclaimed Lord Bryce of Tierra del Fuego, where the breakers roar in upon the coast with a voice that, according to report, can be heard 20 miles inland on a still night. 'The sight of such a coast,' Darwin had written in his diary, 'is enough to make a landsman dream for a week about death, peril, and shipwreck.'

Others claim that the Pacific coast of the United States from northern California to the Straits of Juan de Fuca has a surf as heavy as any in the world. But it seems unlikely that any coast is visited more wrathfully by the sea's waves than the Shetlands and the Orkneys, in the path of the cyclonic storms that pass eastward between Iceland and the British Isles. All the feeling and the fury of such a storm, couched in almost Conradian prose, are contained in the usually prosaic *British Islands Pilot:*

In the terrific gales which usually occur four or five times in every year all distinction between air and water is lost, the nearest objects are obscured by spray, and everything seems enveloped in a thick smoke; upon the open coast the sea rises at once, and striking upon the rocky shores rises in foam for several hundred feet and spreads over the whole country.

The sea, however, is not so heavy in the violent gales of

short continuance as when an ordinary gale has been blowing for many days; the whole force of the Atlantic is then beating against the shores of the Orkneys, rocks of many tons in weight are lifted from their beds, and the roar of the surge may be heard for twenty miles; the breakers rise to the height of 60 feet, and the broken sea on the North Shoal, which lies 12 miles northwestward of Costa Head, is visible at Skail and Birsay.

The first man who ever measured the force of an ocean wave was Thomas Stevenson, father of Robert Louis. Stevenson developed the instrument known as a wave dynamometer and with it studied the waves that battered the coast of his native Scotland. He found that in winter gales the force of a wave might be as great as 6000 pounds to the square foot. Perhaps it was waves of this strength that destroyed the breakwater at Wick on the coast of Scotland in a December storm in 1872. The seaward end of the Wick breakwater consisted of a block of concrete weighing more than 800 tons, bound solidly with iron rods to underlying blocks of stone. During the height of this winter gale the resident engineer watched the onslaught of the waves from a point on the cliff above the breakwater. Before his incredulous eyes, the block of concrete was lifted up and swept shoreward. After the storm had subsided divers investigated the wreckage. They found that not only the concrete monolith but the stones it was attached to had been carried away. The waves had torn loose, lifted, and bodily moved a mass weighing not less than 1350 tons, or 2,700,000 pounds. Five years later it became clear that this feat had been a mere dress rehearsal, for the new pier, weighing about 2600 tons, was then carried away in another storm.

A list of the perverse and freakish doings of the sea can easily be compiled from the records of the keepers of lights on lonely ledges at sea, or on rocky headlands exposed to the full strength of storm surf. At Unst, the most northern of the Shetland Islands, a door in the lighthouse was broken open 195 feet above the sea. At the Bishop Rock Light, on the English Channel, a bell was torn away from its attachment 100 feet above high water during a winter gale. About the Bell Rock Light on the coast of Scotland one November day a heavy ground swell was running, although there was no wind. Suddenly one of the swells rose about the tower, mounted to the gilded ball atop the lantern, 117 feet above the rock, and tore away a ladder that was attached to the tower 86 feet above the water. There have been happenings that, to some minds, are tinged with the supernatural, like that at the Eddystone Light in 1840. The entrance door of the tower had been made fast by strong bolts, as usual. During a night of heavy seas the door was broken open *from within,* and all its iron bolts and hinges were torn loose. Engineers say that such a thing happens as a result of pneumatic action—the sudden back draught created by the recession of a heavy wave combined with an abrupt release of pressure on the outside of the door.

On the Atlantic coast of the United States, the 97-foot tower on Minot's Ledge in Massachusetts is often completely enveloped by masses of water from breaking surf, and an earlier light on this ledge was swept away in 1851. Then there is the often quoted story of the December storm at Trinidad Head Light on the coast of northern California. As the keeper watched the storm from his lantern 196 feet above high water, he could see the near-by Pilot Rock engulfed again and again by waves that swept over its hundred-foot crest. Then a wave, larger than the rest, struck the cliffs at the base of the light. It seemed to rise in a solid wall of water to the level of the lantern, and it hurled its spray completely over the tower. The shock of the blow stopped the revolving of the light.

Along a rocky coast, the waves of a severe storm are likely to be armed with stones and rock fragments, which greatly increase their destructive power. Once a rock weighing 135 pounds was hurled high above the lightkeeper's house on Tillamook Rock on the coast of Oregon, 100 feet above sea level. In falling, it tore a 20-foot hole through the roof. The same day showers of smaller rocks broke many panes of glass in the lantern, 132 feet above the sea. The most amazing of such stories concerns the lighthouse at Dunnet Head, which stands on the summit of a 300-foot cliff at the southwestern entrance to Pentland Firth. The windows of this light have been broken repeatedly by stones swept from the cliff and tossed aloft by waves.

For millennia beyond computation, the sea's waves have battered the coastlines of the world with erosive effect, here cutting back a cliff, there stripping away tons of sand from a beach, and yet again, in a reversal of their destructiveness, building up a bar or a small island. Unlike the slow geologic changes that bring about the flooding of half a continent, the work of the waves is attuned to the brief span of human life, and so the sculpturing of the continent's edge is something each of us can see for ourselves.

The high clay cliff of Cape Cod, rising at Eastham and

running north until it is lost in the sand dunes near Peaked Hill, is wearing back so fast that half of the ten acres which the Government acquired as a site for the Highland Light has disappeared, and the cliffs are said to be receding about three feet a year. Cape Cod is not old, in geologic terms, being the product of the glaciers of the most recent Ice Age, but apparently the waves have cut away, since its formation, a strip of land some two miles wide. At the present rate of erosion, the disappearance of the outer cape is foredoomed; it will presumably occur in another 4000 or 5000 years.

The sea's method on a rocky coast is to wear it down by grinding, to chisel out and wrench away fragments of rock, each of which becomes a tool to wear away the cliff. And as masses of rock are undercut, a whole huge mass will fall into the sea, there to be ground in the mill of the surf and to contribute more weapons for the attack. On a rocky shore this grinding and polishing of rocks and fragments of rocks goes on incessantly and audibly, for the breakers on such a coast have a different sound from those that have only sand to work with—a deep-toned mutter and rumble not easily forgotten, even by one who strolls casually along such a beach. Few people have heard the sounds of the surf mill practically from within the sea, as described by Henwood after his visit to a British mine extending out under the ocean:

> When standing beneath the base of the cliff, and in that part of the mine where but nine feet of rock stood between us and the ocean, the heavy roll of the larger boulders, the ceaseless grinding of the pebbles, the fierce thundering of the billows, with the crackling and boiling as they rebounded, place a tempest in its most appalling form too vividly before me ever to be forgotten. More than once doubting the protection of our rocky shield we retreated in affright; and it was only after repeated trials that we had confidence to pursue our investigations.*

Great Britain, an island, has always been conscious of that 'powerful marine gnawing' by which her coasts are eaten away. An old map dated 1786 and prepared by the county surveyor, John Tuke, gives a long list of lost towns and villages on the Holderness Coast. Among them are notations of Hornsea Burton, Hornsea Beck, and Hartburn— 'washed away by the sea'; of Ancient Withernsea, Hyde, or

* From *Transactions*, Geol. Soc. Cornwall, vol. v, 1843.

Hythe—'lost by the sea.' Many other old records allow comparison of present shorelines with former ones and show astonishing annual rates of cliff erosion on many parts of the coast—up to 15 feet at Holderness, 19 feet between Cromer and Mundesley, and 15 to 45 feet at Southwold. 'The configuration of the coastline of Great Britain,' one of her present engineers writes, 'is not the same for two consecutive days.'

And yet we owe some of the most beautiful and interesting shoreline scenery to the sculpturing effect of moving water. Sea caves are almost literally blasted out of the cliffs by waves, which pour into crevices in the rocks and force them apart by hydraulic pressure. Over the years the widening of fissures and the steady removal of fine rock particles in infinite number result in the excavation of a cave. Within such a cavern the weight of incoming water and the strange suctions and pressures caused by the movements of water in an enclosed space may continue the excavation upward. The roofs of such caves (and of overhanging cliffs) are subjected to blows like those from a battering ram as the water from a breaking wave is hurled upward, most of the energy of the wave passing into this smaller mass of water. Eventually a hole is torn through the roof of the cave, to form a spouting horn. Or, on a narrow promontory, what began as a cave may be cut through from side to side, so that a natural bridge is formed. Later, after years of erosion, the arch may fall, leaving the seaward mass of rock to stand alone—one of the strange, chimneylike formations known as a stack.

The sea waves that have fixed themselves most firmly in the human imagination are the so-called 'tidal waves.' The term is popularly applied to two very different kinds of waves, neither of which has any relation to the tide. One is a seismic sea wave produced by undersea earthquakes; the other is an exceptionally vast wind or storm wave—an immense mass of water driven by winds of hurricane force far above the normal high-water line.

Most of the seismic sea waves, now called 'tsunamis,' are born in the deepest trenches of the ocean floor. The Japanese, Aleutian, and Atacama trenches have each produced waves that claimed many human lives. Such a trench is, by its very nature, a breeder of earthquakes, being a place of disturbed and uneasy equilibrium, of buckling and warping downward of the sea floor to form the deepest pits of all the earth's surface. From the historic records of the ancients down to the modern newspaper, the writings of man contain frequent mention of the devastation of coastal settlements by these great waves that suddenly rise out of the sea. One of the earliest of record rose along the eastern shores of the Mediterranean in A.D. 358, passing completely over islands and low-lying shores, leaving boats on the housetops of Alexandria, and drowning thousands of people. After the Lisbon earthquake of 1755, the coast at Cadiz was visited by a wave said to have been 50 feet higher than the highest tide. This came about an hour after the earthquake. The waves from this same disturbance traveled across the Atlantic and reached the West Indies in 9½ hours. In 1868, a stretch of nearly 3000 miles of the western coast of South America was shaken by earthquakes. Shortly after the most violent shocks, the sea receded from the shore, leaving ships that had been anchored in 40 feet of water stranded in mud; then the water returned in a great wave, and boats were carried a quarter of a mile inland.

This ominous withdrawal of the sea from its normal stand is often the first warning of the approach of seismic sea waves. Natives on the beaches of Hawaii on the first of April 1946 were alarmed when the accustomed voice of the breakers was suddenly stilled, leaving a strange quiet. They could not know that this recession of the waves from the reefs and the shallow coastal waters was the sea's response to an earthquake on the steep slopes of a deep trench off the island of Unimak in the Aleutian chain, more than 2000 miles away; or that in a matter of moments the water would rise rapidly, as though the tide were coming in much too fast, but without surf. The rise carried the ocean waters 25 feet or more above the normal levels of the tide. According to an eyewitness account:

> The waves of the tsunami swept toward shore with steep fronts and great turbulence . . . Between crests the water withdrew from shore, exposing reefs, coastal mudflats, and harbor bottoms for distances up to 500 feet or more from the normal strand-line. The outflow of the water was rapid and turbulent, making a loud hissing, roaring, and rattling noise. At several places houses were carried out to sea, and in some areas even large rocks and blocks of concrete were carried out onto the reefs . . . People and their belongings were swept to sea, some being rescued hours later by boats and life rafts dropped from planes.*

---

* From *Annual Rept.*, Smithsonian Inst., 1947.

In the open ocean the waves produced by the Aleutian quake were only about a foot or two high and would not be noticed from vessels. Their length, however, was enormous, with a distance of about 90 miles between succeeding crests. It took the waves less than five hours to reach the Hawaiian chain, 2300 miles distant, so they must have moved at an average speed of about 470 miles per hour. Along eastern Pacific shores, they were recorded as far into the Southern Hemisphere as Valparaiso, Chile, the distance of 8066 miles from the epicenter being covered by the waves in about 18 hours.

This particular occurrence of seismic sea waves had one result that distinguished it from all its predecessors. It set people to thinking that perhaps we now know enough about such waves and how they behave that a warning system could be devised which would rob them of the terror of the unexpected. Seismologists and specialists on waves and tides co-operated, and now such a system has been established to protect the Hawaiian Islands. A network of stations equipped with special instruments is scattered over the Pacific from Kodiak to Pago Pago and from Balboa to Palau. There are two phases of the warning system. One is based on a new audible alarm at seismograph stations operated by the United States Coast and Geodetic Survey, which calls instant attention to the fact that an earthquake has occurred. If it is found that the epicenter of the quake is under the ocean and so might produce seismic sea waves, a warning is sent to observers at selected tide stations to watch their gauges for evidence of the passage of the racing tsunamis. (Even a very small seismic sea wave can be identified by its peculiar period, and though it may be small at one place, it may reach dangerous heights at another.) When seismologists in Honolulu are notified that an undersea earthquake has occurred and that its waves have actually been recorded at certain stations, they can calculate when the waves will arrive at any point between the epicenter of the quake and the Hawaiian Islands. They can then issue warnings for the evacuation of beaches and waterfront areas. And so, for the first time in history, there is an organized effort to prevent these ominous waves from racing undetected over the empty spaces of the Pacific, to roar up suddenly on some inhabited shore.[12]

The storm waves that sometimes rise over low-lying coast lands in hurricane zones belong in the class of wind waves, but unlike the waves of ordinary winds and storms, they are accompanied by a rise of the general water level, called a storm tide. The rise of water is often so sudden that it leaves no possibility of escape. Such storm waves claim about three-fourths of the lives lost by tropical hurricanes. The most notable disasters from storm waves in the United States have been those at Galveston, Texas, on 8 September, 1900, on the lower Florida Keys on 2 and 3 September, 1935, and the catastrophic rise of water accompanying the New England hurricane of 21 September, 1938. The most fearful destruction by hurricane waves within historic time occurred in the Bay of Bengal on 7 October, 1737, when 20,000 boats were destroyed and 300,000 people drowned.[13]

There are other great waves, usually called 'rollers,' that periodically rise on certain coasts and batter them for days with damaging surf. These, too, are wind waves, but they are related to changes in barometric pressure over the ocean, perhaps several thousand miles distant from the beaches on which the waves eventually arrive. Low-pressure areas—like the one south of Iceland—are notorious storm breeders, their winds lashing the sea into great waves. After the waves leave the storm area they tend to become lower and longer and after perhaps thousands of miles of travel across the sea they become transformed into the undulations known as a ground swell. These swells are so regular and so low that often they are unnoticed as they pass through the short, choppy, new-formed waves of other areas. But when a swell approaches a coast and feels beneath it the gradually shoaling bottom, it begins to 'peak up' into a high, steep wave; within the surf zone the steepening becomes abruptly accentuated, a crest forms, breaks, and a great mass of water plunges downward.

Winter swell on the west coast of North America is the product of storms that travel south of the Aleutians into the Gulf of Alaska. Swell reaching this same coast during the summer has been traced back to its origin in the Southern Hemisphere belt of the 'roaring forties,' several thousand miles south of the equator. Because of the direction of the prevailing winds, the American east coast and the Gulf of Mexico do not receive the swell from far distant storms.

The coast of Morocco has always been particularly at the mercy of swell, for there is no protected harbor from the Strait of Gibraltar southward for some 500 miles. The rollers that visit the Atlantic islands of Ascension, St. Helena, South Trinidad, and Fernando de Noronha are historic. Apparently the same sort of waves occur on the South American coast near Rio de Janeiro, where they are known as *resacas;* others of kindred nature, having run their course from storms in the west-wind belt of the South Pacific, attack the shores of the Paumotos Islands; still others have been responsible for the well-known 'surf days' that plague the Pacific coast of South America. According to Robert Cushman Murphy, it was formerly the custom of shipmasters in the guano trade to demand a special allowance for a certain number of days during which the loading of their vessels would be interrupted by the swell. On such surf days 'mighty rollers come pouring over the sea wall, and have been known to carry away forty-ton freight cars, to uproot concrete piers, and to twist iron rails like wire.'

The slow progression of swell from its place of origin made it possible for the Moroccan Protectorate to establish a service for the prediction of the state of the sea. This was done in 1921, after long and troublesome experience with wrecked vessels and wharves. Daily telegraphic reports of the condition of the sea give advance notice of troublesome surf days. Warned of the approach of swells, ships in port may seek safety in the open sea. Before this service was established, the port of Casablanca had once been paralyzed for seven months, and St. Helena had seen the wreckage of practically all the ships in her harbor on one or more occasions. Modern wave-recording instruments like those now being tested in England and the United States will soon provide even greater security for all such shores.

It is always the unseen that most deeply stirs our imagination, and so it is with waves. The largest and most awe-inspiring waves of the ocean are invisible; they move on their mysterious courses far down in the hidden depths of the sea, rolling ponderously and unceasingly. For many years it was known that the vessels of Arctic expeditions often became almost trapped and made headway only with difficulty in what was called 'dead water'—now recognized as internal waves at the boundary between a thin surface layer of fresh water and the underlying salt water. In the early 1900's several Scandinavian hydrographers called attention to the existence of submarine waves, but another generation was to elapse before science had the instruments to study them thoroughly.

Now, even though mystery still surrounds the causes of these great waves that rise and fall, far below the surface, their oceanwide occurrence is well established. Down in deep water they toss submarines about, just as their surface counterparts set ships to rolling. They seem to break against the Gulf Stream and other strong currents in a deep-sea version of the dramatic meeting of surface waves and opposing tidal currents. Probably internal waves occur wherever there is a boundary between layers of dissimilar water, just as the waves we see occur at the boundary between air and sea. But these are waves such as never moved at the surface of the ocean. The water masses involved are unthinkably great, some of the waves being as high as 300 feet.

Of their effect on fishes and other life of the deep sea we have only the faintest conception. Swedish scientists say that the herring are carried or drawn into some of the fiords of Sweden when the deep internal waves roll over the submerged sills and into the fiords. In the open ocean, we know that the boundary between water masses of different temperatures or salinities is often a barrier that may not be passed by living creatures, delicately adjusted to certain conditions. Do these creatures themselves then move up and down with the roll of the deep waves? And what happens to the bottom fauna of the continental slope, adjusted, it may be, to water of unchanging warmth? What is their fate when the waves move in from a region of arctic cold, rolling like a storm surf against those deep, dark slopes? At present we do not know. We can only sense that in the deep and turbulent recesses of the sea are hidden mysteries far greater than any we have solved.

Wind, Sun, and the Spinning of the Earth

FOR THOUSANDS UPON THOUSANDS OF YEARS THE SUNLIGHT
AND THE SEA AND THE MASTERLESS WINDS HAVE HELD TRYST
TOGETHER.
—LLEWELYN POWYS

As the *Albatross III* groped through fog over Georges Bank
all of one week in the midsummer of 1949, those of us
aboard had a personal demonstration of the power of a great
ocean current. There was never less than a hundred miles of
cold Atlantic water between us and the Gulf Stream, but
the winds blew persistently from the south and the warm
breath of the Stream rolled over the Bank. The combination
of warm air and cold water spelled unending fog. Day after
day the *Albatross* moved in a small circular room, whose
walls were soft gray curtains and whose floor had a glassy
smoothness. Sometimes a petrel flew, with swallow-like flut-
terings, across this room, entering and leaving it by passing
through its walls as if by sorcery. Evenings, the sun, before
it set, was a pale silver disc hung in the ship's rigging, the
drifting streamers of fog picking up a diffused radiance and
creating a scene that set us to searching our memories for
quotations from Coleridge. The sense of a powerful presence felt but not seen, its nearness made manifest but never
revealed, was infinitely more dramatic than a direct encounter with the current.

The permanent currents of the ocean are, in a way, the
most majestic of her phenomena. Reflecting upon them, our
minds are at once taken out from the earth so that we can
regard, as from another planet, the spinning of the globe,
the winds that deeply trouble its surface or gently encompass
it, and the influence of the sun and the moon. For all these
cosmic forces are closely linked with the great currents of the
ocean, earning for them the adjective I like best of all those
applied to them—the planetary currents.

Since the world began, the ocean currents have undoubtedly
changed their courses many times (we know, for example,

125

that the Gulf Stream is no more than about 60 million years old); but it would be a bold writer who would try to describe their pattern in the Cambrian period, for example, or in the Devonian, or in the Jurassic. So far as the brief period of human history is concerned, however, it is most unlikely that there has been any important change in the major patterns of oceanic circulation, and the first thing that impresses us about the currents is their permanence. This is not surprising, for the forces that produce the currents show little disposition to change materially over the eons of earthly time. The primary driving power is supplied by the winds; the modifying influences are the sun, the revolving of the earth ever toward the east, and the obstructing masses of the continents.

The surface of the sea is unequally heated by the sun; as the water is warmed it expands and becomes lighter, while the cold water becomes heavier and more dense. Probably a slow exchange of polar and equatorial waters is brought about by these differences, the heated water of the tropics moving poleward in the upper layers, and polar water creeping toward the equator along the floor of the sea. But these movements are obscured and largely lost in the far greater sweep of the wind-driven currents. The steadiest winds are the trades, blowing diagonally toward the equator from the northeast and southeast. It is the trades that drive the equatorial currents around the globe. On wind and water alike, as on all that moves, be it a ship, a bullet, or a bird, the spinning earth exerts a deflecting force, turning all moving objects to the right in the Northern Hemisphere and to the left in the Southern. Through the combined action of these and other forces, the resulting current patterns are slowly circulating eddies, turning to the right, or clockwise, in the northern oceans, and to the left, or counterclockwise, in the southern.

There are exceptions, and the Indian Ocean, which seems never to be quite like the others, is an important one. Ruled by the capricious monsoons, its currents shift with the seasons. North of the equator, the direction of flow of immense masses of water may be either eastward or westward, depending on which of the monsoons is blowing. In the southern part of this ocean a fairly typical counterclockwise pattern exists: westward under the equator, south along the African coast, east to Australia on the westerly winds, northward by devious and seasonally shifting paths, here giving up water to the Pacific and there receiving contributions from it.

The Antarctic Ocean, being merely a continuous band of

water encircling the globe, is another exception to the typical current pattern. Its waters are driven constantly into the east and the northeast by winds from the west and the southwest, and the currents are given speed by the quantities of fresh water pouring in from melting ice. It is not a closed circulation; water is given off, in surface currents and by deep paths, to the adjacent oceans, and in return other water is received from them.

It is in the Atlantic and Pacific that we see most clearly the interplay of cosmic forces producing the planetary currents.

Perhaps because of the long centuries over which the Atlantic has been crossed and recrossed by trade routes, its currents have been longest known to seafaring men and best studied by oceanographers. The strongly running Equatorial Currents were familiar to generations of seamen in the days of sail. So determined was their set to westward that vessels intending to pass down into the South Atlantic could make no headway unless they had gained the necessary easting in the region of the southeast trades. Ponce de Leon's three ships, sailing south from Cape Canaveral to Tortugas in 1513, sometimes were unable to stem the Gulf Stream, and 'although they had great wind, they could not proceed forward, but backward.' A few years later Spanish shipmasters learned to take advantage of the currents, sailing westward in the Equatorial Current, but returning home via the Gulf Stream as far as Cape Hatteras, whence they launched out into the open Atlantic.

The first chart of the Gulf Stream was prepared about 1769 under the direction of Benjamin Franklin while he was Deputy Postmaster General of the Colonies. The Board of Customs in Boston had complained that the mail packets coming from England took two weeks longer to make the westward crossing than did the Rhode Island merchant ships. Franklin, perplexed, took the problem to a Nantucket sea captain, Timothy Folger, who told him this might very well be true because the Rhode Island captains were well acquainted with the Gulf Stream and avoided it on the westward crossing, whereas the English captains were not. Folger and other Nantucket whalers were personally familiar with the Stream because, he explained,

in our pursuit of whales, which keep to the sides of it but are not met within it, we run along the side and frequently cross it to change our side, and in crossing it have sometimes met and spoke with those packets who were in the middle of it and stemming it. We have informed them that they were stemming a current that was against them to the value of three miles an hour and advised them to cross it, but they were too wise to be counselled by simple American fishermen.*

Franklin, thinking 'it was a pity no notice was taken of this current upon the charts,' asked Folger to mark it out for him. The course of the Gulf Stream was then engraved on an old chart of the Atlantic and sent by Franklin to Falmouth, England, for the captains of the packets, 'who slighted it, however.' It was later printed in France and after the Revolution was published in the *Transactions of the American Philosophical Society*. The thriftiness of the Philosophical Society editors led them to combine in one plate Franklin's chart and a wholly separate figure intended to illustrate a paper by John Gilpin on the 'Annual Migrations of the Herring.' Some later historians have erroneously assumed a connection between Franklin's conception of the Gulf Stream and the insert in the upper left corner (See pp. 130-131).

Were it not for the deflecting barrier of the Panamanian isthmus, the North Equatorial Current would cross into the Pacific, as indeed it must have done through the many geologic ages when the continents of North and South America were separated. After the Panama ridge was formed in the late Cretaceous period, the current was doubled back to the northeast to re-enter the Atlantic as the Gulf Stream. From the Yucatan Channel eastward through the Florida Straits the Stream attains impressive proportions. If thought of in the time-honored conception of a 'river' in the sea, its width from bank to bank is 95 miles. It is a mile deep from surface to river bed. It flows with a velocity of nearly three knots and its volume is that of several hundred Mississippis.

Even in these days of Diesel power, the coastwise shipping off southern Florida shows a wholesome respect for the Gulf Stream. Almost any day, if you are out in a small boat below Miami, you can see the big freighters and tankers moving south in a course that seems surprisingly close to the Keys. Landward is the almost unbroken wall of submerged reefs where the big niggerhead corals send their solid bulks up to within a fathom or two of the surface. To seaward is the Gulf Stream, and while the big boats could fight their way south against it, they would

* From Am. Phil. Soc. *Trans.*, vol. 2, 1786.

consume much time and fuel in doing so. Therefore they pick their way with care between the reefs and the Stream.

The energy of the Stream off southern Florida probably results from the fact that here it is actually flowing downhill. Strong easterly winds pile up so much surface water in the narrow Yucatan Channel and in the Gulf of Mexico that the sea level there is higher than in the open Atlantic. At Cedar Keys, on the Gulf coast of Florida, the level of the sea is 19 centimeters (about 7½ inches) higher than at St. Augustine. There is further unevenness of level within the current itself. The lighter water is deflected by the earth's rotation toward the right side of the current, so that within the Gulf Stream the sea surface actually slopes upward toward the right. Along the coast of Cuba, the ocean is about 18 inches higher than along the mainland, thus upsetting completely our notions that 'sea level' is a literal expression.

Northward, the Stream follows the contours of the continental slope to the offing of Cape Hatteras, whence it turns more to seaward, deserting the sunken edge of the land. But it has left its impress on the continent. The four beautifully sculptured capes of the southern Atlantic coast—Canaveral, Fear, Lookout, Hatteras—apparently have been molded by powerful eddies set up by the passage of the Stream. Each is a cusp projecting seaward; between each pair of capes the beach runs in a long curving arc—the expression of the rhythmically swirling waters of the Gulf Stream eddies.

Beyond Hatteras, the Stream leaves the shelf, turning northeastward, as a narrow, meandering current, always sharply separated from the water on either side. Off the 'tail' of the Grand Banks the line is most sharply drawn between the cold, bottle-green arctic water of the Labrador Current and the warm indigo blue of the Stream. In winter the temperature change across the current boundary is so abrupt that as a ship crosses into the Gulf Stream her bow may be momentarily in water 20° warmer than that at her stern, as though the 'cold wall' were a solid barrier separating the two water masses. One of the densest fog banks in the world lies in this region over the cold water of the Labrador Current—a thick, blanketing whiteness that is the atmospheric response to the Gulf Stream's invasion of the cold northern seas.

Where the Stream feels the rise of the ocean floor known as the 'tail' of the Grand Banks, it bends eastward and begins to spread out into many complexly curving tongues.

Benjamin Franklin's Map of the Gulf Stream

Course of the great, wind-driven current systems of the Atlantic and Pacific oceans. Cold currents appear in white; warm or intermediate ones in black.

Probably the force of the arctic water, the water that has
come down from Baffin Bay and Greenland, freighting its
icebergs, helps push the Stream to the east—that, and the
deflecting force of the earth's rotation, always turning the currents to the right. The Labrador Current itself (being a south-
ward-moving current) is turned in toward the mainland. The
next time you wonder why the water is so cold at certain
coastal resorts of the eastern United States, remember that
the water of the Labrador Current is between you and the
Gulf Stream.

Passing across the Atlantic, the Stream becomes less a
current than a drift of water, fanning out in three main
directions: southward into the Sargasso; northward into the
Norwegian Sea, where it forms eddies and deep vortices;
eastward to warm the coast of Europe (some of it even to
pass into the Mediterranean) and thence as the Canary Current to rejoin the Equatorial Current and close the circuit.[14]

The Atlantic currents of the Southern Hemisphere are
practically a mirror image of those of the Northern. The
great spiral moves counterclockwise—west, south, east, north.
Here the dominant current is in the eastern instead of the
western part of the ocean. It is the Benguela Current, a river
of cold water moving northward along the west coast of
Africa. The South Equatorial Current, in mid-ocean a powerful stream (the *Challenger* scientists said it poured past St.
Paul's Rocks like a millrace) loses a substantial part of its
waters to the North Atlantic off the coast of South America
—about 6 million cubic meters a second. The remainder
becomes the Brazil Current, which circles south and then
turns east as the South Atlantic or Antarctic Current. The
whole is a system of shallow water movements, involving
throughout much of its course not more than the upper hundred fathoms.

The North Equatorial Current of the Pacific is the longest
westerly running current on earth, with nothing to deflect it
in its 9000-mile course from Panama to the Philippines. There,
meeting the barrier of the islands, most of it swings northward as the Japan Current—Asia's counterpart of the Gulf
Stream. A small part persists on its westward course, feeling its way amid the labyrinth of Asiatic islands; part turns
upon itself and streams back along the equator as the Equatorial Countercurrent. The Japan Current—called Kuroshio
or Black Current because of the deep, indigo blue of its
waters—rolls northward along the continental shelf off eastern Asia, until it is driven away from the continent by a
mass of icy water—the Oyashio—that pours out of the Sea

of Okhotsk and Bering Sea. The Japan Current and Oyashio meet in a region of fog and tempestuous winds, as, in the North Atlantic, the meeting of the Gulf Stream and the Labrador Current is marked with fog. Drifting toward America, the Japan Current forms the northern wall of the great North Pacific eddy. Its warm waters become chilled with infusions of cold polar water from Oyashio, the Aleutians, and Alaska. When it reaches the mainland of America it is a cool current, moving southward along the coast of California. There it is further cooled by updrafts of deep water and has much to do with the temperate summer climate of the American west coast. Off Lower California it rejoins the North Equatorial Current.

What with all the immensity of space in the South Pacific, we should expect to find here the most powerfully impressive of all ocean currents, but this does not seem to be true. The South Equatorial Current has its course so frequently interrupted by islands, which are forever deflecting streams of its water into the central basin, that by the time it approaches Asia it is, during most seasons, a comparatively feeble current, lost in a confused and ill-defined pattern around the East Indies and Australia.[15] The West Wind Drift or Antarctic Current—the poleward arc of the spiral—is born of the strongest winds in the world, roaring across stretches of ocean almost unbroken by land. The details of this, as of most of the currents of the South Pacific, are but imperfectly known. Only one has been thoroughly studied—the Humboldt —and this has so direct an effect on human affairs that it overshadows all others.

The Humboldt Current, sometimes called the Peru, flows northward along the west coast of South America, carrying waters almost as cold as the Antarctic from which it comes. But its chill is actually that of the deep ocean, for the current is reinforced by almost continuous upwelling from lower oceanic layers. It is because of the Humboldt that penguins live almost under the equator, on the Galapagos Islands. In these cold waters, rich in minerals, there is an abundance of sea life perhaps unparalleled anywhere else in the world. The direct harvesters of this sea life are not men, but millions of sea birds. From the sun-baked accumulations of guano that whiten the coastal cliffs and islands, the South Americans obtain, at second hand, the wealth of the Humboldt Current.

Robert E. Coker, who studied the Peruvian guano industry at the request of that government, gives a vivid picture of the life of the Humboldt. He writes of

. . . immense schools of small fishes, the anchobetas, which
are followed by numbers of bonitos and other fishes and
by sea lions, while at the same time they are preyed upon
by the flocks of cormorants, pelicans, gannets, and other
abundant sea birds . . . The long files of pelicans, the
low-moving black clouds of cormorants, or the rainstorms
of plunging gannets probably cannot be equaled in any
other part of the world. The birds feed chiefly, almost
exclusively, upon the anchobetas. The anchobeta, then, is
not only . . . the food of the larger fishes, but, as the food
of the birds, it is the source from which is derived each
year probably a score of thousands of tons of high-grade
bird guano.*

Dr. Coker estimated the annual consumption of fish by
the guano-producing birds of Peru as equal to a fourth of the
total production of all United States fisheries. Because of
this diet, which links the birds with all the minerals of the
sea, their excrement is the most valuable and efficient
fertilizer in the world.

Leaving the coast of South America at about the latitude of
Cape Blanco, the Humboldt Current turns westward into the
Pacific, carrying its cool waters almost to the equator. About
the Galapagos Islands it gives rise to a strange mixture of
waters—the cool green of the Humboldt and the blue equatorial waters meeting in rips and foam lines, suggesting hidden movements and conflicts deep in the sea.

The conflict between opposing water masses may, in places,
be one of the most dramatic of the ocean's phenomena.
Superficial hissings and sighings, the striping of the surface
waters with lines of froth, a confused turbulence and boiling,
and even sounds like distant breakers accompany the displacement of the surface layers by deep water. As visible
evidence of the upward movement of the water masses, some
of the creatures that inhabit the deeper places of the sea
may be carried up bodily into the surface, there to set off
orgies of devouring and being devoured such as Robert
Cushman Murphy witnessed one night off the coast of
Columbia from the schooner *Askoy*. The night had been still
and dark, but the behavior of the surface made it clear that
deep water was rising and that some sort of conflict was in
progress among opposing water masses far below the ship. All
about the schooner small, steep waves leaped into being

* From *Bulletin*, U. S. Bureau of Fisheries, vol. xxviii, part 1,
1908, p. 338.

and dissolved in foaming whitecaps, pricked with the blue fire of luminescent organisms. Suddenly,

> On either side, and at a bafflingly uncertain distance from the ship, a dark line, like a wall of advancing water, seemed to be closing in upon us . . . We could hear the splash and murmur of a troubled surface close by . . . Presently we could see a gleam of foam sprinkled with points of luminescence on the slowly approaching swell or head to the left. Vague and unfounded thoughts of marine earthquake bores occurred to Fallon and me together, and we felt peculiarly helpless with a dismantled engine and no breeze to make the craft answer her helm. The dreamlike slowness of all that was going on, moreover, gave me a feeling that I had not yet fully shaken off the bonds of three hours' slumber.
>
> However, when the dark, white-outlined menace reached us, it proved to be nothing more than a field of the dancing water, tossing its little peaks a mere foot or so into the air and beating a tattoo on the steel flanks of 'Askoy' . . .
>
> Presently a sharp hissing sound, different in character from the bursting of small waves, came out of the darkness to starboard, and this was followed by strange sighings and puffings . . . The puffers were blackfish, many scores, or perhaps hundreds of them, rolling and lumbering along and diving to pass beneath 'Askoy' shortly before they reached her bilge . . . We could hear the bacchanalian clamor of their rumblings and belchings. In the long beam of the searchlight, the hissing proved to come from the jumping of small fishes. In all directions as far as the light carried, they were shooting into the air and pouring down like hail . . .
>
> The surface was seething, boiling with life, much of which was *de profundis*. Larvae of clawless lobsters, tinted jellyfish, nurse chains of salps, small herringlike fishes, a silvery hatchetfish with its face bitten off, rudder fishes, hanging head downward, luminous lantern-fishes with shining light pores, red and purple swimming crabs, other creatures which we could not name at sight and much that was too small even to see distinctly . . .
>
> A general holocaust was in progress. The little fishes were eating invertebrates or straining out the plankton; the squids were pursuing and capturing fish of various sizes; and the blackfish were no doubt enjoying the squids . . .
>
> As the night wore on, the amazing manifestations of

abundance and devouring gradually, almost imperceptibly, died away. Eventually, 'Askoy' lay once more in water that seemed as still and dead as oil, and the lap-lap of skipping waves drew off farther and farther into the distance until it was lost.*

Although such exciting displays of upwelling are seen and recognized by comparatively few people, the process takes place regularly off a number of coasts and at many places in the open ocean. Wherever it occurs, it is responsible for a profusion of life. Some of the world's largest fisheries are dependent on upwelling. The coast of Algeria is famous for its sardine fisheries; the sardines are abundant here because upward streams of deep, cold water provide the minerals to support astronomical numbers of diatoms. The west coast of Morocco, the area opposite the Canary and Cape Verde islands, and the southwest coast of Africa are other sites of extensive upwelling and consequent richness of marine life. There is an amazingly abundant fish fauna in the Arabian Sea near Oman and on the Somali Coast near Cape Hafun, both occurring in areas of cold water rising from the depths. In the South Equatorial Current north of Ascension Island is a 'tongue of cold' produced by the rise of sea water from the bottom. It is extraordinarily rich in plankton. Upwelling around the island of South Georgia, east of Cape Horn, makes this one of the world's centers of whaling. On the west coast of the United States the catch of sardines is sometimes as much as a billion pounds in a year, supporting one of the largest fisheries in the world. The fishery could not exist except for upwelling, which sets off the old, familiar biological chain: salts, diatoms, copepods, herring. Down along the west coast of South America, the astonishing profusion of life in the Humboldt is maintained by upwelling, which not only keeps the waters of the current cold in all its 2500-mile course to the Galapagos Islands but brings up the nutrient salts from the deeper layers.

When upwelling takes place along coastlines, it is the result of the interplay of several forces—the winds, the surface currents, the rotation of the earth, and the shape of the hidden slopes of the continent's foundations. When the winds, combined with the deflecting effect of rotation, blow the surface waters offshore, deep water must rise to replace it.

Upwelling may occur in the open sea as well, but from entirely different causes. Wherever two strongly moving currents diverge, water must rise from below to fill the place where the streams separate. One such place lies at the westernmost bounds of the Equatorial Current in the Pacific, where the powerfully moving stream turns and pours part of its waters back into the countercurrent, and part northward toward Japan. These are confused and turbulent waters. There is the strong pull to the north by which the main stream, sensitive to the force of the rotating earth, turns to the right. There are the swirls and eddies by which the lesser stream turns again upon itself and flows back into the eastern Pacific. There is the rushing up from below to fill the otherwise deepening groove between the streams. In the resulting disquietude of the ocean waters, chilled and enriched from below, the smaller organisms of the plankton thrive. As they multiply, they provide food for the larger plankton creatures, which, in turn, provide food for squid and fish. These waters are prodigiously rich in life, and there is evidence that they may have been so for many thousands of years. Swedish oceanographers recently found that under these areas of divergence the sediment layer is exceptionally thick—the layer composed of all that remains of the billions upon billions of minute creatures that have lived and died in this place.

The downward movement of surface water into the depths is an occurrence as dramatic as upwelling, and perhaps it fills the human mind with an even greater sense of awe and mystery, because it cannot be seen but can only be imagined. At several known places the downward flow of enormous quantities of water takes place regularly. This water feeds the deep currents of whose courses we have only the dimmest knowledge. We do know that it is all part of the ocean's system of balances, by which she pays back to one part of her waters what she had latterly borrowed for distribution to another.

The North Atlantic, for example, receives quantities of surface water (some 6 million cubic meters a second) from the South Atlantic via the Equatorial Current. The return payment is made at deep levels, partly in very cold arctic water, and partly in some of the saltiest, warmest water in the world, that of the Mediterranean. There are two places for the down-flow of arctic water. One is in the Labrador Sea. Another is southeast of Greenland. At each the quantity of sinking water is prodigious—some 2 million cubic meters a second. The deep Mediterranean water flows out over the sill that separates the basin of the Mediterranean from the

open Atlantic. This sill lies about 150 fathoms beneath the
surface of the sea. The water that spills over its rocky edge
does so because of the unusual conditions that prevail in
the Mediterranean. The hot sun beating down on its nearly
enclosed water creates an extraordinarily high rate of
evaporation, drawing off into the atmosphere more water than
is added by the inflow of rivers. The water becomes even
saltier and more dense; as evaporation continues the surface
of the Mediterranean falls below that of the Atlantic. To
correct the inequality, lighter water from the Atlantic pours
past Gibraltar in surface streams of great strength.

Now we give the matter little thought, but in the days of
sail, passage out into the Atlantic was a difficult problem because of this surface current. An old ship's log of the year
1855 has this to say of the current and its practical effect:

Weather fine; made 1¼ pt. leeway. At noon, stood in
to Almira Bay, and anchored off the village of Roguetas.
Found a great number of vessels waiting for a chance to
get to the westward, and learned from them that at least a
thousand sail are weather-bound between this and Gibraltar. Some of them have been so for six weeks, and have
even got so far as Malaga, only to be swept back by the
current. Indeed, no vessel has been able to get out into
the Atlantic for three months past.

Later measurements show that these surface currents flow
into the Mediterranean with an average velocity of about
three knots. The bottom current, moving out into the Atlantic,
is even stronger. Its outward flow is so vigorous that it has
been known to wreck oceanographic instruments sent down
to measure it, apparently pounding them against stones on
the bottom; and once the wire of the Falmouth cable near
Gibraltar 'was ground like the edge of a razor, so that it
had to be abandoned and a new one laid well inshore.'

The water that sinks in the arctic regions of the Atlantic,
as well as that spilling over the Gibraltar sill, spreads out
widely into the deeper parts of the ocean basins. Traversing
the North Atlantic, it crosses the equator and continues to
the south, there passing between two layers of water that
are moving northward from the Antarctic Sea. Some of this
antarctic water mingles with the Atlantic water—that from
Greenland and Labrador and the Mediterranean—and with it
returns south. But other antarctic water moves northward
across the equator and has been traced as far as the latitude
of Cape Hatteras.

The flow of these deep waters is hardly a 'flow' at all; its pace is ponderously slow, the measured creep of icy, heavy water. But the volumes involved are prodigious, and the areas covered world-wide. It may even be that the deep ocean water, on such global wanderings, acts to distribute some of the marine fauna—not the surface forms but the dwellers in deep, dark layers. From our knowledge of the source of the currents, it seems significant that some of the same species of deep-water invertebrates and fishes have been collected off the coast of South Africa and off Greenland. And about Bermuda, where a greater variety of deepwater forms has been found than anywhere else, there is a mingling of deep water from the Antarctic, the Arctic, and the Mediterranean. Perhaps in these sunless streams the weird inhabitants of deep waters drift, generation after generation, surviving and multiplying because of the almost changeless character of these slowly moving currents.

There is, then, no water that is wholly of the Pacific, or wholly of the Atlantic, or of the Indian or the Antarctic. The surf that we find exhilarating at Virginia Beach or at La Jolla today may have lapped at the base of antarctic icebergs or sparkled in the Mediterranean sun, years ago, before it moved through dark and unseen waterways to the place we find it now. It is by the deep, hidden currents that the oceans are made one.

The Moving Tides

IN EVERY COUNTRY THE MOON KEEPS EVER THE RULE
OF ALLIANCE WITH THE SEA WHICH IT ONCE FOR ALL HAS
AGREED UPON.
—THE VENERABLE BEDE

There is no drop of water in the ocean, not even in the deepest parts of the abyss, that does not know and respond to the mysterious forces that create the tide. No other force that affects the sea is so strong. Compared with the tide the wind-created waves are surface movements felt, at most, no more than a hundred fathoms below the surface. So, despite their impressive sweep, are the planetary currents, which seldom involve more than the upper several hundred fathoms. The masses of water affected by the tidal movement are enormous, as will be clear from one example. Into one small bay on the east coast of North America—Passamaquoddy—2 billion tons of water are carried by the tidal currents twice each day; into the whole Bay of Fundy, 100 billion tons.

Here and there we find dramatic illustration of the fact that the tides affect the whole ocean, from its surface to its floor. The meeting of opposing tidal currents in the Strait of Messina creates whirlpools (one of them is Charybdis of classical fame) which so deeply stir the waters of the strait that fish bearing all the marks of abyssal existence, their eyes atrophied or abnormally large, their bodies studded with phosphorescent organs, frequently are cast up on the lighthouse beach, and the whole area yields a rich collection of deep-sea fauna for the Institute of Marine Biology at Messina.

The tides are a response of the mobile waters of the ocean to the pull of the moon and the more distant sun. In theory, there is a gravitational attraction between every drop of sea water and even the outermost star of the universe. In practice, however, the pull of the remote stars is so slight as to be obliterated in the vaster movements by which the ocean yields to the moon and the sun. Anyone who has lived near tidewater knows that the moon, far more than the sun, controls the tides. He has noticed that, just as the moon rises later each day by fifty minutes, on the average, than the day before, so, in most places, the time of high tide is correspondingly later each day. And as the moon waxes and wanes in its monthly cycle, so the height of the tide varies. Twice each month, when the moon is a mere thread of silver in the sky, and again when it is full, we have the strongest tidal movements—the highest flood tides and the lowest ebb tides of the lunar month. These are called the spring tides. At these times sun, moon, and earth are directly in line and the pull of the two heavenly bodies is added together to bring the water high on the beaches, and send its surf leaping upward against the sea cliffs, and draw a brimming tide into the harbors so that the boats float high beside their wharfs. And twice each month, at the quarters of the moon, when sun, moon, and earth lie at the apexes of a triangle, and the pull of the sun and moon are opposed, we have the moderate tidal movements called the neap tides. Then the difference between high and lower water is less than at any other time during the month.

That the sun, with a mass 27 million times that of the moon, should have less influence over the tides than a small satellite of the earth is at first surprising. But in the mechanics of the universe, nearness counts for more than distant mass, and when all the mathematical calculations have been made we find that the moon's power over the tides is more than twice that of the sun.

The tides are enormously more complicated than all this would suggest. The influence of sun and moon is constantly changing, varying with the phases of the moon, with the distance of moon and sun from the earth, and with the position of each to north or south of the equator. They are complicated further by the fact that every body of water, whether natural or artificial, has its own period of oscillation. Disturb its waters and they will move with a seesaw or rocking motion, with the most pronounced movement at the ends of the container, the least motion at the center. Tidal scientists now believe that the ocean contains a number of 'basins,' each with its own period of oscillation determined by its length and depth. The disturbance that sets the water in motion is the attracting force of the moon and sun. But the kind of motion, that is, the period of the swing of the water, depends upon the physical dimensions of the basin.

What this means in terms of actual tides we shall presently see.

The tides present a striking paradox, and the essence of it is this: the force that sets them in motion is cosmic, lying wholly outside the earth and presumably acting impartially on all parts of the globe, but the nature of the tide at any particular place is a local matter, with astonishing differences occurring within a very short geographic distance. When we spend a long summer holiday at the seashore we may become aware that the tide in our cove behaves very differently from that at a friend's place twenty miles up the coast, and is strikingly different from what we may have known in some other locality. If we are summering on Nantucket Island our boating and swimming will be little disturbed by the tides, for the range between high water and low is only about a foot or two. But if we choose to vacation near the upper part of the Bay of Fundy, we must accommodate ourselves to a rise and fall of 40 to 50 feet, although both places are included within the same body of water—the Gulf of Maine. Or if we spend our holiday on Chesapeake Bay we may find that the time of high water each day varies by as much as 12 hours in different places on the shores of the same bay.

The truth of the matter is that local topography is all-important in determining the features that to our minds make 'the tide.' The attractive force of the heavenly bodies sets the water in motion, but how, and how far, and how strongly it will rise depend on such things as the slope of the bottom, the depth of a channel, or the width of a bay's entrance.

The United States Coast and Geodetic Survey has a remarkable, robotlike machine with which it can predict the time and height of the tide on any past or future date, for any part of the world, on one essential condition. This is that at some time local observations must have been made to show how the topographic features of the place modify and direct the tidal movements.

Perhaps the most striking differences are in the range of tide, which varies tremendously in different parts of the world, so that what the inhabitants of one place might consider disastrously high water might be regarded as no tide at all by coastal communities only a hundred miles distant. The highest tides in the world occur in the Bay of Fundy, with a rise of about 50 feet in Minas Basin near the head of the Bay at the spring tides. At least half a dozen other places scattered around the world have a tidal range of more than 30 feet—Puerto Gallegos in Argentina and Cook Inlet in Alaska, Frobisher Bay in Davis Strait, the Koksoak River emptying into Hudson Strait, and the Bay of St. Malo in France come to mind. At many other places 'high tide' may mean a rise of only a foot or so, perhaps only a few inches. The tides of Tahiti rise and fall in a gentle movement, with a difference of no more than a foot between high water and low. On most oceanic islands the range of the tide is slight. But it is never safe to generalize about the kinds of places that have high or low tides, because two areas that are not far apart may respond in very different ways to the tide-producing forces. At the Atlantic end of the Panama Canal the tidal range is not more than 1 or 2 feet, but at the Pacific end, only 40 miles away, the range is 12 to 16 feet. The Sea of Okhotsk is another example of the way the height of the tide varies. Throughout much of the Sea the tides are moderate—only about 2 feet—but in some parts of the Sea there is a 10-foot rise, and at the head of one of its arms—the Gulf of Penjinsk—the rise is 37 feet.

What is it about one place that will bring 40 or 50 feet of water rising about its shores, while at another place lying under the same moon and sun, the tide will rise only a few inches? What, for example, can be the explanation of the great tides on the Bay of Fundy, while only a few hundred miles away at Nantucket Island, on the shores of the same ocean, the tide range is little more than a foot?

The modern theory of tidal oscillation seems to offer the best explanation of such local differences—the rocking up and down of water in each natural basin about a central, virtually tideless node. Nantucket is located near the node of its basin, where there is little motion, hence a small tide range. Passing northeastward along the shores of this basin, we find the tides becoming progressively higher, with a 6-foot range at Nauset Harbor on Cape Cod, 8.9 feet at Gloucester, 15.7 feet at West Quoddy Head, 20.9 feet at St. John, and 39.4 feet at Folly Point. The Nova Scotia shore of the Bay of Fundy has somewhat higher tides than the corresponding points on the New Brunswick shore, and the highest tides of all are in Minas Basin at the head of the Bay. The immense movements of water in the Bay of Fundy result from a combination of circumstances. The bay lies at the end of an oscillating basin. Furthermore, the natural period of oscillation of the basin is approximately 12 hours. This very nearly coincides with the period of the ocean tide. Therefore the water movement within the bay is sustained and enormously increased by the ocean tide. The narrowing and shallowing of the bay in its upper reaches, compelling the

huge masses of water to crowd into a constantly diminishing
area, also contribute to the great heights of the Fundy
tides.

The tidal rhythms, as well as the range of tide, vary from
ocean to ocean. Flood tide and ebb succeed each other
around the world, as night follows day, but as to whether
there shall be two high tides and two low in each lunar day,
or only one, there is no unvarying rule. To those who know
best the Atlantic Ocean—either its eastern or western shores
—the rhythm of two high tides and two low tides in each
day seems 'normal.' Here, on each flood tide, the water
advances about as far as the preceding high; and succeeding
ebb tides fall about equally low. But in that great inland
sea of the Atlantic, the Gulf of Mexico, a different rhythm
prevails around most of its borders. At best the tidal rise
here is but a slight movement, of no more than a foot or
two. At certain places on the shores of the Gulf it is a long,
deliberate undulation—one rise and one fall in the lunar
day of 24 hours plus 50 minutes—resembling the untroubled
breathing of that earth monster to whom the ancients attributed all tides. This 'diurnal rhythm' is found in scattered
places about the earth—such as Saint Michael, Alaska, and at
Do Son in French Indo-China—as well as in the Gulf of
Mexico. By far the greater part of the world's coasts—most
of the Pacific basin and the shores of the Indian Ocean—
display a mixture of the diurnal and semidiurnal types of
tide. There are two high and two low tides in a day, but
the succeeding floods may be so unequal that the second
scarcely rises to mean sea level; or it may be the ebb tides
that are of extreme inequality.

There seems to be no simple explanation of why some
parts of the ocean should respond to the pull of sun and
moon with one rhythm and other parts with another, although the matter is perfectly clear to tidal scientists on the
basis of mathematical calculations. To gain some inkling of
the reasons, we must recall the many separate components of
the tide-producing force, which in turn result from the changing relative positions of sun, moon, and earth. Depending on
local geographic features, every part of earth and sea,
while affected in some degree by each component, is more
responsive to some than to others. Presumably the shape
and depths of the Atlantic basin cause it to respond most
strongly to the forces that produce a semidiurnal rhythm.
The Pacific and Indian oceans, on the other hand, are affected
by both the diurnal and semidiurnal forces, and a mixed
tide results.

The island of Tahiti is a classic example of the way even a small area may react to one of the tide-producing forces to the virtual exclusion of the others. On Tahiti, it is sometimes said, you can tell the time of day by looking out at the beach and noticing the stage of the tide. This is not strictly true, but the legend has a certain basis. With slight variations, high tide occurs at noon and at midnight; low water, at six o'clock morning and evening. The tides thus ignore the effect of the moon, which is to advance the time of the tides by 50 minutes each day. Why should the tides of Tahiti follow the sun instead of the moon? The most favored explanation is that the island lies at the axis or node of one of the basins set in oscillation by the moon. There is very little motion in response to the moon at this point, and the waters are therefore free to move in the rhythm induced by the sun.

If the history of the earth's tides should one day be written by some observer of the universe, it would no doubt be said that they reached their greatest grandeur and power in the younger days of Earth, and that they slowly grew feebler and less imposing until one day they ceased to be. For the tides were not always as they are today, and as with all that is earthly, their days are numbered.

In the days when the earth was young, the coming in of the tide must have been a stupendous event. If the moon was, as we have supposed in an earlier chapter, formed by the tearing away of a part of the outer crust of the earth, it must have remained for a time very close to its parent. Its present position is the consequence of being pushed farther and farther away from the earth for some 2 billion years. When it was half its present distance from the earth, its power over the ocean tides was eight times as great as now, and the tidal range may even then have been several hundred feet on certain shores. But when the earth was only a few million years old, assuming that the deep ocean basins were then formed, the sweep of the tides must have been beyond all comprehension. Twice each day, the fury of the incoming waters would inundate all the margins of the continents. The range of the surf must have been enormously extended by the reach of the tides, so that the waves would batter the crests of high cliffs and sweep inland to erode the continents. The fury of such tides would contribute not a little to the general bleakness and grimness and uninhabitability of the young earth.

Under such conditions, no living thing could exist on the shores or pass beyond them, and, had conditions not changed, it is reasonable to suppose that life would have evolved no further than the fishes. But over the millions of years the moon has receded, driven away by the friction of the tides it creates. The very movement of the water over the bed of the ocean, over the shallow edges of the continents, and over the inland seas carries within itself the power that is slowly destroying the tides, for tidal friction is gradually slowing down the rotation of the earth. In those early days we have spoken of, it took the earth a much shorter time—perhaps only about 4 hours—to make a complete rotation on its axis. Since then, the spinning of the globe has been so greatly slowed that a rotation now requires, as everyone knows, about 24 hours. This retarding will continue, according to mathematicians, until the day is about 50 times as long as it is now.

And all the while the tidal friction will be exerting a second effect, pushing the moon farther way, just as it has already pushed it out more than 200,000 miles. (According to the laws of mechanics, as the rotation of the earth is retarded, that of the moon must be accelerated, and centrifugal force will carry it farther away.) As the moon recesses, it will, of course, have less power over the tides and they will grow weaker. It will also take the moon longer to complete its orbit around the earth. When finally the length of the day and of the month coincide, the moon will no longer rotate relatively to the earth, and there will be no lunar tides.

All this, of course, will require time on a scale the mind finds it difficult to conceive, and before it happens it is quite probable that the human race will have vanished from the earth. This may seen, then, like a Wellsian fantasy of a world so remote that we may dismiss it from our thoughts. But already, even in our allotted fraction of earthly time, we can see some of the effects of these cosmic processes. Our day is believed to be several seconds longer than that of Babylonian times. Britain's Astronomer Royal recently called the attention of the American Philosophical Society to the fact that the world will soon have to choose between two kinds of time. The tide-induced lengthening of the day has already complicated the problems of human systems of keeping time. Conventional clocks, geared to the earth's rotation, do not show the effect of the lengthening days. New atomic clocks now being constructed will show actual time and will differ from other clocks.

Although the tides have become tamer, and their range is now measured in tens instead of hundreds of feet, mariners are nevertheless greatly concerned not only with the stages of the tide and the set of the tidal currents, but with the many violent movements and disturbances of the sea that are indirectly related to the tides. Nothing the human mind has invented can tame a tide rip or control the rhythm of the water's ebb and flow, and the most modern instruments cannot carry a vessel over a shoal until the tide has brought a sufficient depth of water over it. Even the *Queen Mary* waits for slack water to come to her pier in New York; otherwise the set of the tidal current might swing her against the pier with enough force to crush it. On the Bay of Fundy, because of the great range of tide, harbor activities in some of the ports follow a pattern as rhythmic as the tides themselves, for vessels can come to the docks to take on or discharge cargo during only a few hours on each tide, leaving promptly to avoid being stranded in mud at low water.

In the confinement of narrow passages or when opposed by contrary winds and swells, the tidal currents often move with uncontrollable violence, creating some of the most dangerous waterways of the world. It is only necessary to read the Coast Pilots and Sailing Directions for various parts of the world to understand the menace of such tidal currents to navigation.

'Vessels around the Aleutians are in more danger from tidal currents than from any other cause, save the lack of surveys,' says the postwar edition of the *Alaska Pilot*. Through Unalga and Akutan passes, which are among the most-used routes for vessels entering Bering Sea from the Pacific, strong tidal currents pour, making their force felt well offshore and setting vessels unexpectedly against the rocks. Through Akun Strait the flood tide has the velocity of a mountain torrent, with dangerous swirls and overfalls. In each of these passes the tide will raise heavy, choppy seas if opposed by wind or swells. 'Vessels must be prepared to take seas aboard,' warns the *Pilot*, for a 15-foot wave of a tide rip may suddenly rise and sweep across a vessel, and more than one man has been carried off to his death in this way.

On the opposite side of the world, the tide setting eastward from the open Atlantic presses between the islands of the Shetlands and Orkneys into the North Sea, and on the ebb returns through the same narrow passages. At certain stages of the tide these waters are dotted with dangerous eddies, with strange upward domings, or with sinister pits or depressions. Even in calm weather boats are warned to avoid the eddies of Pentland Firth, which are known as the Swilkie; and with an ebb tide and a northwest wind the heavy breaking seas of the Swilkie are a menace to vessels 'which few, having once experienced, would be rash enough to encounter a second time.'

Edgar Allan Poe, in his 'Descent into the Maelstrom,' converted one of the more evil manifestations of the tide into literature. Few who have read the story will forget its drama—how the old man led his companion to a mountain cliff high above the sea and let him watch the water far below in the narrow passageway between the islands, with its sinister foam and scum, its uneasy bubbling and boiling, until suddenly the whirlpool was formed before his eyes and rushed with an appalling sound through the narrow waterway. Then the old man told the story of his own descent into the whirlpool and of his miraculous escape. Most of us have wondered how much of the story was fact, how much the creation of Poe's fertile imagination. There actually is a Maelstrom and it exists where Poe placed it, between two of the islands of the Lofoten group off the west coast of Norway. It is, as he described it, a gigantic whirlpool or series of whirlpools, and men with their boats have actually been drawn down into the spinning funnels of water. Although Poe's account exaggerates certain details, the essential facts on which he based his narrative are verified in the *Sailing Directions for the Northwest and North Coasts of Norway,* a practical and circumstantial document:

Though rumor has greatly exaggerated the importance of the Malström, or more properly Moskenstraumen, which runs between Mosken and Lofotodden, it is still the most dangerous tideway in Lofoten, its violence being due, in great measure, to the irregularity of the ground . . . As the strength of the tide increases the sea becomes heavier and the current more irregular, forming extensive eddies or whirlpools (Malström). During such periods no vessel should enter the Moskenstraumen.

These whirlpools are cavities in the form of an inverted bell, wide and rounded at the mouth and narrower toward the bottom; they are largest when first formed and are carried along with the current, diminishing gradually until they disappear; before the extinction of one, two or three more will appear, following each other like so many pits in the sea . . . Fishermen affirm that if they are aware of their approach to a whirlpool and have time to throw an oar or any other bulky body into it they will get over it safely; the reason is that when the continuity is broken and the whirling motion of the sea interrupted by something thrown into it the water must rush suddenly in on all sides and fill up the cavity. For the same reason, in strong breezes, when the waves break, though there may be a whirling round, there can be no cavity. In the Saltström boats and men have been drawn down by these vortices, and much loss of life has resulted.

Among unusual creations of the tide, perhaps the best known are the bores. The world possesses half a dozen or more famous ones. A bore is created when a great part of the flood tide enters a river as a single wave, or at most two or three waves, with a steep and high front. The conditions that produce bores are several: there must be a considerable range of tide, combined with sand bars or other obstructions in the mouth of the river, so that the tide is hindered and held back, until it finally gathers itself together and rushes through. The Amazon is remarkable for the distance its bore travels upstream—some 200 miles—with the result that the bores of as many as 5 flood tides may actually be moving up the river at one time.

On the Tsientang River, which empties into the China Sea, all shipping is controlled by the bore—the largest, most dangerous, and best known in the world. The ancient Chinese used to throw offerings into the river to appease the angry spirit of this bore, whose size and fury appear to have varied from century to century, or perhaps even from decade to decade, as the silting of the estuary has shifted and changed. During most of the month the bore now advances up the river in a wave 8 to 11 feet high, moving at a speed of 12 to 13 knots, its front 'a sloping cascade of bubbling foam, falling forward and pounding on itself and on the river.' Its full ferocity is reserved for the spring tides of the full moon and the new moon, at which times the crest of the advancing wave is said to rise 25 feet above the surface of the river.

There are bores, though none so spectacular, in North America. There is one at Moncton, on New Brunswick's Petitcodiac River, but it is impressive only on the spring tides of the full or new moon. At Turnagain Arm in Cook Inlet, Alaska, where the tides are high and the currents strong, the flood tide under certain conditions comes in as a bore. Its advancing front may be four to six feet high and is recognized as being so dangerous to small craft that boats are beached well above the level of the flats when the bore is approaching. It can be heard about half an hour before its arrival at any point, traveling slowly with a sound as of breakers on a beach.

The influence of the tide over the affairs of sea creatures as well as men may be seen all over the world. The billions upon billions of sessile animals, like oysters, mussels, and barnacles, owe their very existence to the sweep of the tides, which brings them the food which they are unable to go in search of. By marvelous adaptations of form and structure, the inhabitants of the world between the tide lines are enabled to live in a zone where the danger of being dried up is matched against the danger of being washed away, where for every enemy that comes by sea there is another that comes by land, and where the most delicate of living tissues must somehow withstand the assault of storm waves that have the power to shift tons of rock or to crack the hardest granite.

The most curious and incredibly delicate adaptations, however, are the ones by which the breeding rhythm of certain marine animals is timed to coincide with the phases of the moon and the stages of the tide. In Europe it has been well established that the spawning activities of oysters reach their peak on the spring tides, which are about two days after the full or the new moon. In the waters of northern Africa there is a sea urchin that, on the nights when the moon is full and apparently only then, releases its reproductive cells into the sea. And in tropical waters in many parts of the world there are small marine worms whose spawning behavior is so precisely adjusted to the tidal calendar that, merely from observing them, one could tell the month, the day, and often the time of day as well.

Near Samoa in the Pacific, the palolo worm lives out its life on the bottom of the shallow sea, in holes in the rocks and among the masses of corals. Twice each year, during the neap tides of the moon's last quarter in October and November, the worms forsake their burrows and rise to the surface in swarms that cover the water. For this purpose, each worm has literally broken its body in two, half to remain in its rocky tunnel, half to carry the reproductive products to the surface and there to liberate the cells. This happens at dawn on the day before the moon reaches its last quarter, and again on the following day; on the second day of the spawning the quantity of eggs liberated is so great that the sea is discolored.

The Fijians, whose waters have a similar worm, call them 'Mbalolo' and have designated the periods of their spawning 'Mbalolo lailai' (little) for October and 'Mbalolo levu' (large) for November. Similar forms near the Gilbert Islands respond to certain phases of the moon in June and July; in the Malay Archipelago a related worm swarms at the surface on the second and third nights after the full moon of March and April, when the tides are running highest. A Japanese palolo swarms after the new moon and again after the full moon in October and November.

Concerning each of these, the question recurs but remains unanswered: is it the state of the tides that in some unknown way supplies the impulse from which springs this behavior, or is it, even more mysteriously, some other influence of the moon? It is easier to imagine that it is the press and the rhythmic movement of the water that in some way brings about this response. But why is it only certain tides of the year, and why for some species is it the fullest tides of the month and for others the least movements of the waters that are related to the perpetuation of the race? At present, no one can answer.

No other creature displays so exquisite an adaptation to the tidal rhythm as the grunion—a small, shimmering fish about as long as a man's hand. Through no one can say what processes of adaptation, extending over no one knows how many millennia, the grunion has come to know not only the daily rhythm of the tides, but the monthly cycle by which certain tides sweep higher on the beaches than others. It has so adapted its spawning habits to the tidal cycle that the very existence of the race depends on the precision of this adjustment.

Shortly after the full moon of the months from March to August, the grunion appear in the surf on the beaches of California. The tide reaches flood stage, slackens, hesitates, and begins to ebb. Now on these waves of the ebbing tide the fish begin to come in. Their bodies shimmer in the light of the moon as they are borne up the beach on the crest of a wave, they lie glittering on the wet sand for a perceptible moment of time, then fling themselves into the wash of the next wave and are carried back to sea. For about an hour after the turn of the tide this continues, thousands upon thousands of grunion coming up onto the beach, leaving the water, returning to it. This is the spawning act of the species.

During the brief interval between successive waves, the male and female have come together in the wet sand, the one to shed her eggs, the other to fertilize them. When the parent fish return to the water, they have left behind a mass of eggs buried in the sand. Succeeding waves on that night do not wash out the eggs because the tide is already ebbing.

The waves of the next high tide will not reach them, because for a time after the full of the moon each tide will halt its advance a little lower on the beach than the preceeding one. The eggs, then, will be undisturbed for at least a fortnight. In the warm, damp, incubating sand they undergo their development. Within two weeks the magic change from fertilized egg to larval fishlet is completed, the perfectly formed little grunion still confined within the membranes of the egg, still buried in the sand, waiting for release. With the tides of the new moon it comes. Their waves wash over the places where the little masses of the grunion eggs were buried, the swirl and rush of the surf stirring the sand deeply. As the sand is washed away, and the eggs feel the touch of the cool sea water, the membranes rupture, the fishlets hatch, and the waves that released them bear them away to the sea.

But the link between tide and living creature I like best to remember is that of a very small worm, flat of body, with no distinction of appearance, but with one unforgettable quality. The name of this worm is *Convoluta roscoffensis,* and it lives on the sandy beaches of northern Brittany and the Channel Islands. Convoluta has entered into a remarkable partnership with a green alga, whose cells inhabit the body of the worm and lend to its tissues their own green color. The worm lives entirely on the starchy products manufactured by its plant guest, having become so completely dependent upon this means of nutrition that its digestive organs have degenerated. In order that the algal cells may carry on their function of photosynthesis (which is dependent upon sunlight) Convoluta rises from the damp sands of the intertidal zone as soon as the tide has ebbed, the sand becoming spotted with large green patches composed of thousands of the worms. For the several hours while the tide is out, the worms lie thus in the sun, and the plants manufacture their starches and sugars; but when the tide returns, the worms must again sink into the sand to avoid being washed away, out into deep water. So the whole lifetime of the worm is a succession of movements conditioned by the stages of the tide—upward into sunshine on the ebb, downward on the flood.

What I find most unforgettable about Convoluta is this: sometimes it happens that a marine biologist, wishing to study some related problem, will transfer a whole colony of the worms into the laboratory, there to establish them in an aquarium, where there are no tides. But twice each day Convoluta rises out of the sand on the bottom of the aquarium, into the light of the sun. And twice each day it sinks again into the sand. Without a brain, or what we would call a memory, or even any very clear perception, Convoluta continues to live out its life in this alien place, remembering, in every fiber of its small green body, the tidal rhythm of the distant sea.

Part III

MAN AND THE SEA ABOUT HIM

The Global Thermostat

OUT OF THE CHAMBER OF THE SOUTH COMETH THE STORM,
AND COLD OUT OF THE NORTH.
—THE BOOK OF JOB

When the building of the Panama Canal was first suggested, the project was severely criticized in Europe. The French, especially, complained that such a canal would allow the waters of the Equatorial Current to escape into the Pacific, that there would then be no Gulf Stream, and that the winter climate of Europe would become unbearably frigid. The alarmed Frenchmen were completely wrong in their forecast of oceanographic events, but they were right in their recognition of a general principle—the close relation between climate and the pattern of ocean circulation.

There are recurrent schemes for deliberately changing—or attempting to change—the pattern of the currents and so modifying climate at will. We hear of projects for diverting the cold Oyashio from the Asiatic coast, and of others for controlling the Gulf Stream. About 1912 the Congress of the United States was asked to appropriate money to build a jetty from Cape Race eastward across the Grand Banks to obstruct the cold water flowing south from the Arctic. Advocates of the plan believed that the Gulf Stream would then swing in nearer the mainland of the northern United States and would presumably bring us warmer winters. The appropriation was not granted. Even if the money had been provided, there is little reason to suppose that engineers then —or later—could have succeeded in controlling the sweep of the ocean's currents. And fortunately so, for most of these plans would have effects different from those popularly expected. Bringing the Gulf Stream closer to the American east coast, for example, would make our winters worse instead of better. Along the Atlantic coast of North America, the prevailing winds blow eastward, across the land toward the sea. The air masses that have lain over the Gulf Stream seldom reach us. But the Stream, with its mass of warm water, does have something to do with bringing our weather to us. The cold winds of winter are pushed by gravity toward the low-pressure areas over the warm water. The winter of 1916, when Stream temperatures were above normal, was long remembered for its cold and snowy weather along the east coast. If we could move the Stream inshore, the result in winter would be colder, stronger winds from the interior of the continent—not milder weather.

But if the eastern North American climate is not dominated by the Gulf Stream, it is far otherwise for the lands lying 'downstream.' From the Newfoundland Banks, as we have seen, the warm water of the Stream drifts eastward, pushed along by the prevailing westerly winds. Almost immediately, however, it divides into several branches. One flows north to the western shore of Greenland; there the warm water attacks the ice brought around Cape Farewell by the East Greenland Current. Another passes to the southwest coast of Iceland and, before losing itself in arctic waters, brings a gentling influence to the southern shores of that island. But the main branch of the Gulf Stream or North Atlantic Drift flows eastward. Soon it divides again. The southernmost of these branches turns toward Spain and Africa and re-enters the Equatorial Current. The northernmost branch, hurried eastward by the winds blowing around the Icelandic 'low,' piles up against the coast of Europe the warmest water found at comparable latitudes anywhere in the world. From the Bay of Biscay north its influence is felt. And as the current rolls northeastward along the Scandinavian coast, it sends off many lateral branches that curve back westward to bring the breath of warm water to the arctic islands and to mingle with other currents in intricate whirls and eddies. The west coast of Spitsbergen, warmed by one of these lateral streams, is bright with flowers in the arctic summer; the east coast, with its polar current, remains barren and forbidding.

Passing around the North Cape, the warm currents keep open such harbors as Hammerfest and Murmansk, although Riga, 800 miles farther south on the shores of the Baltic, is choked with ice. Somewhere in the Arctic Sea, near the island of Novaya Zemlya, the last traces of Atlantic water disappear, losing themselves at last in the overwhelming sweep of the icy northern sea.

It is always a warm-water current, but the temperature of the Gulf Stream nevertheless varies from year to year, and a seemingly slight change profoundly affects the air temperatures of Europe. The British meteorologist, C. E. P. Brooks, compares the North Atlantic to 'a great bath, with a hot tap and two cold taps.' The hot tap is the Gulf Stream; the cold taps are the East Greenland Current and the Labrador Current. Both the volume and the temperature of the hot-water tap vary. The cold taps are nearly constant in temperature but vary immensely in volume. The adjustment of the three taps determines surface temperatures in the eastern Atlantic and has a great deal to do with the weather of Europe and with happenings in arctic seas. A very slight winter warming of the eastern Atlantic temperatures means, for example, that the snow cover of northwestern Europe will melt earlier, that there will be an earlier thawing of the ground, that spring plowing may begin earlier, and that the harvest will be better. It means, too, that there will be relatively little ice near Iceland in the spring and that the amount of drift ice in the Barents Sea will diminish a year or two later. These relations have been clearly established by European scientists. Some day long-range weather forecasts for the continent of Europe will probably be based in part on ocean temperatures. But at present there are no means for collecting the temperatures over a large enough area, at frequent enough intervals.[16]

For the globe as a whole, the ocean is the great regulator, the great stabilizer of temperatures. It has been described as 'a savings bank for solar energy, receiving deposits in seasons of excessive insolation and paying them back in seasons of want.' Without the ocean, our world would be visited by unthinkably harsh extremes of temperature. For the water that covers three-fourths of the earth's surface with an enveloping mantle is a substance of remarkable qualities. It is an excellent absorber and radiator of heat. Because of its enormous heat capacity, the ocean can absorb a great deal of heat from the sun without becoming what we would consider 'hot,' or it can lose much of its heat without becoming 'cold.'

Through the agency of ocean currents, heat and cold may be distributed over thousands of miles. It is possible to follow the course of a mass of warm water that originates in the trade-wind belt of the Southern Hemisphere and remains recognizable for a year and a half, through a course of more than 7000 miles. This redistributing function of the ocean tends to make up for the uneven heating of the globe by the sun. As it is, ocean currents carry hot equatorial water toward the poles and return cold water equatorward by such surface drifts as the Labrador Current and Oyashio, and even more importantly by deep currents. The redistribution of heat for the whole earth is accomplished about half by the ocean currents, and half by the winds.

At that thin interface between the ocean of water and the ocean of overlying air, lying as they do in direct contact over by far the greater part of the earth, there are continuous interactions of tremendous importance.

The atmosphere warms or cools the ocean. It receives vapors through evaporation, leaving most of the salts in the sea and so increasing the salinity of the water. With the changing weight of that whole mass of air that envelops the earth, the atmosphere brings variable pressure to bear on the surface of the sea, which is depressed under areas of high pressure and springs up in compensation under the atmospheric lows. With the moving force of the winds, the air grips the surface of the ocean and raises it into waves, drives the currents onward, lowers sea levels on windward shores, and raises it on lee shores.

But even more does the ocean dominate the air. Its effect on the temperature and humidity of the atmosphere is far greater than the small transfer of heat from air to sea. It takes 3000 times as much heat to warm a given volume of water 1° as to warm an equal volume of air by the same amount. The heat lost by a cubic meter of water on cooling 1° C. would raise the temperature of 3000 cubic meters of air by the same amount. Or to use another example, a layer of water a meter deep, on cooling .1° could warm a layer of air 33 meters thick by 10°. The temperature of the air is intimately related to atmospheric pressure. Where the air is cold, pressure tends to be high; warm air favors low pressures. The transfer of heat between ocean and air therefore alters the belts of high and low pressure; this profoundly affects the direction and strength of the winds and directs the storms on their paths.

There are six more or less permanent centers of high pressure over the oceans, three in each hemisphere. Not

only do these areas play a controlling part in the climate
of surrounding lands, but they affect the whole world because they are the birthplaces of most of the dominant
winds of the globe. The trade winds originate in high-
pressure belts of the Northern and Southern hemispheres.
Over all the vast extent of ocean across which they blow,
these great winds retain their identity; it is only over the
continents that they become interrupted, confused, and modified.

In other ocean areas there are belts of low pressure,
which develop, especially in winter, over waters that are
then warmer than the surrounding lands. Traveling barometric depressions or cyclonic storms are attracted by these
areas; they move rapidly across them or skirt around their
edges. So winter storms take a path across the Icelandic
'low' and over the Shetlands and Orkneys into the North
Sea and the Norwegian Sea; other storms are directed by
still other low-pressure areas over the Skagerrak and the
Baltic into the interior of Europe. Perhaps more than any
other condition, the low-pressure area over the warm water
south of Iceland dominates the winter climate of Europe.

And most of the rains that fall on sea and land alike
were raised from the sea. They are carried as vapor in
the winds, and then with change of temperature the rains
fall. Most of the European rain comes from evaporation
of Atlantic water. In the United States, vapor and warm
air from the Gulf of Mexico and the tropical waters of
the western Atlantic ride the winds up the wide valley of
the Mississippi and provide rains for much of the eastern
part of North America.

Whether any place will know the harsh extremes of a
continental climate or the moderating effect of the sea depends less on its nearness to the ocean than on the pattern
of currents and winds and the relief of the continents. The
east coast of North America receives little benefit from the
sea, because the prevailing winds are from the west. The
Pacific coast, on the other hand, lies in the path of the
westerly winds that have blown across thousands of miles
of ocean. The moist breath of the Pacific brings climatic
mildness and creates the dense rain forests of British Columbia, Washington, and Oregon; but its full influence is
largely restricted to a narrow strip by the coast ranges that
follow a course parallel to the sea. Europe, in contrast,
is wide open to the sea, and 'Atlantic weather' carries hundreds of miles into the interior.

By a seeming paradox, there are parts of the world that

owe their desert dryness to their nearness to the ocean. The aridity of the Atacama and Kalahari deserts is curiously related to the sea. Wherever such marine deserts occur, there is found this combination of circumstances: a western coast in the path of the prevailing winds, and a cold coastwise current. So on the west coast of South America the cold Humboldt streams northward off the shores of Chile and Peru—the great return flow of Pacific waters seeking the equator. The Humboldt, it will be remembered, is cold because it is continuously being reinforced by the upwelling of deeper water. The presence of this cold water offshore helps create the aridity of the region. The onshore breezes that push in toward the hot land in the afternoons are formed of cool air that has lain over a cool sea. As they reach the land they are forced to rise into the high coastal mountains—the ascent cooling them more than the land can warm them. So there is little condensation of water vapor, and although the cloud banks and the fogs forever seem to promise rain, the promise is not fulfilled so long as the Humboldt rolls on its accustomed course along these shores. On the stretch from Arica to Caldera there is normally less than an inch of rain in a year. It is a beautifully balanced system—as long as it remains in balance. What happens when the Humboldt is temporarily displaced is nothing short of catastrophic.

At irregular intervals the Humboldt is deflected away from the South American continent by a warm current of tropical water that comes down from the north. These are years of disaster. The whole economy of the area is adjusted to the normal aridity of climate. In the years of El Niño, as the warm current is called, torrential rains fall—the downpouring rains of the equatorial regions let loose upon the dust-dry hillsides of the Peruvian coast. The soil washes away, the mud huts literally dissolve and collapse, crops are destroyed. Even worse things happen at sea. The cold-water fauna of the Humboldt sickens and dies in the warm water, and the birds that fish the cold sea for a living must either migrate or starve.

Those parts of the coast of Africa that are bathed by the cool Benguela Current also lie between mountains and sea. The easterly winds are dry, descending winds, and the cool breezes from the sea have their moisture capacity increased by contact with the hot land. Mists form over the cold waters and roll in over the coast, but in a whole year the rainfall is the meagerest token. The mean rainfall at Swakopmund in Walvis Bay is 0.7 inches a year. But again this is true only as long as the Benguela holds sway along the coast, for there are times when the cold stream falters as does the Humboldt, and here also these are years of disaster.

The transforming influence of the sea is portrayed with beautiful clarity in the striking differences between the Arctic and Antarctic regions. As everyone knows, the Arctic is a nearly landlocked sea; the Antarctic, a continent surrounded by ocean. Whether this global balancing of a land pole against a water pole has a deep significance in the physics of the earth is uncertain; but the bearing of the fact on the climates of the two regions is plainly evident.

The ice-covered Antarctic continent, bathed by seas of uniform coldness, is in the grip of the polar anticyclone. High winds blow from the land and repel any warming influence that might seek to penetrate it. The mean temperature of this bitter world is never above the freezing point. On exposed rocks the lichens grow, covering the barrenness of cliffs with their gray or orange growths, and here and there over the snow is the red dust of the hardier algae. Mosses hide in the valleys and crevices less exposed to the winds, but of the higher plants only a few impoverished stands of grasses have managed to invade this land. There are no land mammals; the fauna of the Antarctic continent consists only of birds, wingless mosquitoes, a few flies, and microscopic mites.

In sharp contrast are the arctic summers, where the tundra is bright with many-colored flowers. Everywhere except on the Greenland icecap and some of the arctic islands, summer temperatures are high enough for the growth of plants, packing a year's development into the short, warm, arctic summer. The polar limit of plant growth is set not by latitude, but by the sea. For the influence of the warm Atlantic penetrates strongly within the Arctic Sea, entering, as we have seen, through the one large break in the land girdle, the Greenland Sea. But the streams of warm Atlantic water that enter the icy northern seas bring the gentling touch that makes the Arctic, in climate as well as in geography, a world apart from the Antarctic.

So, day by day and season by season, the ocean dominates the world's climate. Can it also be an agent in bringing about the long-period swings of climatic change that we know have occurred throughout the long history of the earth—the alternating periods of heat and cold, of drought and flood? There is a fascinating theory that it can. This theory links events in the deep, hidden places of the ocean with the cyclic changes of climate and their effects on human history. It was developed by the distinguished Swedish oceanographer, Otto Pettersson, whose almost century-long life closed in 1941. In many papers, Pettersson presented the different facets of his theory as he pieced it together, bit by bit. Many of his fellow scientists were impressed, others doubted. In those days few men could conceive of the dynamics of water movements in the deep sea. Now the theory is being re-examined in the light of modern oceanography and meteorology, and only recently C. E. P. Brooks said, 'It seems that there is good support for Pettersson's theory as well as for that of solar activity, and that the actual variations of climate since about 3000 B.C. may have been to a large extent the result of these two agents.'

To review the Pettersson theory is to review also a pageant of human history, of men and nations in the control of elemental forces whose nature they never understood and whose very existence they never recognized. Pettersson's work was perhaps a natural outcome of the circumstances of his life. He was born—as he died 93 years later—on the shores of the Baltic, a sea of complex and wonderful hydrography. In his laboratory atop a sheer cliff overlooking the deep waters of the Gulmarfiord, instruments recorded strange phenomena in the depths of this gateway to the Baltic. As the ocean water presses in toward that inland sea it dips down and lets the fresh surface water roll out above it; and at that deep level where salt and fresh water come into contact there is a sharp layer of discontinuity, like the surface film between water and air. Each day Pettersson's instruments revealed a strong, pulsing movement of that deep layer—the pressing inward of great submarine waves, of moving mountains of water. The movement was strongest every twelfth hour of the day, and between the 12-hour intervals it subsided. Pettersson soon established a link between these submarine waves and the daily tides. 'Moon waves,' he called them, and as he measured their height and timed their pulsing beat through the months and years, their relation to the ever-changing cycles of the tides became crystal clear.

Some of these deep waves of the Gulmarfiord were giants nearly 100 feet high. Pettersson believed they were formed by the impact of the oceanic tide wave on the submarine ridges of the North Atlantic, as though the waters moving to the pull of the sun and moon, far down in the lower levels of the sea, broke and spilled over in mountains of highly saline water to enter the fiords and sounds of the coast.

From the submarine tide waves, Pettersson's mind moved logically to another problem—the changing fortunes of the Swedish herring fishery. His native Bohuslan had been the site of the great Hanseatic herring fisheries of the Middle Ages. All through the thirteenth, fourteenth, and fifteenth centuries this great sea fishery was pursued in the Sund and the Belts, the narrow passageways into the Baltic. The towns of Skanor and Falsterbo knew unheard-of prosperity, for there seemed no end of the silvery, wealth-bringing fish. Then suddenly the fishery ceased, for the herring withdrew into the North Sea and came no more into the gateways of the Baltic—this to the enrichment of Holland and the impoverishment of Sweden. Why did the herring cease to come? Pettersson thought he knew, and the reason was intimately related to that moving pen in his laboratory, the pen that traced on a revolving drum the movements of the submarine waves far down in the depths of Gulmarfiord.

He had found that the submarine waves varied in height and power as the tide-producing power of the moon and sun varied. From astronomical calculations he learned that the tides must have been at their greatest strength during the closing centuries of the Middle Ages—those centuries when the Baltic herring fishery was flourishing. Then sun, moon, and earth came into such a position at the time of the winter solstice that they exerted the greatest possible attracting force upon the sea. Only about every eighteen centuries do the heavenly bodies assume this particular relation. But in that period of the Middle Ages, the great underwater waves pressed with unusual force into the narrow passages to the Baltic, and with the 'water mountains' went the herring shoals. Later, when the tides became weaker, the herring remained outside the Baltic, in the North Sea.

Then Pettersson realized another fact of extreme significance—that those centuries of great tides had been a period of 'startling and unusual occurrences' in the world of nature. Polar ice blocked much of the North Atlantic. The coasts of the North Sea and the Baltic were laid waste by violent storm floods. The winters were of 'unexplained severity' and in consequence of the climatic rigors political and economic catastrophes occurred all over the populated regions of the earth. Could there be a connection between these events and those moving mountains of unseen water?

Could the deep tides affect the lives of men as well as of herring?

From this germ of an idea, Pettersson's fertile mind evolved a theory of climatic variation, which he set forth in 1912 in an extraordinarily interesting document called *Climatic Variations in Historic and Prehistoric Time.** Marshalling scientific, historic, and literary evidence, he showed that there are alternating periods of mild and severe climates which correspond to the long-period cycles of the oceanic tides. The world's most recent period of maximum tides, and most rigorous climate, occurred about 1433, its effect being felt, however, for several centuries before and after that year. The minimum tidal effect prevailed about A.D. 550, and it will occur again about the year 2400.

During the latest period of benevolent climate, snow and ice were little known on the coast of Europe and in the seas about Iceland and Greenland. Then the Vikings sailed freely over northern seas, monks went back and forth between Ireland and 'Thyle' or Iceland, and there was easy intercourse between Great Britain and the Scandinavian countries. When Eric the Red voyaged to Greenland, according to the Sagas, he 'came from the sea to land at the middle glacier—from thence he went south along the coast to see if the land was habitable. The first year he wintered on Erik's Island . . .' This was probably in the year 984. There is no mention in the Sagas that Eric was hampered by drift ice in the several years of his exploration of the island; nor is there mention of drift ice anywhere about Greenland, or between Greenland and Wineland. Eric's route as described in the Sagas—proceeding directly west from Iceland and then down the east coast of Greenland—is one that would have been impossible during recent centuries. In the thirteenth century the Sagas contain for the first time a warning that those who sail for Greenland should not make the coast too directly west of Iceland on account of the ice in the sea, but no new route is then recommended. At the end of the fourteenth century, however, the old sailing route was abandoned and new sailing directions were given for a more southwesterly course that would avoid the ice.

The early Sagas spoke, too, of the abundant fruit of excellent quality growing in Greenland, and of the number of cattle that could be pastured there. The Norwegian settlements were located in places that are now at the foot of glaciers. There are Eskimo legends of old houses and churches

* *Svenska Hydrog.-Biol. Komm. Skrifter*, No. 5, 1912.

buried under the ice. The Danish Archaeological Expedition sent out by the National Museum of Copenhagen was never able to find all of the villages mentioned in the old records. But its excavations indicated clearly that the colonists lived in a climate definitely milder than the present one.

But these bland climatic conditions began to deteriorate in the thirteenth century. The Eskimos began to make troublesome raids, perhaps because their northern sealing grounds were frozen over and they were hungry. They attacked the western settlement near the present Ameralik Fiord, and when an official mission went out from the eastern colony about 1342, not a single colonist could be found—only a few cattle remained. The eastern settlement was wiped out some time after 1418 and the houses and churches destroyed by fire. Perhaps the fate of the Greenland colonies was in part due to the fact that ships from Iceland and Europe were finding it increasingly difficult to reach Greenland, and the colonists had to be left to their own resources.

The climatic rigors experienced in Greenland in the thirteenth and fourteenth centuries were felt also in Europe in a series of unusual events and extraordinary catastrophes. The seacoast of Holland was devastated by storm floods. Old Icelandic records say that, in the winters of the early 1300's, packs of wolves crossed on the ice from Norway to Denmark. The entire Baltic froze over, forming a bridge of solid ice between Sweden and the Danish islands. Pedestrians and carriages crossed the frozen sea and hostelries were put up on the ice to accommodate them. The freezing of the Baltic seems to have shifted the course of storms originating in the low-pressure belt south of Iceland. In southern Europe, as a result, there were unusual storms, crop failures, famine, and distress. Icelandic literature abounds in tales of volcanic eruptions and other violent natural catastrophes that occurred during the fourteenth century.

What of the previous era of cold and storms, which should have occurred about the third or fourth century B.C., according to the tidal theory? There are shadowy hints in early literature and folklore. The dark and brooding poetry of the Edda deals with a great catastrophe, the Fimbul-winter or Götterdämmerung, when frost and snow ruled the world for generations. When Pytheas journeyed to the seas north of Iceland in 330 B.C., he spoke of the *mare pigrum*, a sluggish, congealed sea. Early history contains striking suggestions that the restless movements of the tribes of northern Europe —the southward migrations of the 'barbarians' who shook the power of Rome—coincided with periods of storms, floods, and other climatic catastrophes that forced their migrations. Large-scale inundations of the sea destroyed the homelands of the Teutons and Cimbrians in Jutland and sent them southward into Gaul. Tradition among the Druids said that their ancestors had been expelled from their lands on the far side of the Rhine by enemy tribes and by 'a great invasion of the ocean.' And about the year 700 B.C. the trade routes for amber, found on the coasts of the North Sea, were suddenly shifted to the east. The old route came down along the Elbe, the Weser, and the Danube, through the Brenner Pass to Italy. The new route followed the Vistula, suggesting that the source of supply was then the Baltic. Perhaps storm floods had destroyed the earlier amber districts, as they invaded these same regions eighteen centuries later.

All these ancient records of climatic variations seemed to Pettersson an indication that cyclic changes in the oceanic circulation and in the conditions of the Atlantic had occurred. 'No geologic alteration that could influence the climate has occurred for the past six or seven centuries,' he wrote. The very nature of these phenomena—floods, inundations, ice blockades—suggested to him a dislocation of the oceanic circulation. Applying the discoveries in his laboratory on Gulmarfiord, he believed that the climatic changes were brought about as the tide-induced submarine waves disturbed the deep waters of polar seas. Although tidal movements are often weak at the surface of these seas, they set up strong pulsations at the submarine boundaries, where there is a layer of comparatively fresh, cold water lying upon a layer of salty, warmer water. In the years or the centuries of strong tidal forces, unusual quantities of warm Atlantic water press into the Arctic Sea at deep levels, moving in under the ice. Then thousands of square miles of ice that normally remain solidly frozen undergo partial thawing and break up. Drift ice, in extraordinary volume, enters the Labrador Current and is carried southward into the Atlantic. This changes the pattern of surface circulation, which is so intimately related to the winds, the rainfall, and the air temperatures. For the drift ice then attacks the Gulf Stream south of Newfoundland and sends it on a more easterly course, deflecting the streams of warm surface water that usually bring a softening effect to the climate of Greenland, Iceland, Spitsbergen, and northern Europe. The position of the low-pressure belt south of Iceland is also shifted, with further direct effect on European climate.

Although the really catastrophic disturbances of the polar regime come only every eighteen centuries, according to Pettersson, there are also rhythmically occurring periods that fall at varying intervals—for example, every 9, 18, or 36 years. These correspond to other tidal cycles. They produce climatic variations of shorter period and of less drastic nature.

The year 1903, for instance, was memorable for its outbursts of polar ice in the Arctic and for the repercussions on Scandinavian fisheries. There was 'a general failure of cod, herring, and other fish along the coast from Finmarken and Lofoten to the Skagerrak and Kattegat. The greater part of the Barents Sea was covered with pack ice up to May, the ice border approaching closer to the Murman and Finmarken coasts than ever before. Herds of arctic seals visited these coasts, and some species of the arctic whitefish extended their migrations to the Christiana Fiord and even entered into the Baltic.' This outbreak of ice came in a year when earth, moon, and sun were in a relative position that gives a secondary maximum of the tide-producing forces. The similar constellation of 1912 was another great ice year in the Labrador Current—a year that brought the disaster of the *Titanic*.

Now in our own lifetime we are witnessing a startling alteration of climate, and it is intriguing to apply Otto Pettersson's ideas as a possible explanation. It is now established beyond question that a definite change in the arctic climate set in about 1900, that it became astonishingly marked about 1930, and that it is now spreading into sub-arctic and temperate regions. The frigid top of the world is very clearly warming up.

The trend toward a milder climate in the Arctic is perhaps most strikingly apparent in the greater ease of navigation in the North Atlantic and the Arctic Sea. In 1932, for example, the *Knipowitsch* sailed around Franz Josef Land for the first time in the history of arctic voyaging. And three years later the Russian ice-breaker *Sadko* went from the northern tip of Novaya Zemlya to a point north of Severnaya Zemlya (Northern Land) and thence to 82° 41' north latitude—the northernmost point ever reached by a ship under its own power.

In 1940 the whole northern coast of Europe and Asia was remarkably free from ice during the summer months, and more than 100 vessels engaged in trade via the arctic routes. In 1942 a vessel unloaded supplies at the west Greenland port of Upernivik (latitude 72° 43' N) during Christmas week 'in almost complete winter darkness.' During the 'forties the season for shipping coal from West Spitsbergen ports lengthened to seven months, compared with three at the beginning of the century. The season when pack ice lies about Iceland became shorter by about two months than it was a century ago. Drift ice in the Russian sector of the Arctic Sea decreased by a million square kilometers between 1924 and 1944, and in the Laptev Sea two islands of fossil ice melted away completely, their position being marked by submarine shoals.

Activities in the nonhuman world also reflect the warming of the Arctic—the changed habits and migrations of many fishes, birds, land mammals, and whales.

Many new birds are appearing in far northern lands for the first time in our records. The long list of southern visitors —birds never reported in Greenland before 1920—includes the American velvet scoter, the greater yellowlegs, American avocet, black-browed albatross, northern cliff swallow, ovenbird, common crossbill, Baltimore oriole, and Canada warbler. Some high-arctic forms, which thrive in cold climates, have shown their distaste for the warmer temperatures by visiting Greenland in sharply decreasing numbers. Such abstainers include the northern horned lark, the grey plover, and the pectoral sandpiper. Iceland, too, has had an extraordinary number of boreal and even subtropical avian visitors since 1935, coming from both America and Europe. Wood warblers, skylarks, and Siberian rubythroats, scarlet grosbeaks, pipits, and thrushes now provide exciting fare for Icelandic bird watchers.

When the cod first appeared at Angmagssalik in Greenland in 1912, it was a new and strange fish to the Eskimos and Danes. Within their memory it had never before appeared on the east coast of the island. But they began to catch it, and by the 1930's it supported so substantial a fishery in the area that the natives had become dependent upon it for food. They were also using its oil as fuel for their lamps and to heat their houses.

On the west coast of Greenland, too, the cod was a rarity at the turn of the century, although there was a small fishery, taking about 500 tons a year, at a few places on the southwest coast. About 1919 the cod began to move north along the west Greenland coast and to become more abundant. The center of the fishery has moved 300 miles farther north, and the catch is now about 15,000 tons a year.

Other fishes seldom or never before reported in Greenland have appeared there. The coalfish or green cod is a European fish so foreign to Greenland waters that when two of them were caught in 1831 they were promptly preserved in salt and sent to the Copenhagen Zoological Museum. But since 1924 this fish has often been found among the cod shoals. The haddock, cusk, and ling, unknown in Greenland waters until about 1930, are now taken regularly. Iceland, too, has strange visitors—warmth-loving southern fishes, like the basking shark, the grotesque sunfish, the six-gilled shark, the swordfish, and the horse mackerel. Some of these same species have penetrated into the Barents and White seas and along the Murman coast.

As the chill of the northern waters has abated and the fish have moved poleward, the fisheries around Iceland have expanded enormously, and it has become profitable for trawlers to push on to Bear Island, Spitsbergen, and the Barents Sea. These waters now yield perhaps two billion pounds of cod a year—the largest catch of a single species by any fishery in the world. But its existence is tenuous. If the cycle turns, the waters begin to chill, and the ice floes creep southward again, there is nothing man can do that will preserve the arctic fisheries.

But for the present, the evidence that the top of the world is growing warmer is to be found on every hand. The recession of the northern glaciers is going on at such a rate that many smaller ones have already disappeared. If the present rate of melting continues others will soon follow them.

The melting away of the snowfields in the Opdal Mountains in Norway has exposed wooden-shafted arrows of a type used about A.D. 400 to 500. This suggests that the snow cover in this region must now be less than it has been at any time within the past 1400 to 1500 years.

The glaciologist Hans Ahlmann reports that most Norwegian glaciers 'are living only on their own mass without receiving any annual fresh supply of snow'; that in the Alps there has been a general retreat and shrinkage of glaciers during the last decades, which became 'catastrophic' in the summer of 1947; and that all glaciers around the Northern Atlantic coasts are shrinking. The most rapid recession of all is occurring in Alaska, where the Muir Glacier receded about 10½ kilometers in 12 years.

At present the vast antarctic glaciers are an enigma; no one can say whether they also are melting away, or at what rate. But reports from other parts of the world show that the northern glaciers are not the only ones that are receding. The glaciers of several East African high volcanoes have been diminishing since they were first studied in the 1800's—very rapidly since 1920—and there is glacial shrinkage in the Andes and also in the high mountains of central Asia.

The milder arctic and sub-arctic climate seems already to have resulted in longer growing seasons and better crops. The cultivation of oats has improved in Iceland. In Norway good seed years are now the rule rather than the exception, and even in northern Scandinavia the trees have spread rapidly above their former timber lines, and both pine and spruce are making a quicker annual growth than they have for some time.

The countries where the most striking changes are taking place are those whose climate is most directly under the control of the North Atlantic currents. Greenland, Iceland, Spitsbergen, and all of northern Europe, as we have seen, experience heat and cold, drought and flood in accordance with the varying strength and warmth of the eastward and northward-moving currents of the Atlantic. Oceanographers who have been studying the matter during the 1940's have discovered many significant changes in the temperature and distribution of great masses of ocean water. Apparently the branch of the Gulf Stream that flows past Spitsbergen has so increased in volume that it now brings in a great body of warm water. Surface waters of the North Atlantic show rising temperatures; so do the deeper layers around Iceland and Spitsbergen. Sea temperatures in the North Sea and along the coast of Norway have been growing warmer since the 1920's.

Unquestionably, there are other agents at work in bringing about the climatic changes in the Arctic and sub-Arctic regions. For one thing, it is almost certainly true that we are still in the warming-up stage following the last Pleistocene glaciation—that the world's climate, over the next thousands of years, will grow considerably warmer before beginning a downward swing into another Ice Age. But what we are experiencing now is perhaps a climatic change of shorter duration, measurable only in decades or centuries. Some scientists say that there must have been a small increase in solar activity, changing the pattern of air circulation and causing the southerly winds to blow more frequently in Scandinavia and Spitsbergen; changes in ocean currents, according to this view, are secondary effects of the shift of prevailing winds.

But if, as Professor Brooks thinks, the Pettersson tidal theory has as good a foundation as that of changing solar radiation, then it is interesting to calculate where our twentieth-century situation fits into the cosmic scheme of the shifting cycles of the tides. The great tides at the close of the Middle Ages, with their accompanying snow and ice, furious winds, and inundating floods, are more than five centuries behind us. The era of weakest tidal movements, with a climate as benign as that of the early Middle Ages, is about four centuries ahead. We have therefore begun to move strongly into a period of warmer, milder weather. There will be fluctuations, as earth and sun and moon move through space and the tidal power waxes and wanes. But the long trend is toward a warmer earth; the pendulum is swinging.

Wealth from the Salt Seas

A SEA CHANGE INTO SOMETHING RICH AND STRANGE.
—SHAKESPEARE

The ocean is the earth's greatest storehouse of minerals. In a single cubic mile of sea water there are, on the average, 166 million tons of dissolved salts, and in all the ocean waters of the earth there are about 50 quadrillion tons. And it is in the nature of things for this quantity to be gradually increasing over the millennia, for although the earth is constantly shifting her component materials from place to place, the heaviest movements are forever seaward.

It has been assumed that the first seas were only faintly saline and that their saltiness has been growing over the eons of time. For the primary source of the ocean's salt is the rocky mantle of the continents. When those first rains came —the centuries-long rains that fell from the heavy clouds enveloping the young earth—they began the processes of wearing away the rocks and carrying their contained minerals to the sea. The annual flow of water seaward is believed to be about 6500 cubic miles, this inflow of river water adding to the ocean several billion tons of salts.

It is a curious fact that there is little similarity between the chemical composition of river water and that of sea water. The various elements are present in entirely different proportions. The rivers bring in four times as much calcium as chloride, for example, yet in the ocean the proportions are strongly reversed—46 times as much chloride as calcium. An important reason for the difference is that immense amounts of calcium salts are constantly being withdrawn from the sea water by marine animals and are used for building shells and skeletons—for the microscopic shells that house the foraminifera, for the massive structures of the coral reefs, and for the shells of oysters and clams and other mollusks. Another reason is the precipitation of calcium from sea water. There is a striking difference, too, in the silicon content of river and sea water—about 500 per cent greater in rivers than in the sea. The silica is required by diatoms to make their shells, and so the immense quantities brought in by rivers are largely utilized by these ubiquitous plants of the sea. Often there are exceptionally heavy growths of diatoms off the mouths of rivers. Because of the enormous total chemical requirements of all the fauna and flora of the sea, only a small part of the salts annually brought in by rivers goes to increasing the quantity of dissolved minerals in the water. The inequalities of chemical make-up are further reduced by reactions that are set in motion immediately the fresh water is discharged into the sea, and by the enormous disparities of volume between the incoming fresh water and the ocean.

There are other agencies by which minerals are added to the sea—from obscure sources buried deep within the earth. From every volcano chlorine and other gases escape into the atmosphere and are carried down in rain onto the surface of land and sea. Volcanic ash and rock bring up other materials. And all the submarine volcanoes, discharging through unseen craters directly into the sea, pour in boron, chlorine, sulphur, and iodine.

All this is a one-way flow of minerals to the sea. Only to a very limited extent is there any return of salts to the land. We attempt to recover some of them directly by chemical extraction and mining, and indirectly by harvesting the sea's plants and animals. There is another way, in the long, recurring cycles of the earth, by which the sea itself gives back to the land what it has received. This happens when the ocean waters rise over the lands, deposit their sediments, and at last withdraw, leaving over the continent another layer of sedimentary rocks. These contain some of the water and salts of the sea. But it is only a temporary loan of minerals to the land and the return payment begins at once by way of the old, familiar channels—rain, erosion, runoff to the rivers, transport to the sea.

There are other curious little exchanges of materials between sea and land. While the process of evaporation, which raises water vapor into the air, leaves most of the salts behind, a surprising amount of salt does intrude itself into the atmosphere and rides long distances on the wind. The so-called 'cyclic salt' is picked up by the winds from the spray of a rough, cresting sea or breaking surf and is blown inland, then brought down in rain and returned by rivers to the ocean. These tiny, invisible particles of sea salt drifting in the atmosphere are, in fact, one of the many forms of atmospheric nuclei around which raindrops form.

Areas nearest the sea, in general, receive the most salt. Published figures have listed 24 to 36 pounds per acre per year for England and more than 100 pounds for British Guiana. But the most astounding example of long-distance, large-scale transport of cyclic salts is furnished by Sambhar Salt Lake in northern India. It receives 3000 tons of salt a year, carried to it on the hot dry monsoons of summer from the sea, 400 miles away.

The plants and animals of the sea are very much better chemists than men, and so far our own efforts to extract the mineral wealth of the sea have been feeble compared with those of lower forms of life. They have been able to find and to utilize elements present in such minute traces that human chemists could not detect their presence until, very recently, highly refined methods of spectroscopic analysis were developed.

We did not know, for example, that vanadium occurred in the sea until it was discovered in the blood of certain sluggish and sedentary sea creatures, the holothurians (of which sea cucumbers are an example) and the ascidians. Relatively huge quantities of cobalt are extracted by lobsters and mussels, and nickel is utilized by various mollusks, yet it is only within recent years that we have been able to recover even traces of these elements. Copper is recoverable only as about a hundredth part in a million of sea water, yet it helps to constitute the life blood of lobsters, entering into their respiratory pigments as iron does in human blood.

In contrast to the accomplishments of invertebrate chemists, we have so far had only limited success in extracting sea salts in quantities we can use for commercial purposes, despite their prodigious quantity and considerable variety. We have recovered about fifty of the known elements by chemical analysis, and shall perhaps find that all the others are there, when we can develop proper methods to discover them. Five salts predominate and are present in fixed proportions. As we would expect, sodium chloride is by far the most abundant, making up 77.8 per cent of the total salts; magnesium chloride follows, with 10.9 per cent; then magnesium sulphate, 4.7 per cent; calcium sulphate, 3.6 per cent; and potassium sulphate, 2.5 per cent. All others combined make up the remaining .5 per cent.

Of all the elements present in the sea, probably none has stirred men's dreams more than gold. It is there—in all the waters covering the greater part of the earth's surface—enough in total quantity to make every person in the world a millionaire. But how can the sea be made to yield it?

The most determined attempt to wrest a substantial quantity of gold from ocean waters—and also the most complete study of the gold in sea water—was made by the German chemist Fritz Haber after the First World War. Haber conceived the idea of extracting enough gold from the sea to pay the German war debt and his dream resulted in the German South Atlantic Expedition of the *Meteor*. The *Meteor* was equipped with a laboratory and filtration plant, and between the years 1924 and 1928 the vessel crossed and recrossed the Atlantic, sampling the water. But the quantity found was less than had been expected, and the cost of extraction far greater than the value of the gold recovered. The practical economics of the matter are about as follows: in a cubic mile of sea water there is about $93,000,000 in gold and $8,500,000 in silver. But to treat this volume of water in a year would require the twice-daily filling and emptying of 200 tanks of water, each 500 feet square and 5 feet deep. Probably this is no greater feat, relatively, than is accomplished regularly by corals, sponges, and oysters, but by human standards it is not economically feasible.

Most mysterious, perhaps, of all substances in the sea is iodine. In sea water it is one of the scarcest of the non-metals, difficult to detect and resisting exact analysis. Yet it is found in almost every marine plant and animal. Sponges, corals, and certain seaweeds accumulate vast quantities of it. Apparently the iodine in the sea is in a constant state of chemical change, sometimes being oxidized, sometimes reduced, again entering into organic combinations. There seem to be constant interchanges between air and sea, the iodine in some form perhaps being carried into the air in spray, for the air at sea level contains detectable quantities, which decrease with altitude. From the time living things first made iodine a part of the chemistry of their tissues, they seem to have become increasingly dependent on it; now we ourselves could not exist without it as a regulator of the basal metabolism of our bodies, through the thyroid gland which accumulates it.

All commercial iodine was formerly obtained from seaweeds; then the deposits of crude nitrate of soda from the high deserts of North Chile were discovered. Probably the original source of this raw material—called 'caliche'—was some prehistoric sea filled with marine vegetation, but that is a subject of controversy. Iodine is obtained also from brine deposits and from the subterranean waters of oil-bearing rocks—all indirectly of marine origin.

A monopoly on the world's bromine is held by the ocean, where 99 per cent of it is now concentrated. The tiny fraction present in rocks was originally deposited there by the sea. First we obtained it from the brines left in subterranean pools by prehistoric oceans; now there are large plants on the seacoasts—especially in the United States—which use ocean water as their raw material and extract the bromine directly. Thanks to modern methods of commercial production of bromine we have high-test gasoline for our cars. There is a long list of other uses, including the manufacture of sedatives, fire extinguishers, photographic chemicals, dyestuffs, and chemical warfare materials.

One of the oldest bromine derivatives known to man was Tyrian purple, which the Phoenicians made in their dyehouses from the purple snail, Murex. This snail may be linked in a curious and wonderful way with the prodigious and seemingly unreasonable quantities of bromine found today in the Dead Sea, which contains, it is estimated, some 850 million tons of the chemical. The concentration of bromine in Dead Sea water is 100 times that in the ocean. Apparently the supply is constantly renewed by underground hot springs, which discharge into the bottom of the Sea of Galilee, which in turn sends its waters to the Dead Sea by way of the River Jordan. Some authorities believe that the source of the bromine in the hot springs is a deposit of billions of ancient snails, laid down by the sea of a bygone age in a stratum long since buried.

Magnesium is another mineral we now obtain by collecting huge volumes of ocean water and treating it with chemicals, although originally it was derived only from brines or from the treatment of such magnesium-containing rocks as dolomite, of which whole mountain ranges are composed. In a cubic mile of sea water there are about 4 million tons of magnesium. Since the direct extraction method was developed about 1941, production has increased enormously. It was magnesium from the sea that made possible the wartime growth of the aviation industry, for every airplane made in the United States (and in most other countries as well) contains about half a ton of magnesium metal. And it has innumerable uses in other industries where a light-weight metal is desired, besides its long-standing utility as an insulating material, and its use in printing inks, medicines, and toothpastes, and in such war implements as incendiary bombs, star shells, and tracer ammunition.

Wherever climate has permitted it, men have evaporated salt from sea water for many centuries. Under the burning sun of the tropics the ancient Greeks, Romans, and Egyptians harvested the salt men and animals everywhere must have in order to live. Even today in parts of the world that are hot and dry and where drying winds blow, solar evaporation of salt is practiced—on the shores of the Persian Gulf, in China, India, and Japan, in the Philippines, and on the coast of California and the alkali flats of Utah.

Here and there are natural basins where the action of sun and wind and sea combine to carry on evaporation of salt on a scale far greater than human industry could accomplish. Such a natural basin is the Rann of Cutch on the west coast of India. The Rann is a flat plain, some 60 by 185 miles, separated from the sea by the island of Cutch. When the southwest monsoons blow, sea water is carried in by way of a channel to cover the plain. But in summer, in the season when the hot northeast monsoon blows from the desert, no more water enters, and that which is collected in pools over the plain evaporates into a salt crust, in some places several feet thick.

Where the sea has come in over the land, laid down its deposits, and then withdrawn, there have been created reservoirs of chemicals, upon which we can draw with comparatively little trouble. Hidden deep under the surface of our earth are pools of 'fossil salt water,' the brine of ancient seas; 'fossil deserts,' the salt of old seas that evaporated away under conditions of extreme heat and dryness; and layers of sedimentary rock in which are contained the organic sediments and the dissolved salts of the sea that deposited them.

During the Permian period, which was a time of great heat and dryness and widespread deserts, a vast inland sea formed over much of Europe, covering parts of the present Britain, France, Germany, and Poland. Rains came seldom and the rate of evaporation was high. The sea became exceedingly salty, and it began to deposit layers of salts. For a period covering thousands of years, only gypsum was deposited, perhaps representing a time when water fresh from the ocean occasionally entered the inland sea to mix with its strong brine. Alternating with the gypsum were thicker beds of salt. Later, as its area shrank and the sea grew still more concentrated, deposits of potassium and magnesium sulphates were formed (this stage representing perhaps 500 years); still later, and perhaps for another 500 years, there were laid down mixed potassium and magnesium chlorides or carnallite. After the sea had completely evaporated, desert conditions prevailed, and soon the salt deposits were buried under sand. The richest beds form the famous deposits of Stassfurt and Alsace; toward the outskirts of the original area of the old sea (as, for example, in England) there are only beds of salt. The Stassfurt beds are about 2500 feet thick; their springs of brine have been known since the thirteenth century, and the salts have been mined since the seventeenth century.

At an even earlier geological period—the Silurian—a great salt basin was deposited in the northern part of the United States, extending from central New York States across Michigan, including northern Pennsylvania and Ohio and part of southern Ontario. Because of the hot, dry climate of that time, the inland sea lying over this place grew so salty that beds of salt and gypsum were deposited over a great area covering about 100,000 square miles. There are seven distinct beds of salt at Ithaca, New York, the uppermost lying at a depth of about half a mile. In southern Michigan some of the individual salt beds are more than 500 feet thick, and the aggregate thickness of salt in the center of the Michigan Basin is approximately 2000 feet. In some places rock salt is mined; in others wells are dug, water is forced down, and the resulting brine is pumped to the surface and evaporated to recover the salt.

One of the greatest stock piles of minerals in the world came from the evaporation of a great inland sea in the western United States. This is Searles Lake in the Mohave Desert of California. An arm of the sea that overlay this region was cut off from the ocean by the thrusting up of a range of mountains; as the lake evaporated away, the water that remained became ever more salty through the inwash of minerals from all the surrounding land. Perhaps Searles Lake began its slow transformation from a landlocked sea to a 'frozen' lake—a lake of solid minerals—only a few thousand years ago; now its surface is a hard crust of salts over which a car may be driven. The crystals of salts form a layer 50 to 70 feet deep. Below that is mud. Engineers have recently discovered a second layer of salts and brine, probably at least as thick as the upper layer, underlying the mud. Searles Lake was first worked in the 1870's for borax; then teams of 20 mules each carried the borax across desert and mountains to the railroads. In the 1930's the recovery of other substances from the lake began—bromine, lithium, and salts of potassium and sodium. Now Searles Lake yields 40 per cent of the production of potassium chloride in the United States and a large share of all the borax and lithium salts produced in the world.

In some future era the Dead Sea will probably repeat the history of Searles Lake, as the centuries pass and evaporation continues. The Dead Sea as we know it is all that remains of a much larger inland sea that once filled the entire Jordan Valley and was about 190 miles long; now it has shrunk to about a fourth of this length and a fourth of its former volume. And with the shrinkage and the evaporation in the hot dry climate has come the concentration of salts that makes the Dead Sea a great reservoir of minerals. No animal life can exist in its brine; such luckless fish as are brought down by the River Jordan die and provide food for the sea birds. It is 1300 feet below the Mediterranean, lying farther below sea level than any other body of water in the world. It occupies the lowest part of the rift valley of the Jordan, which was created by a down-slipping of a block of the earth's crust. The water of the Dead Sea is warmer than the air, a condition favoring evaporation, and clouds of its vapor float, nebulous and half formed, above it, while its brine grows more bitter and the salts accumulate.

Of all legacies of the ancient seas the most valuable is petroleum. Exactly what geologic processes have created the precious pools of liquid deep within the earth no one knows with enough certainty to describe the whole sequence of events. But this much seems to be true: Petroleum is a result of fundamental earth processes that have been operating ever since an abundant and varied life was developed in the sea—at least since the beginning of Paleozoic time, probably longer. Exceptional and catastrophic occurrences may now and then aid its formation but they are not essential; the mechanism that regularly generates petroleum consists of the normal processes of earth and sea—the living and dying of creatures, the deposit of sediments, the advance and retreat of the seas over the continents, the upward and downward foldings of the earth's crust.

The old inorganic theory that linked petroleum formation with volcanic action has been abandoned by most geologists. The origin of petroleum is most likely to be found in the bodies of plants and animals buried under the fine-grained sediments of former seas and there subjected to slow decomposition.

Perhaps the essence of conditions favoring petroleum production is represented by the stagnant waters of the Black Sea or of certain Norwegian fiords. The surprisingly abundant life of the Black Sea is confined to the upper layers; the deeper and especially the bottom waters are devoid of oxygen and are often permeated with hydrogen sulphide. In these poisoned waters there can be no bottom scavengers to devour the bodies of marine animals that drift down from above, so they are entombed in the fine sediments. In many Norwegian fiords the deep layers are foul and oxygenless because the mouth of the fiord is cut off from the circulation of the open sea by a shallow sill. The bottom layers of such fiords are poisoned by the hydrogen sulphide from decomposing organic matter. Sometimes storms drive in unusual quantities of oceanic water and through turbulence of waves stir deeply the waters of these lethal pools; the mixing of the water layers that follows brings death to hordes of fishes and invertebrates living near the surface. Such a catastrophe leads to the deposit of a rich layer of organic material on the bottom.

Wherever great oil fields are found, they are related to past or present seas. This is true of the inland fields as well as of those near the present seacoast. The great quantities of oil that have been obtained from the Oklahoma fields, for example, were trapped in spaces within sedimentary rocks laid down under seas that invaded this part of North America in Paleozoic time.

The search for petroleum has also led geologists repeatedly to those 'unstable belts, covered much of the time by shallow seas, which lie around the margins of the main continental platforms, between them and the great oceanic deeps.'

An example of such a depressed segment of crust lying between continental masses is the one between Europe and the Near East, occupied in part by the Persian Gulf, the Red, Black, and Caspian seas, and the Mediterranean Sea. The Gulf of Mexico and the Caribbean Sea lie in another basin of shallow sea between the Americas. A shallow, island-studded sea lies between the continents of Asia and Australia. Lastly, there is the nearly landlocked sea of the Arctic. In past ages all of these areas have been alternately raised and depressed, belonging at one time to the land, at another to the encroaching sea. During their periods of submersion they have received thick deposits of sediments, and in their waters a rich marine fauna has lived, died, and drifted down into the soft sediment carpet.

There are vast oil deposits in all these areas. In the Near East are the great fields of Saudi Arabia, Iran, and Iraq. The shallow depression between Asia and Australia yields the oil of Java, Sumatra, Borneo, and New Guinea. The American mediterranean is the center of oil production in the Western Hemisphere—half the proved resources of the United States come from the northern shore of the Gulf of

Mexico, and Colombia, Venezuela, and Mexico have rich oil fields along the western and southern margins of the Gulf. The Arctic is one of the unproved frontiers of the petroleum industry, but oil seepages in northern Alaska, on islands north of the Canadian mainland, and along the Arctic coast of Siberia hint that this land recently raised from the sea may be one of the great oil fields of the future.

In recent years, the speculations of petroleum geologists have been focused in a new direction—under sea. By no means all of the land resources of petroleum have been discovered, but probably the richest and most easily worked fields are being tapped, and their possible production is known. The ancient seas gave us the oil that is now being drawn out of the earth. Can the ocean today be induced to give up some of the oil that must be trapped in sedimentary rocks under its floor, covered by water scores or hundreds of fathoms deep?

Oil is already being produced from offshore wells, on the continental shelf. Off California, Texas, and Louisiana, oil companies have drilled into the sediments of the shelf and are obtaining oil. In the United States the most active exploration has been centered in the Gulf of Mexico. Judging from its geologic history, this area has rich promise. For eons of time it was either dry land or a very shallow sea basin, receiving the sediments that washed into it from high lands to the north. Finally, about the middle of the Cretaceous period, the floor of the Gulf began to sink under the load of sediments and in time it acquired its present deep central basin.

By geophysical exploration, we can see that the layers of sedimentary rock underlying the coastal plain tilt steeply downward and pass under the broad continental shelf of the Gulf. Down in the layers deposited in the Jurassic period is a thick salt bed of enormous extent, probably formed when this part of the earth was hot and dry, a place of shrinking seas and encroaching deserts. In Louisiana and Texas, and also, it now appears, out in the Gulf itself, extraordinary features known as salt domes are associated with this deposit. These are fingerlike plugs of salt, usually less than a mile across, pushing up from the deep layer toward the earth's surface. They have been described by geologists as 'driven up through 5000 to 15,000 feet of sediments by earth pressures, like nails through a board.' In the states bordering the Gulf such structures have often been associated with oil. It seems probable that on the continental shelf, also, the salt domes may mark large oil deposits.

In exploring the Gulf for oil, therefore, geologists search for the salt domes where the larger oil fields are likely to live. They use an instrument known as a magnetometer, which measures the variations in magnetic intensity brought about by the salt domes. Gravity meters also help locate the domes by measuring the variation in gravity near them, the specific gravity of salt being less than that of the surrounding sediments. The actual location and outline of the dome are discovered by seismographic exploration, which traces the inclination of the rock strata by recording the reflection of sound waves produced by dynamite explosions. These methods of exploration have been used on land for some years, but only since about 1945 have they been adapted to use in offshore Gulf waters. The magnetometer has been so improved that it will map continuously while being towed behind a boat or carried in or suspended from a plane. A gravity meter can now be lowered rapidly to the bottom and readings made by remote control. (Once an operator had to descend with it in a diving bell.) Seismic crews may shoot off their dynamite charges and make continuous recordings while their boats are under way.

Despite all these improvements which allow exploration to proceed rapidly, it is no simple matter to obtain oil from undersea fields. Prospecting must be followed by the leasing of potential oil-producing areas, and then by drilling to see whether oil is actually there. Offshore drilling platforms rest on piles that must be driven as far as 250 feet into the floor of the Gulf to withstand the force of waves, especially during the season for hurricanes. Winds, storm waves, fogs, the corrosive gnawing of sea water upon metal structures—all these are hazards that must be faced and overcome. Yet the technical difficulties of far more extensive offshore operations than any now attempted do not discourage specialists in petroleum engineering.

So our search for mineral wealth often leads us back to the seas of ancient times—to the oil pressed from the bodies of fishes, seaweeds, and other forms of plant and animal life and then stored away in ancient rocks; to the rich brines hidden in subterranean pools where the fossil water of old seas still remains; to the layers of salts that are the mineral substance of those old seas laid down as a covering mantle over the continents. Perhaps in time, as we learn the chemical secrets of the corals and sponges and diatoms, we shall depend less on the stored wealth of prehistoric seas and shall go more and more directly to the ocean and the rocks now forming under its shallow waters.

The Encircling Sea

A SEA FROM WHICH BIRDS TRAVEL NOT WITHIN A YEAR,
SO VAST IT IS AND FEARFUL.
—HOMER

To the ancient Greeks the ocean was an endless stream that flowed forever around the border of the world, ceaselessly turning upon itself like a wheel, the end of earth, the beginning of heaven. This ocean was boundless; it was infinite. If a person were to venture far out upon it—were such a course thinkable—he would pass through gathering darkness and obscuring fog and would come at last to a dreadful and chaotic blending of sea and sky, a place where whirlpools and yawning abysses waited to draw the traveler down into a dark world from which there was no return.

These ideas are found, in varying form, in much of the literature of the ten centuries before the Christian era, and in later years they keep recurring even through the greater part of the Middle Ages. To the Greeks the familiar Mediterranean was The Sea. Outside, bathing the periphery of the land world, was Oceanus. Perhaps somewhere in its uttermost expanse was the home of the gods and of departed spirits, the Elysian fields. So we meet the ideas of unattainable continents or of beautiful islands in the distant ocean, confusedly mingled with references to a bottomless gulf at the edge of the world—but always around the disc of the habitable world was the vast ocean, encircling all.

Perhaps some word-of-mouth tales of the mysterious northern world, filtering down by way of the early trade routes for amber and tin, colored the conceptions of the early legends, so that the boundary of the land world came to be pictured as a place of fog and storms and darkness. Homer's *Odyssey* described the Cimmerians as dwelling in a distant realm of mist and darkness on the shores of Oceanus, and they told of the shepherds who lived in the land of the long day, where the paths of day and night were closed. And again perhaps the early poets and historians derived some of their ideas of the ocean from the Phoenicians, whose craft roamed the shores of Europe, Asia, and Africa in search of gold, silver, gems, spices, and wood for their commerce with kings and emperors. It may well be that these sailor-merchants were the first ever to cross an ocean, but history does not record the fact. For at least 2000 years before Christ— probably longer—the flourishing trade of the Phoenicians was plied along the shores of the Red Sea to Syria, to Somaliland, to Arabia, even to India and perhaps to China. Herodotus wrote that they circumnavigated Africa from east to west about 600 B.C., reaching Egypt via the Straits of the Pillars and the Mediterranean. But the Phoenicians themselves said and wrote little or nothing of their voyagings, keeping their trade routes and the sources of their precious cargoes secret. So there are only the vaguest rumors, sketchily supported by archaeological findings, that the Phoenicians may have launched out into the open Pacific.

Nor are there anything but rumors and highly plausible suppositions that the Phoenicians, on their coastwise journeys along western Europe, may have sailed as far north as the Scandinavian peninsula and the Baltic, source of the precious amber. There are no definite traces of any such visits by them, and of course the Phoenicians have left no written record of any. Of one of their European voyages, however, there is a secondhand account. This was the expedition under Himlico of Carthage, which sailed northward along the European coast about the year 500 B.C. Himlico apparently wrote an account of this voyage, although his manuscript was not preserved. But his descriptions are quoted by the Roman Avienus, writing nearly a thousand years later. According to Avienus, Himlico painted a discouraging picture of the coastwise seas of Europe:

These seas can scarcely be sailed through in four months . . . no breeze drives the ship forward, so dead is the sluggish wind of this idle sea . . . There is much seaweed among the waves . . . the surface of the earth is barely covered by a little water . . . The monsters of the sea moved continually hither and thither, and the wild beasts swim among the sluggish and slowly creeping ships.

Perhaps the 'wild beasts' are the whales of the Bay of Biscay, later to become a famous whaling ground; the shallow water areas that so impressed Himlico may have been the flats alternately exposed and covered by the ebb and flow

of the great tides of the French coast—a strange phenomenon
to one from the almost tideless Mediterranean. But Himlico
also had ideas of the open ocean to the west, if the account
of Avienus is to be trusted: 'Farther to the west from these
Pillars there is boundless sea . . . None has sailed ships over
these waters, because propelling winds are lacking on these
deeps . . . likewise because darkness screens the light of day
with a sort of clothing, and because a fog always conceals the
sea.' Whether these descriptive details are touches of
Phoenician canniness or merely the old ideas reasserting
themselves it is hard to say, but much the same conceptions
appear again and again in later accounts, echoing down the
centuries to the very threshold of modern times.

So far as historical records are concerned, the first great
voyage of marine exploration was by Pytheas of Massilia
about 330 B.C. Unfortunately his writings, including one
called On the Ocean, are lost and their substance is preserved for us only in fragmentary quotations passed on by
later writers. We know very little of the controlling circumstances of the northward voyage of this astronomer and
geographer, but probably Pytheas wished to see how far the
oecumene or land world extended, to learn the position of
the Arctic Circle, and to see the land of midnight sun. Some
of these things he may have heard of through the merchants
who brought down tin and amber from the Baltic lands by
the overland trade routes.

Since Pytheas was the first to use astronomical measurements to determine the geographic location of a place and
in other ways had proved his competence as an astronomer,
he brought more than ordinary skill to an exploratory voyage.
He seems to have sailed around Great Britain, to have
reached the Shetland Islands, and then to have launched out
into the open ocean to the north, coming at last to 'Thule,'
the land of midnight sun. In this country, he is quoted as
reporting, 'the nights were very short, in some places two, in
others three hours long, so that the sun rose again a short
time after it had set.' The country was inhabited by 'barbarians' who showed Pytheas 'the place where the sun goes
to rest.' The location of 'Thule' is a point much disputed by
later authorities, some believing it to have been Iceland,
while others believe that Pytheas crossed the North Sea to
Norway. Pytheas is also said to have described a 'congealed
sea' lying north of Thule, which accords better with Iceland.

But the Dark Ages were settling down over the civilized
world, and little of the knowledge of distant places acquired

by Pytheas on his voyagings seems to have impressed the learned men who followed him. The geographer Posidonius wrote of the ocean that 'stretched to infinity' and from Rhodes he undertook a journey all the way to Gadir (Cadiz) to see the ocean, measure its tides, and determine the truth of the belief that the sun dropped with the hissing of a red-hot body into the great western sea.

Not for about 1200 years after Pytheas do we have another clear account of marine exploration—this time by the Norwegian Ottar. Ottar described his voyagings in northern seas to King Alfred, who recorded them in a straightforward narrative of geographic exploration strikingly free from sea monsters and other imaginary terrors. Ottar, on the basis of this account, was the first known explorer to round the North Cape, to enter the Polar or Barents Sea, and later to enter the White Sea. He found the coasts of these seas inhabited by people of whom he seems to have heard previously. According to the narrative, he went there 'chiefly to explore the country, and for the sake of the walrus, for they have much valuable bone in their tusks.' This voyage was probably made between A.D. 870 and 890.

Meanwhile the age of the Vikings had dawned. The beginning of their more important expeditions is usually considered to be the end of the eighth century. But long before that time they had visited other countries of northern Europe. 'As early as the third century and until the close of the fifth century,' wrote Fridtjof Nansen, 'the roving Eruli sailed from Scandinavia, sometimes in company with Saxon pirates, over the seas of western Europe, ravaging the coasts of Gaul and Spain, and indeed penetrating in 455 into the Mediterranean as far as Lucca in Italy.' As early as the sixth century the Vikings must have crossed the North Sea to the land of the Franks, and probably to southern Britain. They may have established themselves in Shetland by the beginning of the seventh century, and plundered the Hebrides and northwest Ireland about the same time. Later they sailed to the Faroes and to Iceland; in the last quarter of the tenth century they established two colonies in Greenland, and shortly thereafter they steered across the intervening Atlantic waters to North America. Of the place of these voyages in history Nansen writes:

The shipbuilding and seamanship of the Norwegians mark a new epoch in the history both of navigation and discovery, and with their voyages the knowledge of northern lands and waters was at once completely changed . . .

We find accounts of these voyages of discovery in the old writings and sagas, a large part of which was put into writing in Iceland. A somber undercurrent runs through these narratives of voyages in unknown seas—the silent struggle of hardy men with ice, storms, cold, and want.

They had neither compass, nor astronomical instruments, nor any of the appliances of our time for finding their position at sea; they could only sail by the sun, moon, and stars, and it seems incomprehensible how for days and weeks, when these were invisible, they were able to find their course through fog and bad weather; but they found it, and in the open craft of the Norwegian Vikings, with their square sails, fared north and west over the whole ocean, from Novaya Zemlya and Spitsbergen to Greenland, Baffin Bay, Newfoundland, and North America. . . . It was not until five hundred years later that the ships of other nations were to make their way to the same regions.*

But only the vaguest rumors of any of these things had reached the 'civilized world' of the Mediterranean. While the sagas of the Norsemen were giving clear and factual directions for the passage across oceans, from known to unknown worlds, the writings of the scholars of the medieval world dealt still with that outermost encircling ocean, the dread Sea of Darkness. About the year 1154 the noted Arab geographer Edrisi wrote for the Norman king of Sicily, Roger II, a description of the earth, accompanied by 70 maps, which portrayed on the outside of all the known earth the Dark Sea, forming the limit of the world. He wrote of the sea about the British Isles that it is 'impossible to penetrate very far into this ocean.' He hinted at the existence of far islands but thought the approach to them difficult because of the 'fog and deep darkness that prevails on this sea.' The scholarly Adam of Bremen, writing in the eleventh century, knew of the existence of Greenland and Wineland as distant islands in the great ocean, but could not separate the reality from the old ideas of that sea, 'infinite and fearful to behold, which encompasses the whole world,' that ocean flowing 'endlessly around the circle of the earth.' And even the Norsemen themselves, as they discovered lands across the Atlantic, seem merely to have pushed back the boundaries of the place where still there began that outermost ocean, for the idea of the outer ocean surrounding the disc of the

* From *In Northern Mists*, 1912 edition, A. H. Clark, vol. 1, pp. 234 and 247.

earth appears in such Northern chronicles as the *Kings Mirror* and the *Heimskringla*. And so over that Western Ocean into which Columbus and his men set out there hung still the legend of a dead and stagnant sea, of monsters and entrapping weeds, of fog and gloom and ever present danger.

Yet centuries before Columbus—no one knows how many centuries—men on the opposite side of the world had laid aside whatever fears the ocean may have inspired and were boldly sailing their craft across the Pacific. We know little of the hardships, the difficulties, and the fears that may have beset the Polynesian colonists—we know only that somehow they came from the mainland to those islands, remote from any shore. Perhaps the aspect of these central Pacific waters was kindlier than that of the North Atlantic—it must have been—for in their open canoes they entrusted themselves to the stars and the signposts of the sea and found their way from island to island.

We do not know when the first Polynesian voyages took place. Concerning the later ones, there is some evidence that the last important colonizing voyage to the Hawaiian Islands was made in the thirteenth century, and that about the middle of the fourteenth century a fleet from Tahiti permanently colonized New Zealand. But again, all these things were unknown in Europe, and long after the Polynesians had mastered the art of navigating unknown seas, the European sailors still regarded the Pillars of Hercules as the gateway to a dreaded sea of darkness.

Once Columbus had shown the way to the West Indies and the Americas, once Balboa had seen the Pacific and Magellan had sailed around the globe, there arose, and long persisted, two new ideas. One concerned the existence of a northern passage by sea to Asia; the other had to do with a great southern continent generally believed to lie below the then-known lands.

Magellan, while sailing through the strait that now bears his name, had seen land to the south of him through all the thirty-seven days required for the passage through the strait. At night the lights of many fires glowed from the shores of this land, which Magellan named Tierra del Fuego—Land of Fires. He supposed that these were the near shores of that great land which the theoretical geographers had already decided lie to the south.

Many voyagers after Magellan reported land they assumed to be outlying regions of the sought-for continent, but all proved to be islands. The locations of some, like Bouvet, were so indefinitely described that they were found and lost again many times before being definitely fixed on maps. Kerguelen believed firmly that the bleak, forbidding land he discovered in 1772 was the Southern Continent and so reported it to the French government. When, on a later voyage, he learned that he had found merely another island, Kerguelen unhappily named it 'Isle of Desolation.' Later geographers, however, gave his own name to it.

Discovery of the southern land was one of the objects of Captain Cook's voyages, but instead of a continent, he discovered an ocean. By making an almost complete circumnavigation of the globe in high southern latitudes, Cook revealed the existence of a stormy ocean running completely around the earth south of Africa, Australia, and South America. Perhaps he believed that the islands of the South Sandwich group were part of the Antarctic mainland, but it is by no means sure that he was the first to see these or other islands of the Antarctic Ocean. American sealers had quite possibly been there before him, yet this chapter of Antarctic exploration contains many blank pages. The Yankee sealers did not want their competitors to find the rich sealing grounds, and they kept the details of their voyages secret. Evidently they had operated in the vicinity of the outer Antarctic islands for many years before the beginning of the nineteenth century, because most of the fur seals in these waters had been exterminated by 1820. It was in this year that the Antarctic continent was first sighted, by Captain N. B. Palmer in command of the *Hero,* one of a fleet of eight sealers from Connecticut ports. A century later, explorers were still making fresh discoveries about the nature of that Southern Continent, dreamed of by the old geographers, so long searched for, then branded a myth, and finally established as one of the great continental masses of the earth.

At the opposite pole, meanwhile, the dream of a northern passage to the riches of Asia lured one expedition after another into the frozen seas of the north. Cabot, Frobisher, and Davis sought the passage to the northwest, failed, and turned back. Hudson was left by a mutinous crew to die in an open boat. Sir John Franklin set out with the *Erebus* and *Terror* in 1845, apparently entered the labyrinth of Arctic islands by what later proved a feasible route, but then lost his ships and perished with all his men. Later rescue ships coming from east and west met in Melville Sound and thus the Northwest Passage was established.

Meanwhile there had been repeated efforts to find a way to India by sailing eastward through the Arctic Sea. The Norwegians seem to have hunted walruses in the White

Sea and had probably reached the coasts of Novaya Zemlya by the time of Ottar; they may have discovered Spitsbergen in 1194, although this is usually credited to Barents in 1596. The Russians had hunted seals in the polar seas as early as the sixteenth century, and whalers began to operate out of Spitsbergen soon after Hudson, in 1607, called attention to the great number of whales in the sea between Spitsbergen and Greenland. So at least the threshold of the ice-filled northern ocean was known when the British and Dutch traders began their desperate attempt to find a sea road north of Europe and Asia. There were many attempts, but few got beyond the coasts of Novaya Zemlya; the sixteenth and seventeenth centuries were marked by the wreckage of hopes as well as of vessels, and by the death of such brilliant navigators as William Barents under the hardships met by expeditions ill prepared for arctic winters. Finally the effort was abandoned. It was not until 1879, after the practical need for such a passage had largely disappeared, that Baron Nordenskiöld, in the Swedish *Vega,* passed from Gothenburg to Bering Strait.

So, little by little, through many voyages undertaken over many centuries, the fog and the frightening obscurity of the unknown were lifted from all the surface of the Sea of Darkness. How did they accomplish it—those first voyagers, who had not even the simplest instruments of navigation, who had never seen a nautical chart, to whom the modern miracles of loran, radar, and sonic sounding would have been fantasies beyond belief? Who was the first man to use a mariner's compass, and what were the embryonic beginnings of the charts and the sailing directions that are taken for granted today? None of these questions can be answered with finality; we know only enough to want to know more.

Of the methods of those secretive master mariners, the Phoenicians, we cannot even guess. We have more basis for conjecture about the Polynesians, for we can study their descendants today, and those who have done so find hints of the methods that led the ancient colonizers of the Pacific on their course from island to island. Certainly they seem to have followed the stars, which burned brightly in the heavens over those calm Pacific regions, which are so unlike the stormy and fog-bound northern seas. The Polynesians, considered the stars as moving bands of light that passed across the inverted pit of the sky, and they sailed toward the stars which they knew passed over the islands of their destination. All the language of the sea was understood by them: the varying color of the water, the haze of surf breaking on rocks yet below the horizon, and the cloud patches that hang over every islet of the tropic seas and sometimes seem even to reflect the color of a lagoon within a coral atoll.

Students of primitive navigation believe that the migrations of birds had meaning for the Polynesians, and that they learned much from watching the flocks that gathered each year in the spring and fall, launched out over the ocean, and returned later out of the emptiness into which they had vanished. Harold Gatty believes the Hawaiians may have found their islands by following the spring migration of the golden plover from Tahiti to the Hawaiian chain, as the birds returned to the North American mainland. He has also suggested that the migratory path of the shining cuckoo may have guided other colonists from the Solomons to New Zealand.

Tradition and written records tell us that primitive navigators often carried with them birds which they would release and follow to land. The frigate bird or man-of-war bird was the shore-sighting bird of the Polynesians (even in recent times it has been used to carry messages between islands), and in the Norse Sagas we have an account of the use of 'ravens' by Floki Vilgerdarson to show him the way to Iceland, 'since seafaring men had no loadstone at that time in the north . . . Thence he sailed out to sea with the three ravens . . . And when he let loose the first it flew back astern. The second flew up into the air and back to the ship. The third flew forward over the prow, where they found land.'

In thick and foggy weather, according to repeated statements in the Sagas, the Norsemen drifted for days without knowing where they were. Then they often had to rely on observing the flight of birds to judge the direction of land. The *Landnamabok* says that on the course from Norway to Greenland the voyager should keep far enough to the south of Iceland to have birds and whales from there. In shallow waters it appears that the Norsemen took some sort of soundings, for the *Historia Norwegiae* records that Ingolf and Hjorleif found Iceland 'by probing the waves with the lead.'

The first mention of the use of the magnetic needle as a guide to mariners occurs in the twelfth century after Christ, but as much as a century later scholars were expressing doubt that sailors would entrust their lives to an instrument so obviously invented by the devil. There is fair evidence, however, that the compass was in use in the Mediter-

ranean about the end of the twelfth century, and in northern
Europe within the next hundred years.

For navigating the known seas, there had been the
equivalent of our modern Sailing Directions for a great many
centuries before this. The *portolano* and the *peripli* guided
the mariners of antiquity about the Mediterranean and Black
seas. The *portolano* were harbor-finding charts, designed to
accompany the coast pilots or *peripli*, and it is not known
which of the two was developed first. The *Periplus of Scylax*
is the oldest and most complete of these ancient Coast
Pilots that have survived the hazards of the intervening centuries and are preserved for us. The chart which presumably
accompanied it no longer exists, but the two were, in effect,
a guide to navigation of the Mediterranean in the fourth or
fifth century B.C.

The *periplus* called *Stadiasmus, or circumnavigation of the
great sea* dates from about the fifth century after Christ but
reads surprisingly like a modern Pilot, giving distances between points, the winds with which the various islands
might be approached, and the facilities for anchorage or for
obtaining fresh water. So for example, we read, 'From
Hermaea to Leuce Acte, 20 stadia hereby lies a low islet at
a distance of two stadia from the land, there is anchorage
for cargo boats, to be put into with west wind; but by
the shore below the promontory is a wide anchoring-road
for all kinds of vessels. Temple of Apollo, a famous oracle;
by the temple there is water.'

Lloyd Brown, in his *Story of Maps*, says that no true
mariners' chart of the first thousand years after Christ has
been preserved or is definitely known to have existed. This
he ascribes to the fact that early mariners carefully guarded
the secrets of how they made their passages from place
to place; that sea charts were 'keys to empire' and a 'way
to wealth' and as such were secret, hidden documents.
Therefore, because the earliest specimen of such a chart
now extant was made by Petrus Vesconte in 1311 does not
mean that many had not existed before it.

It was a Dutchman who produced the first collection of
navigational charts bound together in book form—Lucas
Janssz Waghenaer. The *Mariner's Mirror* of Waghenaer, first
published in 1584, covered the navigation of the western
coast of Europe from the Zuyder Zee to Cadiz. Soon it was
issued in several languages. For many years 'Waggoners'
guided Dutch, English, Scandinavian, and German navigators
through eastern Atlantic waters, from the Canaries to Spitsbergen, for succeeding editions had extended the areas cov-

ered to include the Shetland and Faroe islands and even the northern coast of Russia as far as Novaya Zemlya.

In the sixteenth and seventeenth centuries, under the stimulus of fierce competition for the wealth of the East Indies, the finest charts were prepared not by governmental agencies, but by private enterprise. The East India companies employed their own hydrographers, prepared secret atlases, and generally guarded their knowledge of the sailing passages to the East as one of the most precious secrets of their trade. But in 1795 the East India Company's hydrographer, Alexander Dalrymple, became official hydrographer to the Admiralty, and under his direction the British Admiralty began its survey of the coasts of the world from which the modern Admiralty Pilots stem.

Shortly thereafter a young man joined the United States Navy—Matthew Fontaine Maury. In only a few years Lieutenant Maury was to make his influence felt on navigation all over the world, and was to write a book, *The Physical Geography of the Sea,* which is now considered the foundation of the science of oceanography. After a number of years at sea, Maury assumed charge of the Depot of Charts and Instruments—the forerunner of the present Hydrographic Office—and began a practical study of winds and currents from the standpoint of the navigator. Through his energy and initiative a world-wide co-operative system was organized. Ships' officers of all nations sent in the logs of their voyages, from which Maury assembled and organized information, which he incorporated in navigational charts. In return, the co-operating mariner received copies of the charts. Soon Maury's sailing directions were attracting world notice: he had shortened the passage for American east-coast vessels to Rio de Janeiro by 10 days, to Australia by 20 days, and around the Horn to California by 30 days. The co-operative exchange of information sponsored by Maury remains in effect today, and the Pilot Charts of the Hydrographic Office, the lineal descendants of Maury's charts, carry the inscription: 'Founded on the researches of Matthew Fontaine Maury while serving as a Lieutenant in the United States Navy.'

In the modern Sailing Directions and Coast Pilots now issued by every maritime nation of the world we find the most complete information that is available to guide the navigator over the ocean. Yet in these writings of the sea there is a pleasing blend of modernity and antiquity, with unmistakable touches by which we may trace their lineage

back to the sailing directions of the sagas or the *peripli*
of the ancient Mediterranean seamen.

It is surprising, but pleasant, that sailing directions of one
and the same vintage should contain instructions for obtaining position by the use of loran, and should also counsel the
navigator to be guided, like the Norsemen a millennium ago,
by the flight of birds and the behavior of whales in making
land in foggy weather. In the *Norway Pilot* we read as
follows:

> [Of Jan Mayen Island] The presence of sea fowl in
> large numbers will give an indication of the approach to
> land and the noise of their rookeries may be useful in
> locating the shore.
> [Of Bear Island] The sea around the islands teems
> with guillemots. These flocks and the direction of their
> flight on approaching, together with the use of the lead,
> are of great value in making the island when it is foggy.

And the ultra-modern *United States Pilot* for Antarctica
says:

> Navigators should observe the bird life, for deductions
> may often be drawn from the presence of certain species.
> Shags are . . . a sure sign of the close proximity of
> land . . . The snow petrel is invariably associated with ice
> and is of great interest to mariners as an augury of ice
> conditions in their course . . . Blowing whales usually
> travel in the direction of open water.

Sometimes the Pilots for remote areas of the sea can
report only what the whalers or sealers or some old-time
fisherman has said about the navigability of a channel or the
set of the tidal currents; or they must include a chart prepared half a century ago by the last vessel to take soundings
in the area. Often they must caution the navigator not to
proceed without seeking information of those having 'local
knowledge.' In phrases like these we get the feel of the unknown and the mysterious that never quite separates itself
from the sea: 'It is said that there was once an island there
. . . such information as could be secured from reports of
men with local knowledge . . . their position has been disputed . . . a bank reported by an old-time sealer.'

So here and there, in a few out-of-the-way places, the
darkness of antiquity still lingers over the surface of the
waters. But it is rapidly being dispelled and most of the

length and breadth of the ocean is known; it is only in thinking of its third dimension that we can still apply the concept of the Sea of Darkness. It took centuries to chart the surface of the sea; our progress in delineating the unseen world beneath it seems by comparison phenomenally rapid. But even with all our modern instruments for probing and sampling the deep ocean, no one now can say that we shall ever resolve the last, the ultimate mysteries of the sea.

In its broader meaning, that other concept of the ancients remains. For the sea lies all about us. The commerce of all lands must cross it. The very winds that move over the lands have been cradled on its broad expanse and seek ever to return to it. The continents themselves dissolve and pass to the sea, in grain after grain of eroded land. So the rains that rose from it return again in rivers. In its mysterious past it encompasses all the dim origins of life and receives in the end, after, it may be, many transmutations, the dead husks of that same life. For all at last return to the sea—to Oceanus, the ocean river, like the ever-flowing stream of time, the beginning and the end.

1. *The Gray Beginnings, page 20*

Our concept of the age of the earth is constantly undergoing revision as older and older rocks are discovered and as methods of study are refined. The oldest rocks now known in North America are in the Canadian Shield area. Their precise age has not been determined, but some from Manitoba and Ontario are believed to have been formed about 3 billion years ago. Even older rocks have been discovered in the Karelia Peninsula in the U.S.S.R., and in South Africa. Geologists are generally of the opinion that present concepts of geologic time will be considerably lengthened in the future. Tentative adjustments of the length of the various periods have already been made (see chart, pages 26-27) and the age of the Cambrian has been pushed back 100 million years compared with the dating assigned to it a decade ago. It is in that immense and shadowy time that preceded the Cambrian, however, that the greatest uncertainty exists. This is the time of the pre-fossiliferous rocks. Whatever life may have inhabited the earth during that time has left few traces, although by indirect evidence we may infer that life existed in some abundance before its record was written in the rocks.

By studies of the rocks themselves geologists have established a few good benchmarks standing out in those vast stretches of time indicated on the chart as the Proterozoic and Archeozoic Eras. These indicate a billion-year age for the ancient Grenville Mountains of eastern North America. Where these rocks are exposed at the surface, as in Ontario, they contain large amounts of graphite, giving silent testimony to the abundance of plant life when these rocks were forming, for plants are a common source of carbon. An age-reading of 1,700,000,000 years has been obtained in the Penokean Mountains of Minnesota and Ontario, formerly known to geologists as the Killarney Mountains. The remains of these once lofty mountains are still to be seen as low, rolling hills. The discovery of even older rocks in Canada, Russia, and Africa, dating back more than 3 billion years, suggests that the earth itself may have been formed about 4½ billion years ago.

2. *The Sunless Sea, page 48*

Man's dream of personally exploring the deepest recesses of the sea has been realized during the past decade. Persistent effort, imaginative vision, and engineering skill have produced a type of underwater craft capable of withstanding the enormous stresses imposed by the greatest depths of the sea and of carrying human observers into these realms that only a few years ago would have seemed beyond the reach of man.

The pioneer in this area of deep ocean exploration was Professor Auguste Piccard, the Swiss physicist who had already attained fame through his ascent into the stratosphere in a balloon. Professor Piccard proposed a depth-exploring vehicle which, instead of being suspended at the end of a cable like the bathysphere, would move freely, independent of control from the surface. Three such bathyscaphes (depth boats) have now been constructed. Observers ride in a pressure-resisting ball suspended from a metal envelope containing high-octane gasoline, an extremely light, almost incompressible fluid. Silos loaded with iron pellets provide ballast; the pellets are held by electromagnets, to be released by the touch of a button when the divers are ready to return to the surface. The first bathyscaphe, provided by the Fonds National de la Recherche Scientifique, which is the Belgian scientific research fund, was known as the FNRS-2. (The FNRS-1 was the stratosphere balloon, which the Fund also provided for Piccard.) The FNRS-2, in experimental unmanned dives, revealed great promise but also had certain defects which were remedied in the craft built later. The second bathyscaphe, the FNRS-3, was built under a treaty between the Belgian and French governments, under the direction of Piccard and Jacques Cousteau. Before the completion of this bathyscaphe, Professor Piccard went to Italy to begin the building of a third bathyscaphe, to be christened *Trieste*.

The FNRS-3 and the *Trieste* made the history-making descents of the 1950's that carried man to the deepest parts of the abyss. In September 1953, Professor Piccard and his son Jacques descended in the *Trieste* to a depth of 10,395 feet in the Mediterranean. This was more than double the previous record. Then in 1954 two Frenchmen in the FNRS-3, Georges Houot and Pierre-Henri Willm, penetrated even deeper into the sea, to depths of 13,287 feet in the open ocean off Dakar on the coast of Africa. In 1958 the *Trieste* was purchased from the Piccards by the United States Office of Naval Research. The following year the *Trieste* was taken to Guam, in the vicinity of which lies the great Mariana Trench, in which echo soundings have revealed the deepest hole now known in any part of the ocean. On January 23, 1960, manned by Jacques Piccard and Don Walsh, the *Trieste* descended to the bottom of this trench, 35,800 feet (or nearly seven miles) beneath the surface.

3. *The Sunless Sea, page 54*

Even today the mystery of the scattering layer has not been completely resolved. Through an ingenious combination of new techniques, however, the picture is gradually becoming clearer. It now appears that at least in some areas—as over the continental shelf off New England—fishes may compose a substantial part of the layer. This has been determined by studying it with a sound source that embraces many frequencies (the ordinary echo sounder is a single-frequency device). This method not only reveals the vertical migration but brings out the fact that the very nature of the scattering changes with depth. Such changes are best interpreted as originating in the swim bladders of fishes, which are compressed under the increasing pressure of a descent into deeper levels of the sea but which expand with ascent toward the surface and consequent lessening of pressure. The formerly held objection that fishes could not possibly be abundant enough to account for the very widespread occurrence of the scattering layer has melted away in the light of information new techniques have given us. It was formerly supposed that a strong echo implied a very dense concentration of whatever creatures were returning the echo. Now it is realized that the tracings recorded by the echo sounder do not necessarily indicate the density of the animals in the scattering layer, so that actually a dark tracing on the record may be produced by only a few strong scatters passing through the beam in any particular instant of time.

One of the study methods increasingly used during the 1950's was an underwater camera correlated with an echo sounder. All pictures of fishes so obtained have been accompanied by strong echoes. None of these findings rule out the possibility that other organisms may also help to compose the scattering layer. They do furnish rather convincing evidence that fishes compose an important part of a phenomenon that, in all probability, lends itself to no single explanation, but varies as to the species composing it over the vast areas of the ocean.

4. The Sunless Sea, page 55

In 1957 Bruce C. Heezen of the Lamont Geological Observatory published a fascinating compilation of fourteen instances of whales entangled in submarine cables between 1877 and 1955. Ten of these accidents occurred off the Pacific coast of Central and South America, two in the South Atlantic, one in the North Atlantic, and one in the Persian Gulf. All entanglements involved sperm whales and it is possible the concentration of reports off the coasts of Ecuador and Peru may be related to a seasonal migration of these whales. The greatest depth at which a whale was found entangled was 620 fathoms or nearly two-thirds of a mile. More whales were trapped by cables at about 500 fathoms than at any other depth, suggesting that the natural food of the sperm whale may be concentrated at about this level. Two significant details were observed in most of these cases; the entanglement occurred near the site of earlier repairs where slack cable lay on the bottom, and the cable was usually wrapped around the whale's jaw. Heezen suggests that as a whale skims along the ocean bottom in search of food its lower jaw may become entangled in a slack loop of cable lying on the bottom. The struggles of the whale to free itself could easily result in its complete entanglement in the cable.

5. The Sunless Sea, page 61

For years people have speculated as to the function served by sound production on the part of marine species. It has been known for at least 20 years that the bat finds it way about in lightless caves and on dark nights by means of a physiological equivalent of radar, emitting a stream of high-frequency sound, which returns to it as echoes from any obstructions in its path. Could the sounds produced by certain fishes and marine mammals serve a similar purpose, aiding inhabitants of deep waters to swim in darkness and to find prey? Among the early tape recordings of underwater sound obtained by the Woods Hole Oceanographic Institution was a recording of some mysterious calls that emanated from waters so deep as surely to be lightless. They were distinguished by the fact that each call was followed by a faint echo of itself, so that for want of a better name the unknown author of these eerie sounds was christened the "echo fish." Actual evidence of anything similar to the bat's echo location or echo ranging has come only recently in the form of ingenious experiments performed on captive porpoises by W. N. Kellogg of Florida State University. Dr. Kellogg finds that the porpoises emit streams of underwater sound pulses by which they are able to swim accurately through a field of obstructions without collision. They could do this in water too turbid for vision or in darkness. When the experimenters introduced any object into the tank the porpoises gave forth bursts of sound signals by which the animals appeared to be trying to locate the object. Splashing on the surface, as from a hose or a shower of rain, "produced great disturbance, loud sound signals, undulating porpoise 'alarm' whistles, and 'flight' swimming reactions." When food fish were introduced into the tank under such circumstances that they could not be located visually, the porpoises located them by streams of sound signals, turning their heads to right and left as the returning echoes allowed them to fix the exact location of their target.

6. The Sunless Sea, page 62

Latimeria was identified as a coelacanth, or one of an incredibly ancient group of fishes that first appeared in the seas some 300 million years ago. Rocks representing the next 200 million and more years of earth history yielded fossil coelacanths; then, in the Cretaceous, the record of these fishes came to an end. The reappearance of a coelacanth as a live fish off South Africa was at first considered a mysterious and extraordinary incident, not likely to be repeated. An ichthyologist in South Africa, Professor J. L. B. Smith, did not share this view. Believing there must be other coelacanths in the sea, he began a patient search that went on 14 years before it was successful. Then, in December 1952, a second fish of this group was captured near the island of Anjouan, off the northwestern tip of Madagascar. The search was then taken up by Professor J. Millot, Director of the Research Institute in Madagascar. By 1958 Professor Millot had obtained ten more specimens, consisting of seven males and three females.

A plausible explanation of the sixty-million-year gap in the occurrence of fossil coelacanths has been put forward by Dr. Bobb Schaeffer of the American Museum of Natural History. Dr. Schaeffer points out that the earliest coelacanths, from pre-Jurassic time, seem to have inhabited a variety of environments, including fresh-water swamps as well as seas. From the Jurassic to the present time, on the other hand, they seem to have been exclusively marine. At the close of the Cretaceous, the great withdrawal of the sea from the continental areas it had overflowed may have confined the coelacanths to the permanent ocean basins. There, in the bottom sediments, their fossils would be so inaccessible that the chance of their discovery would be exceedingly remote.

7. Hidden Lands, page 64

The range of echo-sounding instruments has now been so greatly extended that under ideal conditions the most powerful of them are capable of sounding the maximum depths of the sea. Factors such as the nature of the underlying bottom and conditions in the intervening water layers influence the effectiveness with which the sounding devices operate under actual conditions at sea. Nevertheless, the potential range necessary for charting all parts of the sea is now at the command of oceanographers.

8. Hidden Lands, page 67

In the ten years that have elapsed since this account of the canyons was written much more has been learned about them, but it may still be said that there is no general agreement about their origin. Many of the resources of the modern oceanographer have been brought to bear on the problem. Divers have engaged in direct exploration of the shallow heads of some of the California canyons, collecting samples of their walls and photographing them. Other canyons have been studied by oceanographers using deep-sea corers or dredges to obtain samples of rocks and sediments. Precision depth recorders have given much new information about their shapes. As a result of these studies it is now known that there are at least five types of canyons, so different in their characteristics that almost certainly they have different origins. No single theory may be expected to explain all of them. Professor Francis S. Shepard, the marine geologist who originally put forward the theory that the canyons had been cut by rivers and later submerged, now feels this explanation is adequate for some canyons but not for others. For example, some marine valleys, trough-shaped and straight-walled and occurring in areas where the earth's crust is in a state of unrest, probably represent a fault or fracture of the rocky floor. The theory that some of the canyons have been cut by vast sediment flows called turbidity currents has gained support as a result of new concepts of dynamic activity on the floor of the sea. Further detailed study of all types of these extraordinarily fascinating features of the sea floor should not only clarify their own history but add greatly to our understanding of the history of the earth.

9.   Hidden Lands, page 69

Somewhat greater depths have more recently been recorded in the Mariana Trench off the island of Guam, the trench into which the bathyscaphe *Trieste* made its record-breaking descent to the bottom. In this trench the *Challenger* in 1951 recorded a depth of 10,863 meters or about 6.7 miles. Since the exact location of the *Challenger* echo sounding was given, this depth is capable of verification and so is regarded as the maximum depth of which we have authentic record. In 1958, however, Russian scientists aboard the *Vitiaz* reported a finding of slightly greater depths (11,034 meters or 6.8 miles) also in the Mariana Trench, but at an unspecified location.

10.   Hidden Lands, page 70

The supposition that the Atlantic Ridge may extend across the Arctic basin has been confirmed in exciting new developments in marine geology. Indeed, it is now suggested by some geologists that the whole mid-Atlantic ridge is part of a continuous range of mountains that runs for 40,000 miles across the bottom of the Alantic, the Arctic, the Pacific, and the Indian Oceans (see Preface).

As for the exploration of the Arctic basin itself—the charting of details so long unknown and merely guessed at—the revolutionary development that made it possible to substitute fact for theory was the use of American nuclear-powered submarines to pass beneath the ice cover and directly explore the depths of this ocean. In 1957 the *Nautilus* (bearing the same name as Wilkin's conventional submarine) first penetrated beneath Arctic ice in a preliminary exploration designed to discover whether it was feasible to explore these regions by submarines. The *Nautilus* remained submerged for 74 hours and covered a distance of almost 1000

miles. A vast amount of data was collected, including depth soundings and measurements of the thickness of the overlying ice. Then
in 1958 the *Nautilus* crossed the entire Arctic basin from Point
Barrow in Alaska to the North Pole and thence to the Atlantic.
In the course of this historic voyage it made the first continuously
recorded echo-sounder profile across the center of the Arctic basin.
Other nuclear submarines have subsequently contributed to our
knowledge of the Arctic. It is now clear, from the work of the
nuclear submarines and from other, more conventional explorations,
that the bottom topography of the Arctic Ocean is for the most
part that of a normal oceanic basin, with flat abyssal plains, scattered sea mounts, and rugged mountains. The greatest depth so
far discovered is somewhat more than three miles. The shelf break
(from which a steeper descent begins) falls at the unusually shallow depth of 35 fathoms off Alaska. From samplings by coring
tubes and dredges and from deep-sea photography it was discovered
during the International Geophysical Year that the bottom is widely
covered with rocks, pebbles, and shells, the latter chiefly of shallow-
water forms. The present ice cover seems to be carrying little or
no material such as rock fragments and sand, so the material now
found in bottom samples must have come from ice rafted in from
surrounding continents during some past geologic time, when the
Arctic was relatively open water.

Russian scientists, who have done rather extensive work in marine
biology, obtained interesting data which seem to disprove Nansen's
earlier belief that the waters of the central Arctic are extremely
poor in both plant and animal life. Data collected from the drifting station "North Pole" indicate that both plant and animal
plankton in great variety exist in the region of the Pole. Little-
studied organisms develop on the surface of the ice; these contain
much fat and tint the ice shades of yellow and red. Diatoms are
not found on the surface of the ice but develop (along with other
plankton) in the lakes that form on the surface of the ice as it
melts. By absorbing a great amount of energy from the sun, the
abundant diatom colonies contribute to further melting of the ice
cover. The wealth of plankton during the Arctic summer attracts
numbers of birds and various mammals.

11. *The Long Snowfall, page 80*

Now that the sediments have been measured over much greater
areas of the ocean floor, the reaction of oceanographers is one of
considerable amazement—but their surprise concerns the fact that
on the whole the mantle of sediments is so much thinner than
related facts would lead them to expect. Over vast areas of the
Pacific the average thickness of the sediments (unconsolidated sediments plus sedimentary rock) is only about a quarter of a mile. It
is little thicker over much of the Atlantic. (These are average

figures; some much deeper deposits of course exist.) In some areas there has been almost no sedimentation. A few years ago several oceanographers obtained photographs of manganese nodules lying on the floor of the Atlantic at great depths and of others on the Easter Island Ridge of the southeast Pacific. Sharks' teeth dating from the Tertiary, hence possibly as much as 70 million years old, sometimes form the nuclei of these nodules. Certainly their growth, by deposit of successive layers around these nuclei, must be very slow. Hans Petterson has estimated a growth of about 1 mm. per thousand years. Yet during the period these nodules have lain on the ocean floor, sediments deep enough to cover them have not been accumulated.

Some idea of the rate of sedimentation during post-glacial time has been gained by observation of the rate of radioactive decay of some of the components of the sediments. If this sedimentation rate had prevailed during the supposed life of the oceans, the average thickness of the sediments would be enormously greater than it now appears to be. Did much of the deposited sediments dissolve? Were most of the present land masses submerged for far greater periods than we now assume, with consequently long periods of slight erosion? These and other explanations of the mystery of the sediments have been suggested, but none seems wholly satisfying. Possibly the dramatic project of boring holes in the floor of the ocean down to the Mohorovicic discontinuity (Project Mohole; see Preface) will provide the explanation that is now lacking.

12. Wind and Water, page 121

From the time of its establishment up to 1960, the warning system has issued eight alerts warning residents of the Hawaiian Islands of the approach of seismic waves. On three of these occasions, waves of major proportions have in fact struck the islands. None have been so large or so destructive, however, as those of May 23, 1960, which spread out across the Pacific from their place of origin in violent earthquakes on the coast of Chile. Without such warning the loss of life would almost certainly have been enormous. As soon as the seismograph at the Honolulu Observatory recorded the first of the Chilean quakes the system went into operation. Reports from the scattered tide stations gave ample notice that a seismic wave had formed and was spreading out across the Pacific. By early news bulletins and later by an official "sea wave warning" the Observatory alerted residents of the area and predicted the time the wave would arrive and the areas to be affected. These predictions proved to be accurate within reasonable limits, and although property damage was heavy, loss of life was limited to the few who disregarded the warnings. Sea wave activity was reported as far west as New Zealand and as far north as Alaska. The Japanese coasts were struck by heavy waves. Although the

United States warning system does not now include other nations, officials at Honolulu sent to Japan warnings of the wave, which, unfortunately, were disregarded.

The warning system now (in 1960) consists of eight seismograph stations at points on both eastern and western shores of the Pacific and on certain islands, and of twenty widely scattered wave stations, four of which are equipped with automatic wave detectors. The Coast and Geodetic Survey feels that additional wave-reporting tide stations would improve the effectiveness of the system. Its principal defect now, however, is the fact that it is not possible to predict the height of a wave as it reaches any particular shore, and therefore the same alert must be issued for all approaching seismic waves. Research on methods of forecasting wave height is therefore needed. Even with its present limitations, however, the system has filled so great a need that there is strong international interest in extending it to other parts of the world.

13. *Wind and Water, page 122*

The flood of ocean waters that overwhelmed the coast of the Netherlands on February 1, 1953, deserves a place in the history of great storm waves. A winter gale that formed west of Iceland swept across the Atlantic and into the North Sea. All its force was ultimately brought to bear on the first land mass to obstruct the course of its center—the southwestern corner of Holland. The storm-driven waves and tides battered against the dikes in such bitter violence that these ancient defenses were breached in a hundred places, through which the flood rushed in to inundate farms and villages. The storm struck on Saturday, January 31, and by midday of Sunday one-eighth of Holland was under water. The toll included about half a million acres of Holland's best agricultural land— ravaged by water and permeated with salt—thousands of buildings, hundreds of thousands of live stock, and an estimated 1400 people. In all the long history of Holland's struggle against the sea, there has been no comparable assault by ocean waters.

14. *Wind, Sun, and the Spinning of the Earth, page 134*

It is now the fashion among oceanographers to speak of the Gulf Stream System, reflecting the discovery that east of Cape Hatteras there is no longer a continuous river of warm water but a "series of overlapping currents arranged somewhat like the shingles on a roof." Not only do the streams "overlap" but they are narrow and swift. The main branches of the stream that have long been recognized east of the Grand Banks are now known to originate far to westward of the Banks, developing not as branches in the ordinary sense but as a series of new currents, each to the north of the next older one.

As oceanographers study more about the dynamics of circulation in the sea, they are more and more struck by parallels between the ocean of water and the ocean of air. One of the leading students of the Gulf Stream, Columbus Iselin, has commented on the branching of the Stream in terms of a fascinating analogy: "Much the same phenomena seem to be present in the jet streams found at high elevations in the great belts of prevailing westerly winds of mid-latitudes," he says, "although each atmospheric jet has greater dimensions than the overlapping subdivision of the Gulf Stream System."

15.   Wind, Sun, and the Spinning of the Earth, page 135

One of the most exciting recent events in oceanography was the discovery of a powerful current running under the South Equatorial current but in the opposite direction. The core of the counter current lies about 300 feet below the surface (although shallower near its eastern terminal in the vicinity of the Galapagos Islands). This subsurface current is about 250 miles wide and it flows at least 3500 miles eastward along the equator at a speed of about 3 knots. (The speed of the surface current is only about one knot.) The existence of the current was discovered in 1952 by Townsend Cromwell in the course of a U. S. Fish and Wildlife Service investigation of methods of tuna fishing. Cromwell observed that long lines set for tuna at the equator did not move westward with the surface current, as would be expected, but drifted rapidly in the opposite direction. It was not until 1958, however, that an extensive survey of the current was made by the Scripps Institution of Oceanography and its impressive dimensions measured. This same survey gave further proof that the deep circulation of the ocean is far more complicated than has generally been realized, for beneath the swift-flowing eastward current was still another, flowing to the west. In only the uppermost half mile of Pacific equatorial waters, therefore, there are three great rivers of water, one above the other, each flowing on its own course independent of the other. When such surveys can be extended all the way to the floor of the ocean an even more complex picture will undoubtedly be revealed.

Only a year before the detailed charting of this Pacific current, British and American oceanographers discovered a south-flowing counter current running from the North to the South Atlantic under the Gulf Stream and the Brazil Current. The techniques that make such discoveries possible have only very recently become available to oceanographers. As their use becomes more widespread our almost complete ignorance of the deep circulation of the ocean will be dispelled.

16. *The Global Thermostat, page 158*

During the 1950's enormous advances were made in the development of instruments for the recording of water temperatures. A continuous recording of water temperatures to a depth of several hundred feet may be obtained by towing a thermistor chain behind a vessel. The electronic bathythermograph is potentially capable of obtaining temperatures at any depth, depending on the length of cable available. It is a vast improvement over the original bathythermograph because a recorder on deck traces a continuous graph of the temperatures being registered while the vessel is under way. An even more revolutionary development in the study of sea temperatures is the airborne radiation thermometer which, while flown above the sea, registers the surface temperature with an accuracy of a fraction of a degree. Oceanographers regard this instrument as still in the developmental stage, with further refinement of accuracy possible. However, in such work as tracing the edge of the Gulf Stream these airborne thermometers have already proven themselves enormously useful. During a 1960 survey of the Gulf Stream conducted by the Woods Hole Oceanographic Institution, a low-flying plane covered some 30,000 miles, obtaining surface temperatures in various areas of the Stream.

SUGGESTIONS FOR FURTHER READING *

General Information About the Ocean and Its Life.

Bigelow, Henry B. and Edmonson, W. T. *Wind Waves at Sea, Breakers and Surf,* U.S. Navy, Hydrographic Office Pub. no. 602, Washington, U.S. Government Printing Office, 1947. 177 pp. *Extremely readable; full of interesting and practical information about waves at sea and along coasts.*

Johnson, Douglas W. *Shore Processes and Shoreline Development.* New York, John Wiley and Sons, 1919. 584 pp. *Primarily for geologists and engineers concerned with shoreline changes, yet the chapter, The Work of Waves, is unmatched for sheer interest. Out of print.*

Marmer, H. A. *The Tide.* New York, D. Appleton and Co., 1926. 282 pp. *In this book the late outstanding American authority on tidal phenomena explains the complex behavior of the tides. Out of print.*

Maury, Matthew Fontaine. *Physical Geography of the Sea.* New York, Harper and Brothers, 1855. 287 pp. *Marks the foundation of the science of oceanography, as the first book to consider the sea as a dynamic whole. Out of print.*

Murray, Sir John, and Hjort, Johan. *The Depths of the Ocean.* London, Macmillan, 1912. 822 pp. *Based chiefly on the work of the Norwegian research vessel Michael Sars in the North Atlantic, this work was for many years the bible of oceanography. It is now out of print and copies are rare.*

Ommaney, F. D. *The Ocean.* London, Oxford University Press, 1949. 238 pp. *A thoughtful and pleasantly written account of the ocean and its life, for the general reader.*

Russell, F. S. and Yonge, C. M. *The Seas.* London, Frederick Warne and Co., 1928. 379 pp. *Written chiefly from the biological point of view, this is one of the best general treatments of the subject.*

Sverdrup, H. U., Fleming, Richard, and Johnson, Martin W. *The Oceans.* New York, Prentice-Hall, Inc., 1942. 1087 pp. *The standard modern textbook of oceanography.*

* Many of the old basic works on the sea are now out of print but they are well worth pursuing in libraries for the excellent background they provide.

Some of the most rewarding sources of information about the sea are the Sailing Directions of the U. S. Hydrographic Office (for waters outside of the United States) and the Coast Pilots of the U. S. Coast and Geodetic Survey (for United States shores). Besides giving detailed accounts of the coastlines and coastal waters of the world, these books are repositories of fascinating information on icebergs and sea ice, storms, and fog at sea. Some approach the character of regional geographies. Those dealing with remote and inaccessible coasts are especially interesting. They may be purchased from the issuing agency. The British Admiralty publishes a similar series, as do the appropriate authorities of most maritime nations.

Sea Life in Relation to Its Surrounding.

Hardy, Alister. *The Open Sea.* Part I, The World of Plankton. Boston, Houghton Mifflin Co., 1956. 335 pp. Part II, Fish and Fisheries, Boston, Houghton Mifflin Co., 1959. 322 pp. *A two-part study of marine biology, describing first the little-known creatures of the true sea world beyond the coastal areas, and then the fishes that depend on them.*

Hesse, Richard, Allee, W. C., and Schmidt, Karl P. *Ecological Animal Geography.* New York, John Wiley and Sons (2nd Ed., 1951). 597 pp. *This is an excellent source of information on the intricate relations of living things to their environment, with profuse references to source material. About a fourth of the book is concerned with marine animals.*

Murphy, Robert Cushman. *Oceanic Birds of South America.* New York, Macmillan, 1948. 1245 pp. 2 vols. (originally issued by American Museum of Natural History, 1936). *Highly recommended for an understanding of the relation of birds to the sea and of marine organisms to their environment. It describes little-known shores and islands in extremely readable prose, and contains an extensive bibliography.* Out of print.

Wallace, Alfred Russell. *Island Life.* London, Macmillan, 1880. 526 pp. *Deals in interesting fashion with the basic biology of island life.* Out of print.

Yonge, C. M. *The Sea Shore.* London, Collins, 1949. 311 pp. *For the general reader, a charming and authoritative account of the life of the shore; based chiefly on British localities.* Out of print.

Ricketts, E. F. and Calvin, Jack. *Between Pacific Tides.* Stanford, Stanford University Press, 1948. 365 pp. *An ideal companion for exploring American Pacific shores.*

Exploration and Discovery.

Babcock, William H. *Legendary Islands of the Atlantic; a study in medieval geography.* New York, American Geographical Society, 1922, 385 pp. *Deals with early exploration of the sea and the search for distant lands.* Out of print.

Beebe, William. *Half Mile Down.* New York, Harcourt Brace, 1934. 344 pp. *Stands alone as a vivid eyewitness account of the sea half a mile below the surface.*

Brown, Lloyd A. *The Story of Maps.* Boston, Little, Brown, 1940. 397 pp. *Contains, especially in the chapter, The Haven Finding Art, much of interest about early voyages.*

Challenger Staff. *Report on the Scientific Results of the Exploring Voyage* of H. M. S. Challenger, 1873-76. 40 vols. *See especially volume 1, parts 1 and 2—Narrative of the Cruise— which gives an interesting account of this historic expedition. Consult in libraries.*

Cousteau, Jacques-Yves and Frederic Dumas. *The Silent World.* New York, Harper and Brothers, 1953. 288 pp. *A fascinating book in which the reader shares Cousteau's long and remarkable experience undersea.*

Darwin, Charles. *The Diary of the Voyage of* H. M. S. Beagle. Edited from the manuscript by Nora Barlow. Cambridge, Cambridge University Press, 1934. 451 pp. *A fresh and charming account, as Darwin actually set it down in the course of the* Beagle *voyage.*

Dugan, James. *Man Under the Sea.* New York, Harper and Brothers, 1956. 322 pp. *An interesting and useful account of man's explorations undersea during the past 5000 years.*

Heycrdahl, Thor. *Kon-Tiki.* Chicago, Rand McNally & Co., 1950. 304 pp. *The Odyssey of six modern Vikings who crossed the Pacific on a primitive raft—one of the great books of the sea.*

History of Earth and Sea.

Brooks, C. E. P. *Climate Through the Ages.* New York, McGraw-Hill, 1949. 395 pp. *Interprets clearly and readably the climatic changes of past ages.* Out of print.

Coleman, A. P. *Ice Ages, Recent and Ancient.* New York, Macmillan, 1926. 296 pp. *An account of Pleistocene glaciation, and also of earlier glacial epochs.* Out of print.

Daly, Reginald. *The Changing World of the Ice Age.* New Haven, Yale University Press, 1934. 271 pp. *A fresh, stimulating, and vigorous treatment of the subject, more easily read, however, against some background of geology.* Out of print.

Our Mobile Earth. New York, Charles Scribner's Sons, 1926. 342 pp. *For the general reader; an excellent picture of the earth's continuing development.* Out of print.

Hussy, Russell C. *Historical Geology: The Geological History of North America.* New York and London, McGraw-Hill, 1947. 465 pp. Out of print.

Miller, William J. *An Introduction to Historical Geology, with Special Reference to North America.* New York, D. Van Nostrand Co., 6th Ed. 1952. 499 pp.

Schuchert, Charles, and Dunbar, Carl O. *Outlines of Historical Geology*. New York, John Wiley and Sons, 1941. 291 pp. *Any one of these three books will give the general reader a good conception of this fascinating subject; the treatment by the various authors differs enough that all may read with profit.*

Shepard, Francis P. *Submarine Geology*. New York, Harper and Brothers, 1948. 348 pp. *The first textbook in a field which is still in the pioneering stages.*

Outstanding Sea Prose.

These books are listed because each, in one way or another, captures the sea's varied and always changing moods; all are among my own favorite volumes.

Beston, Henry. *The Outermost House: A Year of Life on the Great Beach of Cape Cod*. New York, Rinehart and Company, 1949. 222 pp.

Conrad, Joseph. *The Mirror of the Sea*. New York, Doubleday, Anchor Books, 1960. 304 pp. (Combined with Conrad's *A Personal Record*.)

Hughes, Richard. *In Hazard*. New York, Harper and Brothers, 1938. 279 pp. (also published by Penguin Books, 1943).

Melville, Herman. *Moby Dick*. Available in many editions, as Modern Library, New American Library, Pocket Books.

Nordhoff, Charles, and Hall, James Norman. *Men Against the Sea*. Boston, Little, Brown, 1934. 251 pp. (also published by Pocket Books, 1946).

Tomlinson, H. M. *The Sea and the Jungle*. New York, Modern Library, 1928. 322 pp. *Paper: Dutton* (Everyman).

INDEX

213

SIGNET and MENTOR Books of Interest

Recommended Reading from MENTOR and SIGNET

☐ **THE LIMITS TO GROWTH: A Report for the Club of Rome's Project on the Predicament of Mankind,** Donella H. Meadows, Dennis L. Meadows, Jorgen Randers, and William H. Behrens III. The headline-making report on the imminent global disaster facing humanity—and what we can do about it before time runs out. "One of the most important documents of our age!"—Anthony Lewis, *The New York Times*   (#J8985—$1.95)

☐ **BLUEPRINT FOR SURVIVAL by the Editors of** *The Ecologist.* Introduction by Paul Ehrlich. Inspired by the warnings of THE LIMITS TO GROWTH, the first positive plan for solving the dire problems of our world energy crisis. "A storehouse of information about what needs to be done if we are to avoid turning the planet into a clinker."—*Washington Post*
(#W7830—$1.50)†

☐ **THE ORIGIN OF SPECIES by Charles Darwin, Introduction by Julian Huxley.** The famous classic on evolution that exploded into public controversy and revolutionized the course of science.   (#ME1690—$2.50)

☐ **THE DOUBLE HELIX by James D. Watson.** A "behind-the-scenes" account of the work that led to the discovery of DNA. "It is a thrilling book from beginning to end—delightful, often funny, vividly observant, full of suspense and mounting tension . . . so directly candid about the brilliant and abrasive personalities and institutions involved . . ."—*Eliot Fremont-Smith, New York Times.* Illustrated.
(#ME1823—$1.75)

☐ **THE CLONING OF MAN: A Brave New Hope—Or Horror? edited by Martin Ebon.** Martin Ebon tells the complete, astonishing story of cloning, its theory and practice, and its history, as cloning moved from the realms of myth and literature into scientific reality.   (#J8426—$1.95)*

* Price slightly higher in Canada
† Not available in Canada

Buy them at your local

bookstore or use coupon

on next page for ordering.

MENTOR and SIGNET Books You'll Enjoy

☐ **RED GIANTS AND WHITE DWARFS: Man's Descent from the Stars by Robert Jastrow.** Revised Edition. A fascinating discussion of the most fundamental questions regarding the origins of the universe and the appearance of life on this planet. Revised to include the results of the moon landings and Mars flights. (#J8270—$1.95)

☐ **THE NEXT TEN THOUSAND YEARS: A Vision of Man's Future in the Universe by Adrian Berry. With an Introduction by Robert Jastrow.** What lies ahead: a devastated earth, or a galaxy-wide expansion to claim the resources of the stars? (#ME1601—$2.25)*

☐ **FROM KNOW-HOW TO NOWHERE: The Development of American Technology by Elting E. Morrison.** An exploration of the ways in which machines have been shaped by and in turn shaped American society over the past two hundred years. (#MJ1539—$1.95)

☐ **THE BIOLOGICAL TIME BOMB by Gordon Rattray Taylor.** The author discusses the new discoveries for the manipulation of life which are being made in biology, supplies a wealth of social problems that will occur, and submits that things have gone too far too quickly. (#MW1457—$1.50)

☐ **THE WEB OF LIFE by John H. Storer.** An easy-to-understand introduction to the science of ecology showing how all living things—bacteria, insects, plants, birds, and mammals—are related to each other and to their environment, and how man can help maintain the delicate balance of nature. Illustrated. (#MW1644—$1.50)

* Not available in Canada

Buy them at your local bookstore or use this convenient coupon for ordering.

THE NEW AMERICAN LIBRARY, INC.,
P.O. Box 999, Bergenfield, New Jersey 07621

Please send me the SIGNET and MENTOR BOOKS I have checked above. I am enclosing $_____(please add 50¢ to this order to cover postage and handling). Send check or money order—no cash or C.O.D.'s. Prices and numbers are subject to change without notice.

Name _____

Address _____

City_____ State _____ Zip Code_____
Allow 4-6 weeks for delivery.
This offer is subject to withdrawal without notice.